BOOKKEEPING WITH SAGE AND SPREADSHEETS WITH EXCEL

Workbook (with Sage and Excel data files on CD)

In this April 2008 edition

- Layout designed to be easy on the eye – and easy to use
- Clear language and presentation
- Practical exercises – with data supplied on CD-ROM for use with Sage Line 50 (now called Sage 50) or Sage Instant (you must have access to Sage software to use this data)
- Exercises using Microsoft Excel and Microsoft Word
- Designed to cover the skills required at the Association of Accounting Technicians (AAT) Foundation level

BPP LEARNING MEDIA

First edition May 2003
Sixth edition April 2008

ISBN 9780 7517 4647 1 (previous 9780 7517 4494 1)

British Library Cataloguing-in-Publication Data
A catalogue record for this book
is available from the British Library

Published by

BPP Learning Media Ltd
BPP House, Aldine Place
London W12 8AA

www.bpp.com/learningmedia

Printed in Great Britain by

WM Print
45-47 Frederick Street
Walsall
West Midlands
WS2 9NE

Your learning materials, published by BPP Learning Media Ltd, are printed on paper sourced from sustainable, managed forests.

All our rights reserved. No part of this publication may be reproduced, stored in a retrieval system or transmitted, in any form or by any means, electronic, mechanical, photocopying, recording or otherwise, without the prior written permission of BPP Learning Media Ltd.

We are grateful to the Lead Body for Accounting for permission to reproduce extracts from the Standards of Competence for Accounting, and to the AAT for permission to reproduce extracts from the mapping and Guidance Notes.

©
BPP Learning Media Ltd
2008

Contents

Introduction

How to use this Workbook and CD-ROM – Foundation qualification structure – Information Technology and the Foundation AAT Standards of competence – Assessment – Building your portfolio

	Page	Answers to activities

PART A Spreadsheets

| 1 | Using spreadsheets | 3 | 169 |

PART B Using accounting software

2	Introducing the case study	41	171
3	Supplier invoices and credit notes	61	172
4	Customer invoices and credit notes	81	173
5	Payments to suppliers	105	176
6	Receipts from customers	123	177
7	Other cash transactions	139	178
8	Other credit transactions	151	179

PART C Assignments

1	Supplier invoices and credit notes	183	219
2	Customer invoices and credit notes	187	223
3	Payments to suppliers	195	231
4	Receipts from customers	199	237
5	Other cash transactions	205	243
6	Other credit transactions	213	249

CONTENTS

Page   Answers to assignments

PART D   Appendices

1   The Blitz nominal ledger – account codes 257
2   Shortcut keys 261

Index 265

Review form

Introduction

How to use this Workbook and CD-ROM

Aims of this Workbook and CD-ROM

> To provide knowledge that will assist students display competency in information technology skills as required at AAT Foundation Level.

To pass the assessment successfully you need a thorough understanding in all areas covered by the standards of competence.

> To tie in with the other components of the BPP Effective Study Package to ensure you have the best possible chance of success.

This Workbook

Foundation Level papers require you to provide evidence of your practical computing skills. This Workbook and the accompanying CD contains practical exercises using Sage accounting software, Microsoft Excel and Microsoft Word.

Interactive Texts and Practice and Revision Kits

Computer skills and computerised systems are relevant in Foundation Units 1-4 and Unit 21. To ensure you have the knowledge you need for Foundation Level skills tests ensure you study the relevant BPP Interactive Texts and Revision Kits for these units. This Workbook and CD-ROM provides additional, practical knowledge and examples.

Passcards

These short memorable notes are focused on key topics for the Foundation Units, designed to remind you of what the Interactive Text has taught you.

INTRODUCTION

The Case Study in this Workbook

The case study is about a newly-established company of contract cleaners, Blitz Limited. The company has been operating for just over one month when the assignments in the book begin. The case starts in August 2000.

The data for each assignment is held in a separate Sage back-up file on the CD-ROM that accompanies this book. The files allow you to attempt 'later' assignments (eg Assignment 4) without having to do earlier assignments (eg Assignments 1, 2 and 3) first.

The book and CD contain six assignments covering credit and cash transactions and a variety of simple word processing and spreadsheet exercises. Guidance is given on how to carry out the tasks in each assignment using Sage or Microsoft Word or Microsoft Excel.

How much prior knowledge is needed?

Some basic knowledge of accounting is presumed. You should have an understanding of the logic behind the processing of accounting transactions. This book does not explain ledgers, accounts, invoices, credit notes and so on. These are explained in other study material (eg for AAT Units 1-4).

Explanations are given for each assignment about how the computerised accounting system is being used, and why. It is important to understand what the computerised processing being performed means in accounting terms.

Using the Sage data with your Sage software

Sage software is produced by the Sage Group plc, the leading producer of accounting software in the UK. The CD packaged with this book contains data only. To make use of this data **you need to have access to Sage software**.

The CD contains data compatible with:

- **Sage Line 50 (now called Sage 50) versions 10, 11, 12, 13 ('2007') and 14 ('2008')**
- **Sage Instant Accounts versions 10, 11, 12 and 14 ('2008')**

See the section 'Loading the Sage data' in Chapter 2 for detailed instructions regarding how to use the Sage data held on the CD.

Foundation qualification structure

The competence-based Education and Training Scheme of the Association of Accounting Technicians is based on an analysis of the work of accounting staff in a wide range of industries and types of organisation. The Standards of Competence for Accounting which students are expected to meet are based on this analysis.

The AAT Standards identify the key purpose of the accounting occupation, which is to operate, maintain and improve systems to record, plan, monitor and report on the financial activities of an organisation, and a number of key roles of the occupation. Each key role is subdivided into units of competence, which are further divided into elements of competences.

By successfully completing assessments in specified units of competence, students can gain qualifications at NVQ/SVQ levels 2, 3 and 4, which correspond to the AAT Foundation, Intermediate and Technician stages of competence respectively.

Whether you are competent in a Unit is demonstrated by means of:

- *Either* an Exam Based Assessment (set and marked by AAT assessors)
- *Or* a Skills Based Assessment (where competence is judged by an Approved Assessment Centre to whom responsibility for this is devolved)
- Or *both* Exam *and* Skills Based Assessment

In the following pages we set out the overall structure of the Foundation (NVQ/SVQ Level 2) stage, indicating how competence in each Unit is assessed. In the next section there is more detail about the computerised aspect of the Foundation Units.

All units are assessed by Skills Based Assessment, and Unit 3 is also assessed by Exam Based Assessment.

INTRODUCTION

NVQ/SVQ Level 2 – Foundation

Unit 1 Recording Income and Receipts	Element 1.1	Process documents relating to goods and services supplied
	Element 1.2	Process receipts

Unit 2 Making and Recording Payments	Element 2.1	Process documents relating to goods and services received
	Element 2.2	Process payments

Unit 3 Preparing Ledger Balances and an Initial Trial Balance	Element 3.1	Balance bank transactions
	Element 3.2	Prepare ledger balances and control accounts
	Element 3.3	Draft an initial trial balance

Unit 4 Supplying Information for Management Control	Element 4.1	Code and extract information
	Element 4.2	Provide comparisons on costs and income

*Unit 21 Working with Computers	Element 21.1	Use computer systems and software
	Element 21.2	Maintain the security of data

*Unit 22 Contribute to the Maintenance of a Healthy, Safe and Productive Working Environment	Element 22.1	Contribute to the maintenance of a healthy, safe and productive working environment
	Element 22.2	Monitor and maintain an effective and efficient working environment

Unit 23 Achieving Personal Effectiveness	Element 23.1	Plan and organise your own work
	Element 23.2	Maintain good working relationships
	Element 23.3	Improve your own performance

* Students that have direct entry to subsequent Levels must demonstrate competence in Units 21 and 22 at those Levels.

Information Technology and the Foundation Standards of Competence

The Standards of Competence provide details relating to the amount of evidence a candidate is required to produce to prove competence in the Information Technology (IT) aspects at Foundation level.

This is done through the range statements.

Unit 4, Supplying Information for Management Control, requires candidates to produce a word processed report and a spreadsheet.

Unit 21, Working with Computers, requires candidates to prove competence in the generic tasks of using a computer and maintaining the security of data. Many of the competencies in this unit can be evidenced through observation whilst the candidate is producing evidence for units 1-4.

Evidence requirements

The Knowledge and Understanding for each of **Units 1-3** require candidates to understand:

- The operation of computerised accounting systems, including output

The extent of this knowledge is determined by the evidence requirements stipulated in the range statements. Therefore, candidates should be able to produce the following computerised evidence. (Different accounting packages use different terminology for the following evidence, but the essence of the requirements should not be affected.)

For Unit 1:
- Sales day book
- Sales returns day book
- Subsidiary sales ledger
- Main ledger
- Cash book
- Statements of account

For Unit 2:
- Purchases day book
- Purchases returns day book
- Subsidiary purchases ledger
- Main ledger
- Cash book
- Petty cash book

For Unit 3:
- Cash book
- Main ledger
- Subsidiary ledgers
- Bank reconciliation statement
- Journal
- Control accounts: sales ledger; purchases ledger; non-trade debtors and petty cash
- Trial balance

The Knowledge and Understanding for **Unit 4** requires the candidate to know and understand:
- Methods of analysing information in spreadsheets (Element 4.2)
- Methods of presenting information, including word-processed documents (Element 4.2)
- House style for different types of documents, including word-processed documents (Element 4.2)

INTRODUCTION

The extent of this knowledge is determined by the evidence requirements stipulated in the range statements. The range statement for element 4.2 also specifies word processed documents. Therefore, candidates should be able to produce the following evidence:

- The performance criteria 'Provide comparisons to the appropriate person in the required format' includes the format of a word-processed report
- The Knowledge and Understanding regarding spreadsheets requires candidates to analyse information in a spreadsheet, in the contexts of providing comparisons on costs and income

The depth of knowledge required for **word-processed reports** is, in the context of providing comparisons, to be able to produce a short informal report using:

- Different font sizes
- Embolden
- Italicise
- Table

The depth of knowledge required for **spreadsheets**, in the context of analysing information in respect of costs and income, is to be able to produce a spreadsheet which has the following features:

- Title
- Labels and figures
- Simple formulae

Assessment

The computerised aspect of units 1, 2, 3 and 4 should be assessed through skills testing. However, as Unit 3 is also examined, candidates should also be prepared for a question on computerised accounting in the Initial Trial Balance exam.

Details of possible assessment methods can be found in the guidance notes for units 1–4 and 21 (these are reproduced in the front pages of the relevant BPP Interactive Texts). However, the opportunity exists for many of the competencies of Unit 21 to be evidenced whilst computerised evidence is being produced for Units 1–4.

Where the Approved Assessment Centre is a **college or training organisation**, skills testing will involve a combination of the following.

(a) Documentary evidence of activities carried out at the workplace, collected by you in an **accounting portfolio**

(b) Realistic **simulations** of workplace activities; these simulations may take the form of case studies and in-tray exercises and involve the use of primary documents and reference sources

(c) **Projects and assignments** designed to assess the Standards of Competence

If you are unable to provide workplace evidence, you will be able to complete the assessment requirements by the alternative methods listed above.

Students and Assessment Centres should be aware of the opportunity that exists for many of the competences of Unit 21 to be evidenced whilst computerised evidence is being produced for units 1–4 (and 7). The most powerful evidence will come from observation, but witness testimony from the workplace, personal report/checklists will also be valuable pieces of evidence. This coupled with the output produced and evidence of questioning should enable centres to ensure all performance criteria, range and knowledge and understanding are evidenced in a variety of ways.

Computer related evidence in the portfolio may be distributed through the various units or may be filed in the Unit 21 section. Either way, the use of cross-referencing in the portfolio will be of paramount importance.

Building your portfolio

What is a portfolio?

A portfolio is a collection of work that demonstrates what the owner can do. In AAT language the portfolio demonstrates **competence**.

A painter will have a collection of his paintings to exhibit in a gallery, an advertising executive will have a range of advertisements and ideas that she has produced to show to a prospective client. Both the collection of paintings and the advertisements form the portfolio of that artist or advertising executive.

Your portfolio will be unique to you just as the portfolio of the artist will be unique because no one will paint the same range of pictures in the same way. It is a very personal collection of your work and should be treated as a **confidential** record.

What evidence should a portfolio include?

No two portfolios will be the same but by following some simple guidelines you can decide which of the following suggestions will be appropriate in your case.

(a) **Your current CV**

This should be at the front. It will give your personal details as well as brief descriptions of posts you have held with the most recent one shown first.

(b) **References and testimonials**

References from previous employers may be included especially those of which you are particularly proud.

(c) **Your current job description**

You should emphasise financial **responsibilities and duties**.

(d) **Your student record sheets**

These should be supplied by AAT when you begin your studies, and your training provider should also have some if necessary.

(e) **Evidence from your current workplace**

This could take many forms including **letters, memos, reports** you have written, **copies of accounts** or **reconciliations** you have prepared, **discrepancies** you have investigated etc. Remember to obtain permission to include the evidence from your line manager because some records may be sensitive. Discuss the performance criteria that are listed in your Student Record Sheets with your training provider and employer, and think of other evidence that could be appropriate to you.

(f) **Evidence from your social activities**

For example you may be the treasurer of a club in which case examples of your cash and banking records could be appropriate.

(g) **Evidence from your studies**

Few students are able to satisfy all the requirements of competence by workplace evidence alone. They therefore rely on simulations to provide the remaining evidence to complete a unit. If you are not working or not working in a relevant post, then you may need to rely more heavily on simulations as a source of evidence.

(h) **Additional work**

Your training provider may give you work that specifically targets one or a group of performance criteria in order to complete a unit. It could take the form of questions, presentations or demonstrations. Each training provider will approach this in a different way.

(i) **Evidence from a previous workplace**

This evidence may be difficult to obtain and should be used with caution because it must satisfy the 'rules' of evidence, that is, it must be current. Only rely on this as evidence if you have changed jobs recently.

(j) **Prior achievements**

For example you may have already completed the health and safety unit during a previous course of study, and therefore there is no need to repeat this work. Advise your training provider who will check to ensure that it is the same unit and record it as complete if appropriate.

How should it be presented?

As you assemble the evidence remember to **make a note** of it on your Student Record Sheet in the space provided and **cross reference** it. In this way it is easy to check to see if your evidence is **appropriate**. Remember one piece of evidence may satisfy a number of performance criteria so remember to check this thoroughly and discuss it with your training provider if in doubt. Keep all your evidence together in a ring binder or lever arch file for safe storage.

When should evidence be assembled?

You should begin to assemble evidence **as soon as you have registered as a student**. **Don't leave it all** until the last few weeks of your studies, because you may miss vital deadlines and your resulting certificate sent by the AAT may not include all the units you have completed. Give yourself and your training provider time to examine your portfolio and report your results to AAT at regular intervals. In this way the task of assembling the portfolio will be spread out over a longer period of time and will be presented in a more professional manner.

What are the key criteria that the portfolio must fulfil?

As you assemble your evidence bear in mind that it must be:

- **Valid**. It must relate to the Standards.
- **Authentic**. It must be your own work.
- **Current**. It must refer to your current or most recent job.
- **Sufficient**. It must meet all the performance criteria by the time you have completed your portfolio.

Finally

Remember that the portfolio is **your property** and **your responsibility**. Not only could it be presented to the external verifier before your award can be confirmed; it could be used when you are seeking **promotion** or applying for a more senior and better paid post elsewhere. How your portfolio is presented can say as much about you as the evidence inside.

> For further information about portfolios, BPP have produced a book *Building Your Portfolio*. It can be ordered using the order form at the back of this book or at *www.bpp.com/aat*.

INTRODUCTION

PART A

Spreadsheets

chapter 1

Using Spreadsheets

Contents

1 Introduction
2 What is a spreadsheet?
3 Examples of spreadsheet formulae
4 Basic skills
5 Spreadsheet construction
6 Formulae with conditions
7 Charts and graphs
8 Spreadsheet format and appearance
9 Other issues: printing; controls; using spreadsheets with word processing software
10 Three dimensional (multi-sheet) spreadsheets

Knowledge and understanding

Methods of analysing information in spreadsheets

PART A   SPREADSHEETS

1 Introduction

The vast majority of people who work in an accounting environment are required to use spreadsheets to perform their duties. This fact is reflected in the AAT Standards, which require candidates to be able to produce clear, well-presented spreadsheets, that utilise basic spreadsheet functions such as simple formulae.

2 What is a spreadsheet?

A spreadsheet is essentially an electronic piece of paper divided into **rows** (horizontal) and **columns** (vertical). The rows are numbered 1, 2, 3 . . . etc and the columns lettered A, B C . . . etc. Each individual area representing the intersection of a row and a column is called a '**cell**'. A cell address consists of its row and column reference. For example, in the spreadsheet below the word '*Jan*' is in cell B2. The cell that the cursor is currently in or over is known as the 'active cell'.

The main examples of spreadsheet packages are Lotus 1 2 3 and Microsoft Excel. We will be referring to **Microsoft Excel**. The examples use **Excel 2003** rather than Excel 2007, as at the time of publication Excel 2003 is more widely used than Excel 2007.

A simple spreadsheet is shown below.

	A	B	C	D	E	F
1	BUDGETED SALES FIGURES					
2		Jan	Feb	Mar	Total	
3		£'000	£'000	£'000	£'000	
4	North	2,431	3,001	2,189	7,621	
5	South	6,532	5,826	6,124	18,482	
6	West	895	432	596	1,923	
7	Total	9,858	9,259	8,909	28,026	
8						

2.1 Why use spreadsheets?

Spreadsheets provide a tool for calculating, analysing and manipulating numerical data. Spreadsheets make the calculation and manipulation of data easier and quicker. For example, the spreadsheet above has been set up to calculate the totals **automatically**. If you changed your estimate of sales in February for the North region to £3,296, when you input this figure in cell C4 the totals (in E4 and C7) would change accordingly.

2.1.1 Uses of spreadsheets

Spreadsheets can be used for a wide range of tasks. Some common applications of spreadsheets are:

- Management accounts
- Cash flow analysis and forecasting
- Reconciliations
- Revenue analysis and comparison
- Cost analysis and comparison
- Budgets and forecasts

2.1.2 Cell contents

The contents of any cell can be one of the following.

(a) **Text**. A text cell usually contains **words**. Numbers that do not represent numeric values for calculation purposes (eg a Part Number) may be entered in a way that tells Excel to treat the cell contents as text. To do this, enter an apostrophe before the number eg '451.

(b) **Values**. A value is a **number** that can be used in a calculation.

(c) **Formulae**. A formula **refers to other cells** in the spreadsheet, and performs some sort of computation with them. For example, if cell C1 contains the formula =A1-B1, cell C1 will display the result of the calculation subtracting the contents of cell B1 from the contents of cell A1. In Excel, a formula always begins with an equals sign: = . There are a wide range of formulae and functions available.

2.1.3 Formula bar

The following illustration shows the formula bar. (If the formula bar is not visible, choose **View**, **Formula bar** from Excel's main menu.)

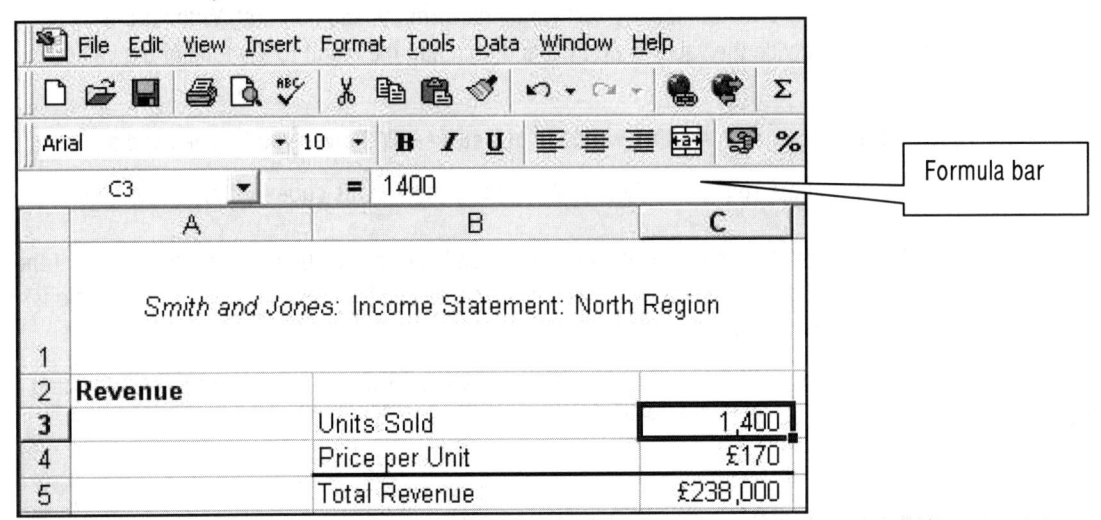

	A	B	C
1		Smith and Jones: Income Statement: North Region	
2	**Revenue**		
3		Units Sold	1,400
4		Price per Unit	£170
5		Total Revenue	£238,000

The formula bar allows you to see and edit the contents of the active cell. The bar also shows the cell address of the active cell (C3 in the example above).

PART A   SPREADSHEETS

3 Examples of spreadsheet formulae

Formulas in Microsoft Excel follow a specific syntax. All Excel formulae start with the equals sign =, followed by the elements to be calculated (the operands) and the calculation operators. Each operand can be a value that does not change (a constant value), a cell or range reference, a label, a name, or a worksheet function.

Formulae can be used to perform a variety of calculations. Here are some examples.

(a) =C4*5. This formula **multiplies** the value in C4 by 5. The result will appear in the cell holding the formula.

(b) =C4*B10. This **multiplies** the value in C4 by the value in B10.

(c) =C4/E5. This **divides** the value in C4 by the value in E5. (* means multiply and / means divide by.)

(d) =C4*B10–D1. This **multiplies** the value in C4 by that in B10 and then subtracts the value in D1 from the result. Note that generally Excel will perform multiplication and division before addition or subtraction. If in any doubt, use brackets (parentheses): =(C4*B10)–D1.

(e) =C4*117.5%. This **adds** 17.5% to the value in C4. It could be used to calculate a price including 17.5% VAT.

(f) =(C4+C5+C6)/3. Note that the **brackets** mean Excel would perform the addition first. Without the brackets, Excel would first divide the value in C6 by 3 and then add the result to the total of the values in C4 and C5.

(g) = 2^2 gives you 2 **to the power** of 2, in other words 2^2. Likewise = 2^3 gives you 2 cubed and so on.

(h) = 4^ (1/2) gives you the **square root** of 4. Likewise 27^(1/3) gives you the cube root of 27 and so on.

Excel calculates a formula from left to right. You can control how calculation is performed by changing the syntax of the formula. For example, the formula =5+2*3 gives a result of 11 because Excel calculates multiplication before addition. Excel would multiply 2 by 3 (resulting in 6) and would then add 5.

You may use parentheses to change the order of operations. For example =(5+2)*3 would result in Excel firstly adding the 5 and 2 together, then multiplying that result by 3 to give 21.

3.1 Displaying the formulae held in your spreadsheet

It is sometimes useful to see all formulae held in your spreadsheet to enable you to see how the spreadsheet works. There are two ways of making Excel **display the formulae** held in a spreadsheet.

(a) You can 'toggle' between the two types of display by pressing **Ctrl +`** (the latter is the key above the Tab key). Press Ctrl + ` again to get the previous display back.

(b) You can also click on Tools, then on Options, then on View and tick the box next to 'Formulas'.

In the following paragraphs we provide examples of how spreadsheets and formulae may be used in an accounting context.

Example: formulae

	A	B	C	D	E	F
1	BUDGETED SALES FIGURES					
2		Jan	Feb	Mar	Total	
3		£'000	£'000	£'000	£'000	
4	North	2,431	3,001	2,189	7,621	
5	South	6,532	5,826	6,124	18,482	
6	West	895	432	596	1,923	
7	Total	9,858	9,259	8,909	28,026	
8						

(a) In the spreadsheet shown above, which of the cells have had a number typed in, and which cells display the result of calculations (ie which cells contain a formula)?

(b) What formula would you put in each of the following cells?

    (i)   Cell B7.
    (ii)   Cell E6.
    (iii) Cell E7.

(c) If the February sales figure for the South changed from £5,826 to £5,731, what other figures would change as a result? Give cell references.

Solution

(a) Cells into which you would need to enter a value are: B4, B5, B6, C4, C5, C6, D4, D5 and D6. Cells which would perform calculations are B7, C7, D7, E4, E5, E6 and E7.

(b) (i)   =B4+B5+B6 *or better* =SUM(B4:B6)

     (ii)   =B6+C6+D6 *or better* =SUM(B6:D6)

     (iii) =E4+E5+E6 *or better* =SUM(E4:E6) Alternatively, the three monthly totals could be added across the spreadsheet: = SUM (B7: D7)

(c) The figures which would change, besides the amount in cell C5, would be those in cells C7, E5 and E7. (The contents of E7 would change if any of the sales figures changed.)

PART A SPREADSHEETS

Activity 1.1

The following spreadsheet shows sales of two products, the Ego and the Id, for the period July to September.

	A	B	C	D	E	F	G
1	Sigmund Ltd						
2	Sales analysis - Q3 X7						
3		M7	M8	M9	Total		
4		£	£	£	£		
5	Ego	3000	4000	2000	9000		
6	Id	2000	1500	4000	7500		
7	Total	5000	5500	6000	16500		
8							
9							
10							

Devise a suitable formula for each of the following cells.

(a) Cell B7.
(b) Cell E6.
(c) Cell E7.

Note: In this Workbook, Answers to Activities follow Chapter 8.

Activity 1.2

The following spreadsheet shows sales, exclusive of VAT, in row 6.

	A	B	C	D	E	F	G	H
1	Taxable Supplies plc							
2	Sales analysis - Branch C							
3	Six months ended 30 June XX							
4		Jan	Feb	Mar	Apr	May	Jun	Total
5		£	£	£	£	£	£	£
6	Net sales	2,491.54	5,876.75	3,485.01	5,927.70	6,744.52	3,021.28	27,546.80
7	VAT							
8	Total							
9								
10								

Your manager has asked you to insert formulae to calculate VAT at 17½% in row 7 and also to produce totals.

(a) Devise a suitable formula for cell B7 and cell E8.
(b) How could the spreadsheet be better designed?

8

Activity 1.3

The following balances have been taken from the books of Ed Sheet, a sole trader, at 31 December 200X.

	Dr £	Cr £
Plant and machinery (NBV)	20,000	
Motor vehicles (NBV)	10,000	
Stock	2,000	
Debtors	1,000	
Cash	1,500	
Creditors		2,500
Overdraft		1,500
Drawings	1,000	
Capital (1 Jan 20XX)		28,000
Profit for year	3,500	

Your manager has started to prepare a balance sheet using Microsoft Excel. The basic structure of the spreadsheet has been set up, and the required numbers have been input. You have been asked to insert the formulae required in the cells highlighted with a border.

	A	B	C
1	**Ed Sheet**		
2	*Balance sheet as at 31 Dec 200X*		
3		£	£
4	*Fixed assets*		
5	Plant	20000	
6	Vehicles	10000	
7			
8	*Current assets*		
9	Stock	2000	
10	Debtors	1000	
11	Cash	1500	
12			
13	*Current liabilities*		
14	Creditors	2500	
15	Overdraft	1500	
16			
17	Net current assets		
18	Net assets		
19			
20	*Represented by:*		
21	Opening capital		28000
22	Profit for year		3500
23	Drawings		1000
24	Closing capital		
25			
26			

Devise the formulae required to go in the cells C7, B12, B16, C17, C18 and C24.

PART A   SPREADSHEETS

4 Basic skills

In this section we explain some **basic spreadsheeting skills**. We give instructions for Microsoft Excel, the most widely used package. Our examples should be valid with all versions of Excel released since 1997.

You should read this section while sitting at a computer and trying out the skills we describe **'hands-on'**.

4.1 Examples of useful spreadsheet skills

Start Microsoft Excel by double-clicking on the Excel **icon** or button (it will look like an X), or by choosing Excel from the **Start** menu (maybe from within the **Microsoft Office** option).

4.1.1 Moving about

The F5 key is useful for moving around within large spreadsheets. If you press the function key **F5**, a **Go To** dialogue box will allow you to specify the cell address you would like to move to. Try this out.

Also experiment by holding down Ctrl and pressing each of the direction arrow keys in turn to see where you end up. Try using the **Page Up** and **Page Down** keys and also try **Home** and **End** and Ctrl + these keys. Try **Tab** and **Shift + Tab**, too. These are all useful shortcuts for moving quickly from one place to another in a large spreadsheet.

4.1.2 Editing cell contents

Suppose cell A2 currently contains the value 456. If you wish to **change the entry** in cell A2 from 456 to 123456 there are four options – as shown below.

(a)   Activate cell A2, **type** 123456 and press **Enter**.

   To undo this and try the next option press **Ctrl + Z**: this will always undo what you have just done.

(b)   **Double-click** in cell A2. The cell will keep its thick outline but you will now be able to see a vertical line flashing in the cell. You can move this line by using the direction arrow keys or the Home and the End keys. Move it to before the 4 and type 123. Then press Enter.

   When you have tried this press Ctrl + Z to undo it.

(c)   **Click once** before the number 456 in the formula bar. Again you will get the vertical line and you can type in 123 before the 4. Then press Enter. Undo this before moving onto (d).

(d)   Press the **function key F2**. The vertical line cursor will be flashing in cell A2 at the *end* of the figures entered there (after the 6). Press Home to get to a position before the 4 and then type in 123 and press Enter, as before.

4.1.3 Deleting cell contents

You may delete the contents of a cell simply by making the cell the active cell and then pressing **Delete**. The contents of the cell will disappear. You may also highlight a range of cells to delete and then delete the contents of all cells within the range.

For example, enter any value in cell A1 and any value in cell A2. Move the cursor to cell A2. Now hold down the **Shift** key (the one above the Ctrl key) and keeping it held down press the ↑ arrow. Cell A2 will stay white but cell A1 will go black. What you have done here is **selected** the range A1 and A2. Now press the Delete key. The contents of cells A1 and A2 will be deleted.

4.1.4 Filling a range of cells

Start with a blank spreadsheet. Type the number 1 in cell A1 and the number 2 in cell A2. Now select cells A1: A2, this time by positioning the mouse pointer over cell A1, holding down the left mouse button and moving the pointer down to cell A2. When cell A2 is highlighted release the mouse button.

Now position the mouse pointer at the **bottom right hand corner** of cell A2. When you have the mouse pointer in the right place it will turn into a **black cross**.

Then, hold down the left mouse button again and move the pointer down to cell A10. You will see an outline surrounding the cells you are trying to 'fill'.

Release the mouse button when you have the pointer over cell A10. You will find that the software **automatically** fills in the numbers 3 to 10 below 1 and 2.

Try the following variations of this technique.

(a) Delete what you have just done and type in **Jan** in cell A1. See what happens if you select cell A1 and fill down to cell A12: you get the months **Feb, Mar, Apr** and so on.

(b) Type the number 2 in cell A1. Select A1 and fill down to cell A10. What happens? The cells should fill up with 2's.

(c) Type the number 2 in cell A1 and 4 in cell A2. Then select A1: A2 and fill down to cell A10. What happens? You should get 2, 4, 6, 8, and so on.

(d) Try **filling across** as well as down.

(e) If you click on the bottom right hand corner of the cell using the **right mouse button**, drag down to a lower cell and then release the button you should see a menu providing a variety of options for filling the cells.

4.1.5 The Sum button Σ

We will explain how to use the SUM button by way of a simple example. Start with a blank spreadsheet, then enter the following figures in cells A1:B5.

	A	B
1	400	582
2	250	478
3	359	264
4	476	16
5	97	125

Make cell B6 the active cell and click once on the **sum button** (the button with a Σ symbol on the Excel toolbar - the Σ symbol is the mathematical sign for 'the sum of'). A formula will appear in the cell saying =SUM(B1:B5). Above cell B6 you will see a flashing dotted line encircling cells B1:B5. Accept the suggested formula by hitting the Enter key.

PART A   SPREADSHEETS

The formula =SUM(B1:B5) will be entered, and the number 1465 will be appear in cell B6.

Next, make cell A6 the active cell and **double-click** on the sum button. The number 1582 should appear in cell A6.

4.1.6 Multiplication

Continuing on with our example, next select cell C1. Type in an = sign then click on cell A1. Now type in an **asterisk *** (which serves as a **multiplication sign**) and click on cell B1. Watch how the formula in cell C1 changes as you do this. (Alternatively you can enter the cell references by moving the direction arrow keys.) Finally press Enter. Cell C1 will show the result (232,800) of multiplying the figure in Cell A1 by the one in cell B1.

Your next task is to select cell C1 and **fill in** cells C2 to C5 automatically using the **dragging technique** described above. If you then click on each cell in column C and look above at the line showing what the cell contains you will find that the software has automatically filled in the correct cell references for you: A2*B2 in cell C2, A3*B3 in cell C3 and so on.

(**Note**: The forward slash **/** is used to represent division in spreadsheet formulae.)

4.1.7 Inserting columns and rows

Suppose we also want to add each row, for example cells A1 and B1. The logical place to do this would be cell C1, but column C already contains data. We have three options that would enable us to place this total in column C.

(a)   Highlight cells C1 to C5 and position the mouse pointer on one of the **edges**. (It will change to an arrow shape.) Hold down the **left** mouse button and drag cells C1 to C5 into column D. There is now space in column C for our next set of sums. Any **formulae** that need to be changed as a result of moving cells using this method should be changed **automatically** – but always check them.

(b)   The second option is to highlight cells C1 to C5 as before, position the mouse pointer anywhere **within** column C and click on the **right** mouse button. A menu will appear offering you an option **Insert...** . If you click on this you will be asked where you want to shift the cells that are being moved. In this case you want to move them to the right so choose this option and click on OK.

(c)   The third option is to **insert a whole new column**. You do this by clicking on the letter at the top of the column (here C) to highlight the whole of it then proceeding as in (b). The new column will always be inserted to the left of the one you highlight.

You can now display the sum of each of the rows in column C.

You can also insert a new row in a similar way (or stretch rows).

(a)   To **insert** one row, perhaps for headings, click on the row number to highlight it, click with the right mouse button and choose insert. One row will be inserted **above** the one you highlighted. Try putting some headings above the figures in columns A to C.

(b)   To insert **several** rows click on the row number immediately **below** the point where you want the new rows to appear and, holding down the left mouse button highlight the number of rows you wish to insert. Click on the highlighted area with the right mouse button and choose Insert (or if you prefer, choose **Insert**, **Rows** from the main menu).

4.1.8 Changing column width

You may occasionally find that a cell is not wide enough to display its contents. When this occurs, the cell displays a series of hashes ######. There are two options available to solve this problem.

(a) One is to **decide for yourself** how wide you want the columns to be. Position the mouse pointer at the head of column A directly over the little line dividing the letter A from the letter B. The mouse **pointer** will change to a sort of **cross**. Hold down the left mouse button and, by moving your mouse, stretch Column A to the right, to about the middle of column D, until the words you typed fit. You can do the same for column B. Then make your columns too narrow again so you can try option (b).

(b) Often it is easier to **let the software decide for you**. Position the mouse pointer over the little dividing line as before and get the cross symbol. Then double-click with the left mouse button. The column automatically adjusts to an appropriate width to fit the widest cell in that column.

You can either adjust the width of each column individually or you can do them all in one go. To do the latter click on the button in the top left hand corner to **select the whole sheet** and then **double-click** on just one of the dividing lines: all the columns will adjust to the **'best fit'** width.

4.1.9 Keyboard shortcuts and toolbar buttons

Here are a few tips to improve the **appearance** of your spreadsheets and speed up your work. To do any of the following to a cell or range of cells, first **select** the cell or cells and then:

(a) Press Ctrl + B to make the cell contents **bold.**
(b) Press Ctrl + I to make the cell contents *italic.*
(c) Press **Ctrl + C** to **copy** the contents of the cells.
(d) Move the cursor and press **Ctrl + V** to **paste** the cell you just copied into the new active cell or cells.

There are also **buttons** in the Excel toolbar (shown below) that may be used to carry out these and other functions. The best way to learn about these features is to use them - enter some numbers and text into a spreadsheet and experiment with keyboard shortcuts and toolbar buttons.

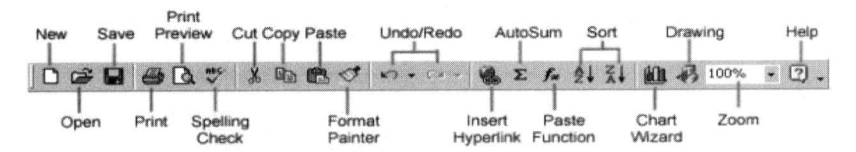

5 Spreadsheet construction

Spreadsheet models that will be used mainly as a calculation tool for various scenarios should ideally be constructed in **three sections**, as follows.

1. An inputs section containing the variables (eg the amount of a loan and the interest rate).
2. A calculations section containing formulae (eg the loan term and interest rate).
3. The results section, showing the outcome the calculations.

PART A   SPREADSHEETS

Here is an example arranged in this way.

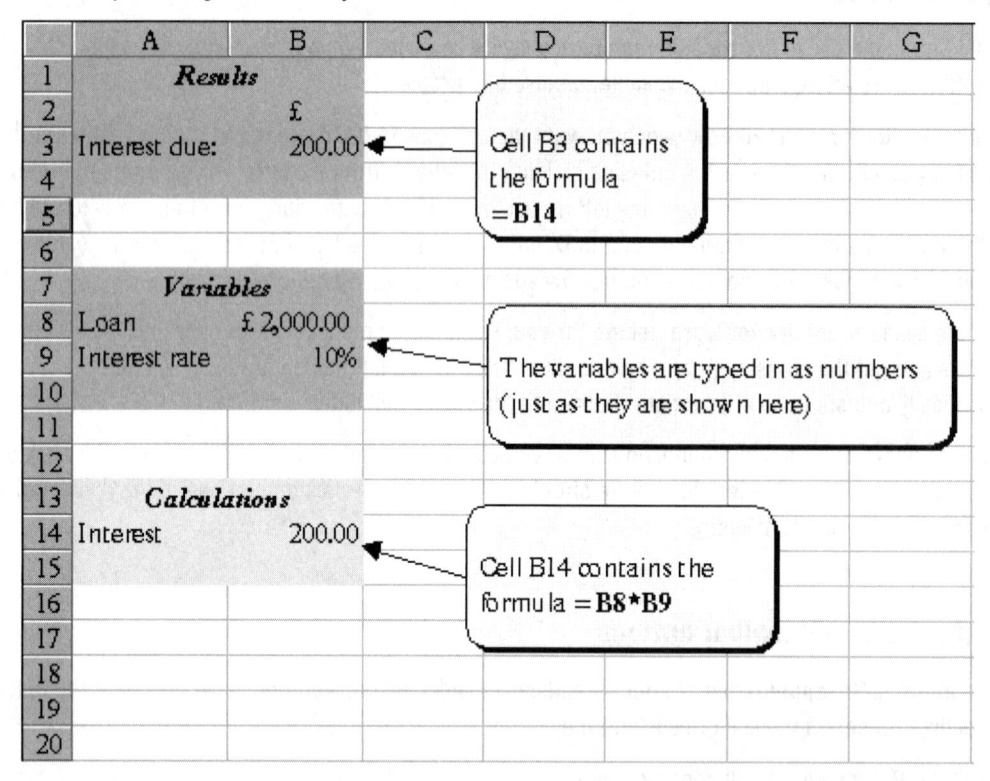

	A	B	C	D	E	F	G
1	*Results*						
2		£					
3	Interest due:	200.00		Cell B3 contains the formula =B14			
4							
5							
6							
7	*Variables*						
8	Loan	£2,000.00					
9	Interest rate	10%		The variables are typed in as numbers (just as they are shown here)			
10							
11							
12							
13	*Calculations*						
14	Interest	200.00		Cell B14 contains the formula =B8*B9			
15							
16							
17							
18							
19							
20							

In practice, in many situations it is often **more convenient** to combine the results and calculations areas as follows.

	A	B	C	D	E	F	G
1	*Results*						
2		£					
3	Interest due:	200.00		Cell B3 contains the formula =B8*B9			
4							
5							
6							
7	*Variables*						
8	Loan	£2,000.00					
9	Interest rate	10.00%		The variables are typed in as numbers (just as they are shown here)			
10							
11							
12							
13							
14							
15							

If we took out another loan of £4,789 at an interest rate of 7.25% we would simply need to **overwrite the figures in the variable section** of the spreadsheet with the new figures to calculate the interest.

After the activity below, we look at a more complicated example. Work through this example at a PC with Excel loaded.

Activity 1.4

Answer questions (a) and (b) below, which relate to the following spreadsheet.

	A	B	C	D	E
1	**Boilermakers Ltd**				
2	*Department B*				
3					
4	*Production data*	Machine A	Machine B	Machine C	
5	Shift 1	245.84	237.49	231.79	
6	Shift 2	241.14	237.62	261.31	
7	Shift 3	244.77	201.64	242.71	
8	Shift 4	240.96	238.18	234.50	
9					
10					
11	*Usage data*	Machine A	Machine B	Machine C	
12	Maintenance	35	71	6	
13	Operational	8.47	7.98	9.31	
14	Idle	1.42	2.4	0.87	
15	Recovery	0	15	4	
16					
17					
18					
19					
20					

(a) Cell B9 needs to contain an average of all the preceding numbers in column B. Suggest a formula which would achieve this.

(b) Cell C16 contains the formula

=C12+C13/C14-C15

What would the result be, displayed in cell C16?

5.1 Example: Constructing a cash flow projection

Suppose you wanted to set up a simple six-month cash flow projection, in such a way that you could use it to estimate how the **projected cash balance** figures will **change** in total when any **individual item** in the projection is **altered**. You have the following information.

(a) Sales were £45,000 per month in 20X5, falling to £42,000 in January 20X6. Thereafter they are expected to increase by 3% per month (ie February will be 3% higher than January, and so on).

(b) Debts are collected as follows.

   (i) 60% in month following sale.
   (ii) 30% in second month after sale.

PART A   SPREADSHEETS

    (iii)   7% in third month after sale.
    (iv)   3% remains uncollected.
(c) Purchases are equal to cost of sales, set at 65% of sales.
(d) Overheads were £6,000 per month in 20X5, rising by 5% in 20X6.
(e) Opening cash is an overdraft of £7,500.
(f) Dividends: £10,000 final dividend on 20X5 profits payable in May.
(g) Capital purchases: plant costing £18,000 will be ordered in January. 20% is payable with order, 70% on delivery in February and the final 10% in May.

5.1.1 Headings and layout

The first step is to put in the various **headings** required for the cash flow projection. At this stage, your spreadsheet might look as follows.

	A	B	C	D	E	F	G
1	**EXCELLENT PLC**						
2	*Cash flow projection - six months ending 30 June X6*						
3		*Jan*	*Feb*	*Mar*	*Apr*	*May*	*Jun*
4		£	£	£	£	£	£
5	Sales						
6	*Cash receipts*						
7	1 month in arrears						
8	2 months in arrears						
9	3 months in arrears						
10	Total operating receipts						
11							
12	Cash payments						
13	Purchases						
14	Overheads						
15	Total operating payments						
16							
17	Dividends						
18	Capital purchases						
19	Total other payments						
20							
21	Net cash flow						
22	Cash balance b/f						
23	Cash balance c/f						
24							

Note the following points.

(a) We have **increased the width** of column A to allow longer pieces of text to be inserted. Had we not done so, only the first part of each caption would have been displayed (and printed). If you skipped Section 2 of this chapter but you don't know how to widen a column, you had better go back and read it now.

(b) We have developed a **simple style for headings**. Headings are essential, so that users can identify what a spreadsheet does. We have **emboldened** the company name and *italicised* other headings.

(c) When **text** is entered into a cell it is usually **left-aligned** (as for example in column A). We have **centred** the headings above each column by highlighting the cells and using the relevant buttons at the top of the screen.

(d) **Numbers** should be **right-aligned** in cells.

(e) We have left **spaces** in certain rows (after blocks of related items) to make the spreadsheet **easier to use and read**.

5.1.2 Inserting formulae

The next step is to enter the **formulae** required. For example, in cell B10 you want total operating receipts, =SUM(B7:B9).

Look for a moment at cell C7. We are told that sales in January were £42,000 and that 60% of customers settle their accounts one month in arrears. We could insert the formula =B5*0.6 in the cell and fill in the other cells along the row so that it is replicated in each month. However, consider the effect of a change in payment patterns to a situation where, say, 55% of customer debts are settled after one month. This would necessitate a **change to each and every cell** in which the 0.6 ratio appears.

An alternative approach, which makes **future changes much simpler** to execute, is to put the relevant ratio (here, 60% or 0.6) in a cell **outside** the main table and cross-refer each cell in the main table to that cell. This means that, if the percentage changes, the change need only be reflected in **one cell**, following which all cells which are dependent on that cell will **automatically use the new percentage**. We will therefore input such values in separate parts of the spreadsheet, as follows. Look at the other assumptions which we have inserted into this part of the spreadsheet.

	A	B	C	D	E	F	G
24							
25							
26	This table contains the key variables for the		X6 cash flow projections				
27							
28	Sales growth factor per month		1.03				
29	Purchases as % of sales		-0.65				
30							
31	Debts paid within 1 month		0.6				
32	Debts paid within 2 months		0.3				
33	Debts paid within 3 months		0.07				
34	Bad debts		0.03				
35							
36	Increase in overheads		1.05				
37							
38	Dividends (May)		-10000				
39							
40	Capital purchases		-18000				
41	January		0.2				
42	February		0.7				
43	May		0.1				
44							
45							
46	This table contains relevant opening balance data as at Jan X6						
47							
48	Monthly sales X5		45000				
49	January X6 sales		42000				
50	Monthly overheads X5		-6000				
51	Opening cash		-7500				
52							

PART A   SPREADSHEETS

Now we can go back to cell C7 and input =B5*C31 and then fill this in across the '1 month in arrears' row. (Note that, as we have no December sales figure, we will have to deal with cell B7 separately.) If we assume for the moment that we are copying to cells D7 through to G7 and follow this procedure, the contents of cell D7 would be shown as =C5*D31, and so on, as shown below.

	A	B	C	D	E	F	G
3		Jan	Feb	Mar	Apr	May	Jun
4		£	£	£	£	£	£
5	Sales						
6	*Cash receipts*						
7	1 month in arrears		=B5*C31	=C5*D31	=D5*E31	=E5*F31	=F5*G31
8	2 months in arrears						
9	3 months in arrears						
10	Total operating receipts						

You may have noticed a problem. While the formula in cell C7 is fine - it multiplies January sales by 0.6 (the 1 month ratio stored in cell C31) - the remaining formulae are useless, as they **refer to empty cells** in row 31. This is what the spreadsheet would look like (assuming, for now, constant sales of £42,000 per month).

	A	B	C	D	E	F	G
3		Jan	Feb	Mar	Apr	May	Jun
4		£	£	£	£	£	£
5	Sales	42000	42000	42000	42000	42000	42000
6	*Cash receipts*						
7	1 month in arrears		25200	0	0	0	0
8	2 months in arrears						
9	3 months in arrears						
10	Total operating receipts						

This problem highlights the important distinction between **relative** cell references and **absolute** cell references. Usually, cell references are **relative**. A formula of =SUM(B7:B9) in cell B10 is relative. It does not really mean 'add up the numbers in cells B7 to B9'; it actually means '**add up the numbers in the three cells above this one**'. If this formula was copied to cell C10 (as we will do later), it would become =SUM(C7:C9).

This is what is causing the problem encountered above. The spreadsheet thinks we are asking it to 'multiply the number two up and one to the left by the number twenty-four cells down', and that is indeed the effect of the instruction we have given. But we are actually intending to ask it to 'multiply the number two up and one to the left by the number in cell C31'. This means that we need to create an **absolute** (unchanging) **reference** to cell C31.

Absolute cell references use **dollar signs** ($). A dollar sign before the column letter makes the column reference absolute, and one before the row number makes the row number absolute. You do not need to type the dollar signs - add them as follows.

(a) Make cell C7 the active cell and press F2 to edit it.

(b) Note where the cursor is flashing: it should be after the 1. If it is not move it with the direction arrow keys so that it is positioned somewhere next to or within the cell reference C31.

(c) Press F4.

The **function key F4** adds dollar signs to the cell reference: it becomes $C$31. Press F4 again: the reference becomes C$31. Press it again: the reference becomes $C31. Press it once more, and the simple relative reference is restored: C31.

(a) A dollar sign **before a letter** means that the **column** reference stays the same when you copy the formula to another cell.

(b) A dollar sign **before a number** means that the **row** reference stays the same when you copy the formula to another cell.

In our example we have now altered the reference in cell C7 and filled in across to cell G7, overwriting what was there previously. This is the result.

(a) Formulae

	A	B	C	D	E	F	G
3		Jan	Feb	Mar	Apr	May	Jun
4		£	£	£	£	£	£
5	Sales	42000	42000	42000	42000	42000	42000
6	*Cash receipts*						
7	1 month in arrears		=B5*$C$31	=C5*$C$31	=D5*$C$31	=E5*$C$31	=F5*$C$31
8	2 months in arrears						
9	3 months in arrears						
10	Total operating receipts						

(b) Numbers

	A	B	C	D	E	F	G
3		Jan	Feb	Mar	Apr	May	Jun
4		£	£	£	£	£	£
5	Sales	42000	42000	42000	42000	42000	42000
6	*Cash receipts*						
7	1 month in arrears		25200	25200	25200	25200	25200
8	2 months in arrears						
9	3 months in arrears						
10	Total operating receipts						

Other formulae required for this projection are as follows.

(a) **Cell B5** refers directly to the information we are given - **sales of £42,000** in January. We have input this variable in cell C49. The other formulae in row 5 (sales) reflect the predicted sales growth of 3% per month, as entered in cell C28.

(b) Similar formulae to the one already described for row 7 are required in rows 8 and 9.

(c) **Row 10** (total operating receipts) will display simple **subtotals**, in the form =SUM(B7:B9).

(d) **Row 13 (purchases)** requires a formula based on the data in row 5 **(sales)** and the value in cell C29 (**purchases** as a % of sales). This model assumes no changes in stock levels from month to month, and that stocks are sufficiently high to enable this. The formula is B5 * $C$29. Note that C29 is negative.

(e) **Row 15** (total operating payments), like row 10, requires **formulae** to create **subtotals**.

(f) **Rows 17 and 18** refer to the **dividends and capital purchase data** input in cells C38 and C40 to 43.

(g) **Row 21** (net cash flow) requires a **total** in the form =B10 + B15 + B21.

(h) **Row 22** (balance b/f) requires the contents of the **previous month's closing cash** figure.

(i) **Row 23** (balance b/f) requires the **total** of the **opening cash** figure and the **net cash flow** for the month.

PART A SPREADSHEETS

The following image shows the formulae that should now be present in the spreadsheet.

	A	B	C	D	E	F	G
1	EXCELLENT PLC						
2	Cash flow projection - six months						
3		Jan	Feb	Mar	Apr	May	Jun
4		£	£	£	£	£	£
5	Sales	=C49	=B5*$C$28	=C5*$C$28	=D5*$C$28	=E5*$C$28	=F5*$C$28
6	Cash receipts						
7	1 month in arrears	=$C$48*$C$31	=B5*$C$31	=C5*$C$31	=D5*$C$31	=E5*$C$31	=F5*$C$31
8	2 months in arrears	=$C$48*$C$32	=$C$48*$C$32	=B5*$C$32	=C5*$C$32	=D5*$C$32	=E5*$C$32
9	3 months in arrears	=$C$48*$C$33	=$C$48*$C$33	=$C$48*$C$33	=B5*$C$33	=C5*$C$33	=D5*$C$33
10	Total operating receipts	=SUM(B7:B9)	=SUM(C7:C9)	=SUM(D7:D9)	=SUM(E7:E9)	=SUM(F7:F9)	=SUM(G7:G9)
11							
12	Cash payments						
13	Purchases	=B5*$C$29	=C5*$C$29	=D5*$C$29	=E5*$C$29	=F5*$C$29	=G5*$C$29
14	Overheads	=$C$50*$C$36	=$C$50*$C$36	=$C$50*$C$36	=$C$50*$C$36	=$C$50*$C$36	=$C$50*$C$36
15	Total operating payments	=SUM(B13:B14)	=SUM(C13:C14)	=SUM(D13:D14)	=SUM(E13:E14)	=SUM(F13:F14)	=SUM(G13:G14)
16							
17	Dividends	0	0	0	0	=C38	0
18	Capital purchases	=C40*C41	=C40*C42	0	0	=C40*C43	0
19	Total other payments	=SUM(B17:B18)	=SUM(C17:C18)	=SUM(D17:D18)	=SUM(E17:E18)	=SUM(F17:F18)	=SUM(G17:G18)
20							
21	Net cash flow	=B10+B15+B19	=C10+C15+C19	=D10+D15+D19	=E10+E15+E19	=F10+F15+F19	=G10+G15+G19
22	Cash balance b/f	=C51	=B23	=C23	=D23	=E23	=F23
23	Cash balance c/f	=SUM(B21:B22)	=SUM(C21:C22)	=SUM(D21:D22)	=SUM(E21:E22)	=SUM(F21:F22)	=SUM(G21:G22)
24							

Be careful to ensure you use the correct sign (negative or positive) when manipulating numbers. For example, if total operating payments in row 15 are shown as **positive**, you would need to **subtract** them from total operating receipts in the formulae in row 23. However if you have chosen to make them **negative**, to represent outflows, then you will need to **add** them to total operating receipts.

Here is the spreadsheet in its normal 'numbers' form.

	A	B	C	D	E	F	G
1	EXCELLENT PLC						
2	Cash flow projection - six months ending 30 June X6						
3		Jan	Feb	Mar	Apr	May	Jun
4		£	£	£	£	£	£
5	Sales	42000	43260	44558	45895	47271	48690
6	Cash receipts						
7	1 month in arrears	27000	25200	25956	26735	27537	28363
8	2 months in arrears	13500	13500	12600	12978	13367	13768
9	3 months in arrears	3150	3150	3150	2940	3028	3119
10	Total operating receipts	43650	41850	41706	42653	43932	45250
11							
12	Cash payments						
13	Purchases	-27300	-28119	-28963	-29831	-30726	-31648
14	Overheads	-6300	-6300	-6300	-6300	-6300	-6300
15	Total operating payments	-33600	-34419	-35263	-36131	-37026	-37948
16							
17	Dividends					-10000	
18	Capital purchases	-3600	-12600			-1800	
19	Total other payments	-3600	-12600			-11800	
20							
21	Net cash flow	6450	-5169	6443	6521	-4894	7302
22	Cash balance b/f	-7500	-1050	-6219	224	6746	1852
23	Cash balance c/f	-1050	-6219	224	6746	1852	9154
24							

5.1.3 Tidy the spreadsheet up

Our spreadsheet needs a little **tidying up**. We will do the following.

(a) Add in **commas** to denote thousands of pounds.

(b) Put **zeros** in the cells with no entry in them.

(c) Change **negative numbers** from being displayed with a **minus sign** to being displayed in **brackets**.

	A	B	C	D	E	F	G
1	EXCELLENT PLC						
2	Cash flow projection - six months ending 30 June X6						
3		Jan	Feb	Mar	Apr	May	Jun
4		£	£	£	£	£	£
5	Sales	42,000	43,260	44,558	45,895	47,271	48,690
6	Cash receipts						
7	1 month in arrears	27,000	25,200	25,956	26,735	27,537	28,363
8	2 months in arrears	13,500	13,500	12,600	12,978	13,367	13,768
9	3 months in arrears	3,150	3,150	3,150	2,940	3,028	3,119
10	Total operating receipts	43,650	41,850	41,706	42,653	43,932	45,250
11							
12	Cash payments						
13	Purchases	(27,300)	(28,119)	(28,963)	(29,831)	(30,726)	(31,648)
14	Overheads	(6,300)	(6,300)	(6,300)	(6,300)	(6,300)	(6,300)
15	Total operating payments	(33,600)	(34,419)	(35,263)	(36,131)	(37,026)	(37,948)
16							
17	Dividends	0	0	0	0	(10,000)	0
18	Capital purchases	(3,600)	(12,600)	0	0	(1,800)	0
19	Total other payments	(3,600)	(12,600)	0	0	(11,800)	0
20							
21	Net cash flow	6,450	(5,169)	6,443	6,521	(4,894)	7,302
22	Cash balance b/f	(7,500)	(1,050)	(6,219)	224	6,746	1,852
23	Cash balance c/f	(1,050)	(6,219)	224	6,746	1,852	9,154
24							

5.1.4 Changes in assumptions (what if? analysis)

We referred to earlier to the need to design a spreadsheet so that **changes in assumptions** do **not** require **major changes** to the spreadsheet. This is why we set up two separate areas of the spreadsheet, one for 20X6 assumptions and one for opening balances. Consider each of the following.

(a) Negotiations with suppliers and gains in productivity have resulted in cost of sales being reduced to 62% of sales.

(b) The effects of a recession have changed the cash collection profile so that receipts in any month are 50% of prior month sales, 35% of the previous month and 10% of the month before that, with bad debt experience rising to 5%.

(c) An insurance claim made in 20X5 and successfully settled in December has resulted in the opening cash balance being an overdraft of £3,500.

(d) Sales growth will only be 2% per month.

PART A SPREADSHEETS

All of these changes can be made quickly and easily. The two tables are revised as follows.

	A	B	C	D	E	F	G
25							
26	*This table contains the key variables for the X6 cash flow projections*						
27							
28	Sales growth factor per month		1.02				
29	Purchases as % of sales		-0.62				
30							
31	Debts paid within 1 month		0.5				
32	Debts paid within 2 months		0.35				
33	Debts paid within 3 months		0.1				
34	Bad debts		0.05				
35							
36	Increase in overheads		1.05				
37							
38	Dividends (May)		-10000				
39							
40	Capital purchases		-18000				
41	January		0.2				
42	February		0.7				
43	May		0.1				
44							
45							
46	*This table contains relevant opening balance data as at Jan X6*						
47							
48	Monthly sales X5		45000				
49	January X6 sales		42000				
50	Monthly overheads X5		-6000				
51	Opening cash		-3500				
52							

The resulting (recalculated) spreadsheet would look like this.

	A	B	C	D	E	F	G
1	**EXCELLENT PLC**						
2	*Cash flow projection - six months ending 30 June X6*						
3		Jan	Feb	Mar	Apr	May	Jun
4		£	£	£	£	£	£
5	Sales	42,000	42,840	43,697	44,571	45,462	46,371
6	*Cash receipts*						
7	1 month in arrears	22,500	21,000	21,420	21,848	22,285	22,731
8	2 months in arrears	15,750	15,750	14,700	14,994	15,294	15,600
9	3 months in arrears	4,500	4,500	4,500	4,200	4,284	4,370
10	Total operating receipts	42,750	41,250	40,620	41,042	41,863	42,701
11							
12	*Cash payments*						
13	Purchases	-26,040	-26,561	-27,092	-27,634	-28,187	-28,750
14	Overheads	-6,300	-6,300	-6,300	-6,300	-6,300	-6,300
15	Total operating payments	-32,340	-32,861	-33,392	-33,934	-34,487	-35,050
16							
17	Dividends	0	0	0	0	-10,000	0
18	Capital purchases	-3,600	-12,600	0	0	-1,800	0
19	Total other payments	-3,600	-12,600	0	0	-11,800	0
20							
21	Net cash flow	6,810	-4,211	7,228	7,109	-4,423	7,650
22	Cash balance b/f	-3,500	3,310	-901	6,327	13,436	9,012
23	Cash balance c/f	3,310	-901	6,327	13,436	9,012	16,663
24							

Example: Commission calculations

The following four telesales people each earn a basic salary of £14,000 pa. They also earn a commission of 2% of sales. The following spreadsheet has been created to process their commission and total earnings. Give an appropriate formula for each of the following cells.

(a) Cell D4.

(b) Cell E6.

(c) Cell D9.

(d) Cell E9.

	A	B	C	D	E
1	Sales team salaries and commissions – 200X				
2	Name	Sales	Salary	Commission	Total earnings
3		£	£	£	£
4	Northington	284,000	14,000	5,680	19,680
5	Souther	193,000	14,000	3,860	17,860
6	Weston	12,000	14,000	240	14,240
7	Easterman	152,000	14,000	3,040	17,040
8					
9	Total	641,000	56,000	12,820	68,820
10					
11					
12	Variables				
13	Basic Salary	14,000			
14	Commission rate	0.02			
15					

Solution

Possible formulae are as follows.

(a) =B4*$B$14.

(b) =C6+D6.

(c) =SUM(D4:D7).

(d) There are a number of possibilities here, depending on whether you set the cell as the total of the earnings of each salesman (cells E4 to E7) or as the total of the different elements of remuneration (cells C9 and D9). Even better, would be a formula that checked that both calculations gave the same answer. A suitable formula for this purpose would be:

=IF(SUM(E4:E7)=SUM(C9:D9),SUM(E4:E7),"ERROR")

We will explain this formula in more detail after the next example.

PART A   SPREADSHEETS

Example: actual sales compared with budget sales

A business will often need to compare its results with budgets or targets to see how far it has exceeded, or fallen short of, its expectations. It is useful to express **variations as a percentage of the original budget**, for example sales may be 10% higher than predicted.

Continuing the example of the insurance salesmen, a spreadsheet could be set up as follows showing differences between actual sales and target sales, and expressing the difference as a percentage of target sales.

	A	B	C	D	E	F
1	Sales team comparison of actual against budget sales					
2	Name	Sales (Budget)	Sales (Actual)	Difference	% of budget	
3		£	£	£	£	
4	Northington	275,000	284,000	9,000	3.27	
5	Souther	200,000	193,000	(7,000)	(3.50)	
6	Weston	10,000	12,000	2,000	20.00	
7	Easterman	153,000	152,000	(1,000)	(0.65)	
8						
9	Total	638,000	641,000	3,000	0.47	
10						

Give a suitable formula for each of the following cells.

(a)   Cell D4.
(b)   Cell E6.
(c)   Cell E9.

Try this for yourself, before looking at the solution.

Solution

(a)   =C4-B4.
(b)   =(D6/B6)*100.
(c)   =(D9/B9)*100. Note that in (c) you **cannot simply add up the individual percentage differences**, as the percentages are based on different quantities.

6 Formulae with conditions

Suppose the company employing the salesmen in the above example awards a bonus to those salesmen who exceed their target by more than £1,000. The spreadsheet could work out who is entitled to the bonus.

To do this we would enter the appropriate formula in cells F4 to F7. For salesperson Easterman, we would enter the following in cell F7:

=IF(D4>1000,"BONUS"," ")

We will now explain this formula.

IF statements follow the following structure (or syntax).

=IF(logical_test,value_if_true,value_if_false)

The logical_test is any value or expression that can be evaluated to Yes or No. For example, D4>1000 is a logical expression; if the value in cell D4 is over 1000, the expression evaluates to Yes. Otherwise, the expression evaluates to No.

Value_if_true is the value that is returned if the answer to the logical_test is Yes. For example, if the answer to D4>1000 is Yes, and the value_if_true is the text string "BONUS", then the cell containing the IF function will display the text "BONUS".

Value_if_false is the value that is returned if the answer to the logical_test is No. For example, if the value_if_false is two sets of quote marks "" this means display a blank cell if the answer to the logical test is No. So in our example, if D4 is not over 1000, then the cell containing the IF function will display a blank cell.

Note the following symbols which can be used in formulae with conditions:

<	less than (like L (for 'less') on its side)
<=	less than or equal to
=	equal to
>=	greater than or equal to
>	greater than
<>	not equal to

Care is required to ensure **brackets** and **commas** are entered in the right places. If, when you try out this kind of formula, you get an error message, it may well be a simple mistake, such as leaving a comma out.

6.1 Examples of formulae with conditions

A company offers a discount of 5% to customers who order more than £1,000 worth of goods. A spreadsheet showing what customers will pay might look like this.

	A	B	C	D	E	F
1	Discount Traders Ltd					
2	*Sales analysis - April 200X*					
3	Customer	Sales	5% discount	Sales (net)		
4		£	£	£		
5	Arthur	956.00	0.00	956.00		
6	Dent	1423.00	71.15	1351.85		
7	Ford	2894.00	144.70	2749.30		
8	Prefect	842.00	0.00	842.00		
9						
10						

The formula in cell C5 is: =IF(B5>1,000,(0.05*B5),0). This means, if the value in B5 is greater than £1,000 multiply it by 0.05, otherwise the discount will be zero. Cell D5 will calculate the amount net of discount, using the formula: =B5-C5. The same conditional formula with the cell references changed will be found in cells C6, C7 and C8. **Strictly**, the variables £1,000 and 5% should be entered in a **different part** of the spreadsheet.

PART A SPREADSHEETS

Here is another example. Suppose the pass mark for an examination is 50%. You have a spreadsheet containing candidate's scores in column B. If a score is held in cell B10, an appropriate formula for cell C10 would be:

=IF(B10<50,"FAILED","PASSED").

7 Charts and graphs

Using Microsoft Excel, It is possible to display data held in a range of spreadsheet cells in a variety of charts or graphs. We will use the Discount Traders Ltd spreadsheet shown below to generate a chart.

	A	B	C	D	E
1	Discount Traders Ltd				
2	Sales analysis - April 200X				
3	Customer	Sales	5% discount	Sales (net)	
4		£	£	£	
5	Arthur	956.00	0.00	956.00	
6	Dent	1423.00	71.15	1351.85	
7	Ford	2894.00	144.70	2749.30	
8	Prefect	842.00	0.00	842.00	
9					
10					

The data in the spreadsheet could be used to generate a chart, such as those shown below. We explain how later in this section.

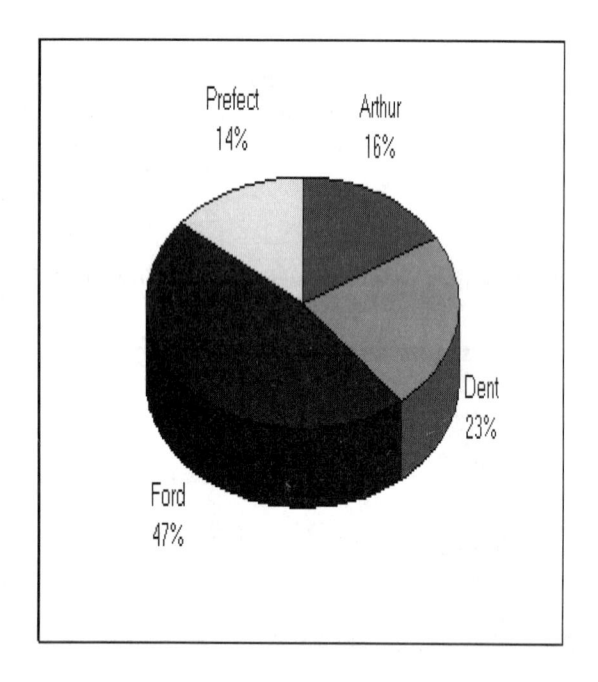

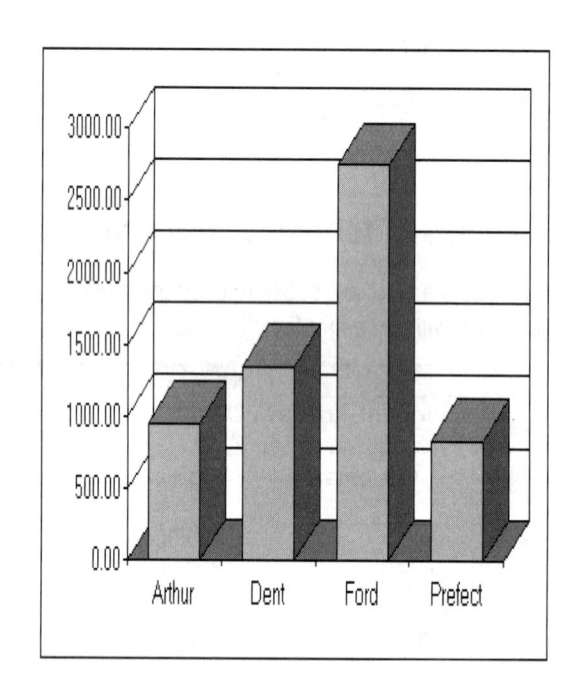

The Chart Wizard, which we explain in a moment, may also be used to generate a line graph. A line graph would normally be used to track a trend over time. For example, the chart below graphs the Total Revenue figures shown in Row 7 of the following spreadsheet.

	A	B	C	D	E	F
1			Revenue 2000-2003			
2						
3						
4	**Net revenue:**	2000	2001	2002	**2003**	
5	Products	24,001	27,552	34,823	**39,205**	
6	Services	5,306	5,720	6,104	**6,820**	
7	Total Revenue	29,307	33,272	40,927	**46,025**	

Total Revenue 2000-2003

(Line graph showing total revenue rising from approximately 29,307 in 2000 to 46,025 in 2003, with y-axis labelled £ from 0 to 50000, and x-axis labelled Year.)

PART A   SPREADSHEETS

7.1 The Chart Wizard

Charts and graphs may be generated simply by **selecting the range** of figures to be included, then using Excel's Chart Wizard. The Discount Traders spreadsheet referred to earlier is shown again below.

	A	B	C	D	E
1	Discount Traders Ltd				
2	Sales analysis - April 200X				
3	Customer	Sales	5% discount	Sales (net)	
4		£	£	£	
5	Arthur	956.00	0.00	956.00	
6	Dent	1423.00	71.15	1351.85	
7	Ford	2894.00	144.70	2749.30	
8	Prefect	842.00	0.00	842.00	
9					
10					

To chart the **net sales** of the different **customers**, follow the following steps.

Step 1   Highlight cells A5:A8, then move your pointer to cell D5, hold down **Ctrl** and drag to also select cells D5:D8.

Step 2   Look at the **toolbar** at the top of your spreadsheet. You should see an **icon** that looks like a small bar chart. Click on this icon to start the 'Chart Wizard'.

The appearance of the Excel Chart Wizard (shown below) may differ slightly if you are using a different version of Excel.

Step 3   Pick the type of chart you want. We will choose chart type **Column** and then select the sub-type we think will be most effective. (To produce a graph, select a type such as **Line**.)

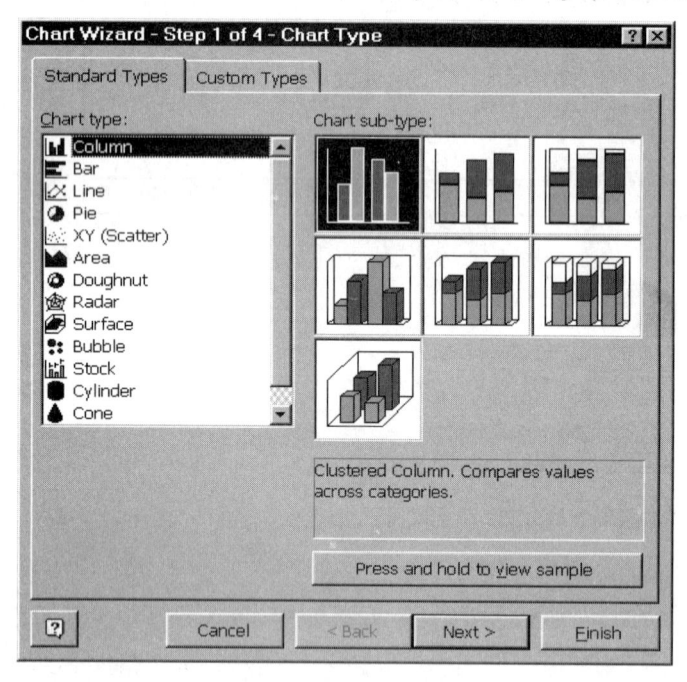

1: USING SPREADSHEETS

Step 4 This step gives us the opportunity to confirm that the data we selected earlier was correct and to decide whether the chart should be based on **columns** (eg Customer, Sales, Discount etc) or **rows** (Arthur, Dent etc). We can accept the default values and click Next.

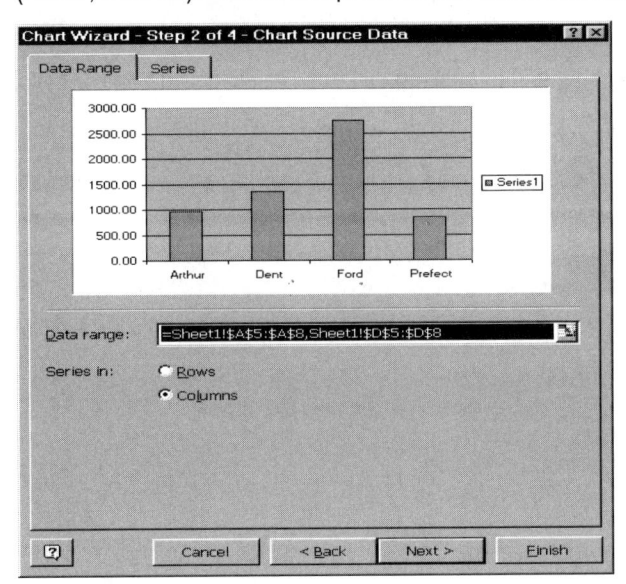

Step 5 Next, specify your chart **title** and axis **labels**. Incidentally, one way of remembering which is the **X axis** and which is the **Y axis** is to look at the letter Y: it is the only letter that has a vertical part pointing straight up, so it must be the vertical axis! Click Next to move on.

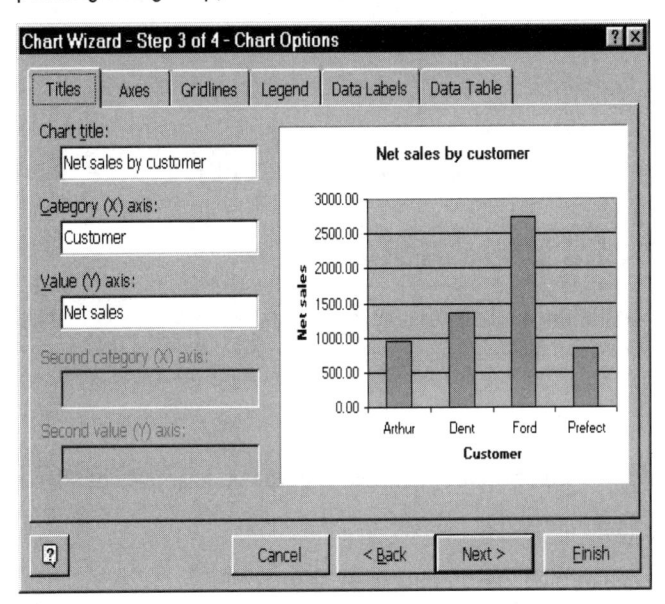

As you can see, there are other index tabs available. You can see the effect of selecting or deselecting each one in **preview** - experiment with these options as you like then click Next.

Step 6 The final step is to choose whether you want the chart to appear on the same worksheet as the data or on a separate sheet of its own. This is a matter of personal preference – for this example choose to place the chart as an object within the existing spreadsheet.

PART A   SPREADSHEETS

7.2 Changing existing charts

Even after your chart is 'finished' you may change it in a variety of ways.

(a) You can **resize it** simply by selecting it and dragging out its borders.

(b) You can change **each element** by **double clicking** on it then selecting from the options available.

(c) You could also select any item of **text** and alter the wording, size or font, or change the **colours** used.

(d) In the following illustration, the user has double-clicked on the Y axis to enable them to **change the scale**.

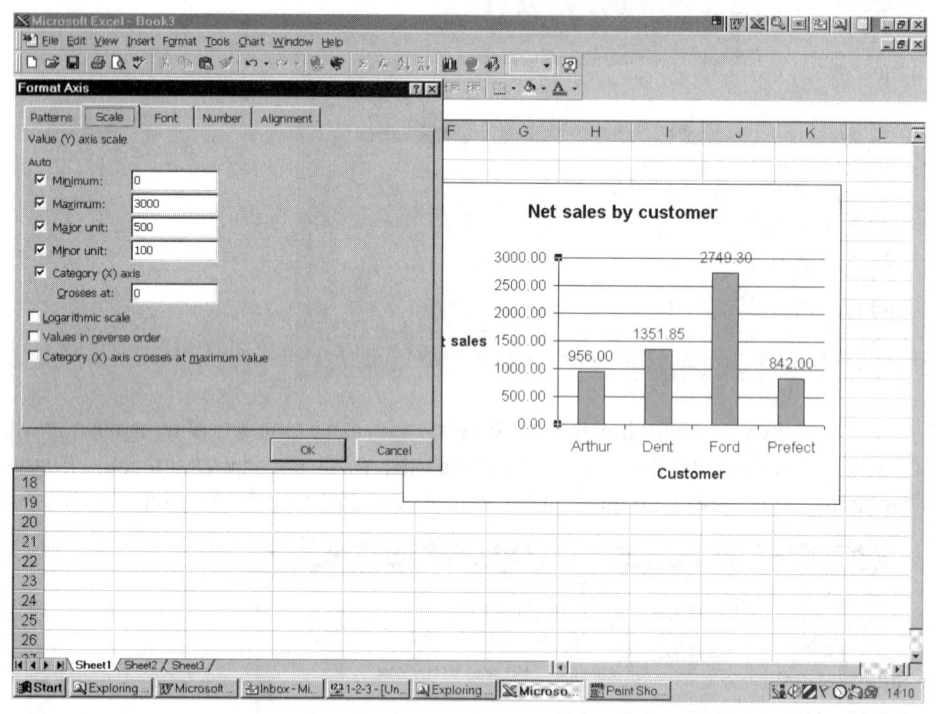

8 Spreadsheet format and appearance

Good presentation can help people understand the contents of a spreadsheet.

8.1 Titles and labels

A spreadsheet should be headed up with a title which **clearly defines its purpose**. Examples of titles are follows.

(a) Trading, profit and loss account for the year ended 30 June 200X.

(b) (i) Area A: Sales forecast for the three months to 31 March 200X.
    (ii) Area B: Sales forecast for the three months to 31 March 200X.
    (iii) Combined sales forecast for the three months to 31 March 200X.

(c) Salesmen: Analysis of earnings and commission for the six months ended 30 June 200X.

Row and **column** headings (or labels) should clearly identify the contents of the row/column. Any assumptions made that have influenced the spreadsheet contents should be clearly stated.

8.2 Formatting

There are a wide range of options available under the **Format** menu. Some of these functions may also be accessed through toolbar **buttons**. Formatting options include the ability to:

(a) Add **shading** or **borders** to cells.

(b) Use **different sizes of text** and different **fonts**.

(c) Choose from a range of options for presenting values, for example to present a number as a **percentage** (eg 0.05 as 5%), or with commas every third digit, or to a specified number of **decimal places** etc.

Experiment with the various formatting options yourself.

8.2.1 Formatting numbers

Most spreadsheet programs contain facilities for presenting numbers in a particular way. In Excel you simply click on **Format** and then **Cells** ...to reach these options.

(a) **Fixed format** displays the number in the cell rounded off to the number of decimal places you select.

(b) **Currency format** displays the number with a '£' in front, with commas and not more than two decimal places, eg £10,540.23.

(c) **Comma format** is the same as currency format except that the numbers are displayed without the '£'.

(d) **General format** is the format assumed unless another format is specified. In general format the number is displayed with no commas and with as many decimal places as entered or calculated that fit in the cell.

(e) **Percent format** multiplies the number in the display by 100 and follows it with a percentage sign. For example the number 0.548 in a cell would be displayed as 54.8%.

(f) **Hidden format** is a facility by which values can be entered into cells and used in calculations but are not actually displayed on the spreadsheet. The format is useful for hiding sensitive information.

8.3 Gridlines

One of the options available under the **Tools**, **Options** menu, on the **View** tab, is an option to remove the gridlines from your spreadsheet.

Compare the following two versions of the same spreadsheet. Note how the formatting applied to the second version has improved the spreadsheet presentation.

	A	B	C	D	E	F
1	Sales team salaries and commissions - 200X					
2	Name	Sales	Salary	Commi	Total earnings	
3		£	£	£	£	
4	Northingto	284000	14000	5680	19680	
5	Souther	193000	14000	3860	17860	
6	Weston	12000	14000	240	14240	
7	Easterman	152000	14000	3040	17040	
8						
9	Total	641000	56000	12820	68820	
10						

	A	B	C	D	E
1	Sales team salaries and commissions - 200X				
2	Name	Sales	Salary	Commission	Total earnings
3		£	£	£	£
4	Northington	284,000	14,000	5,680	19,680
5	Souther	193,000	14,000	3,860	17,860
6	Weston	12,000	14,000	240	14,240
7	Easterman	152,000	14,000	3,040	17,040
8					
9	Total	641,000	56,000	12,820	68,820
10					

8.4 Rounding errors

The ability to display numbers in a variety of formats (eg to no decimal places) can result in a situation whereby totals that are correct may actually look incorrect.

Example: Rounding errors

The following example shows how apparent rounding errors can arise.

	A	B	C	D
1	*Petty cash*			
2	*Week ended 16 August 200X*			
3		£		
4	Opening balance	231		
5	Receipts	33		
6	Payments	-105		
7	Closing balance	160		
8				

	A	B	C	D
1	*Petty cash*			
2	*Week ended 16 August 200X*			
3		£		
4	Opening balance	231.34		
5	Receipts	32.99		
6	Payments	(104.67)		
7	Closing balance	159.66		
8				

Cell B7 contains the formula =SUM(B4:B6). The spreadsheet on the left shows that 231 + 33 - 105 is equal to 160, which is not true (check it). The **reason for the discrepancy** is that both spreadsheets actually contain the values shown in the spreadsheet on the right.

However, the spreadsheet on the left has been formatted to display numbers with **no decimal places**. So, individual numbers display as the nearest whole number, although the actual value held by the spreadsheet and used in calculations includes the decimals.

Solution

One solution, that will prevent the appearance of apparent errors, is to use the **ROUND function.** The ROUND function has the following structure: ROUND (value, places). 'Value' is the value to be rounded. 'Places' is the number of places to which the value is to be rounded.

The difference between using the ROUND function and formatting a value to a number of decimal places is that using the ROUND function actually **changes** the **value**, while formatting only changes the **appearance** of the value.

In the example above, the ROUND function could be used as follows. The following formulae could be inserted in cells C4 to C7.

C4 = ROUND(B4,0)   C5 = ROUND(B5,0)   C6 = ROUND(B6,0)   C7 = SUM(C4:C6)

Column B could then be hidden by highlighting the whole column (by clicking on the B at the top of the column), then selecting Format, Column, Hide from the main menu. Try this for yourself, hands-on.

Note that using the ROUND function to eliminate decimals results in slightly inaccurate calculation totals (in our example 160 is actually 'more correct' than the 159 obtained using ROUND. For this reason, some people prefer not to use the function, and to make users of the spreadsheet aware that small apparent differences are due to rounding.

9 Other issues: printing; controls; using spreadsheets with word processing software

9.1 Printing spreadsheets

The print options for your spreadsheet may be accessed by selecting **File** and then **Page Setup**. The various Tabs contain a range of options. You specify the area of the spreadsheet to be printed in the Print area box on the Sheet tab. Other options include the ability to repeat headings on all pages and the option to print gridlines if required (normally they wouldn't be!)

Experiment with these options including the options available under Header/Footer.

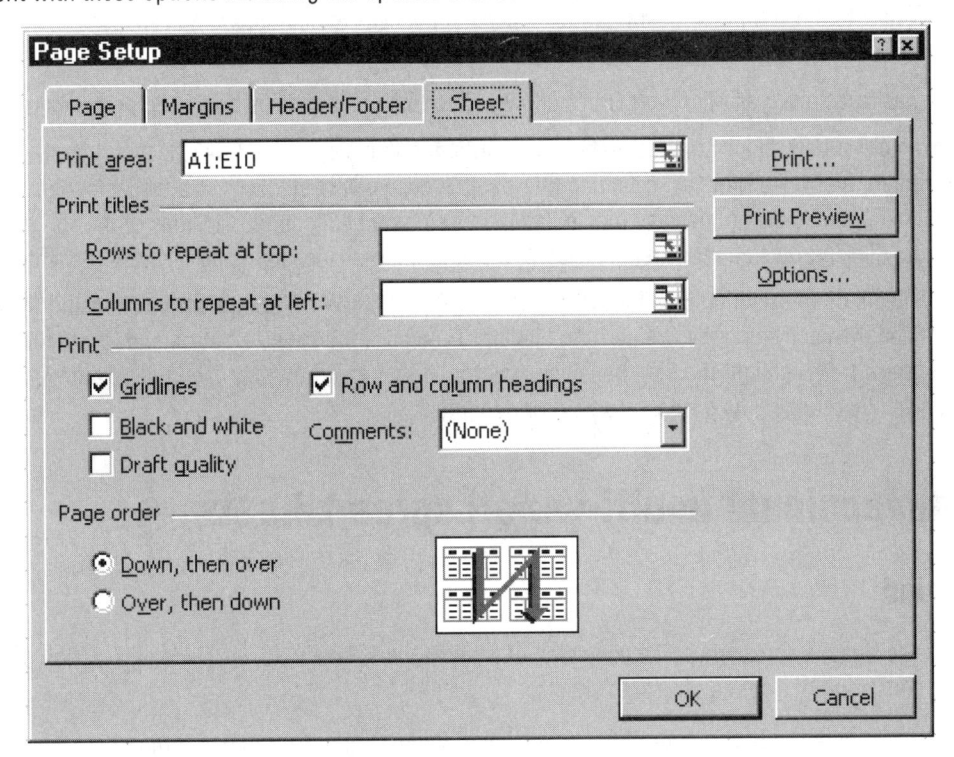

9.2 Controls

There are facilities available in spreadsheet packages which can be used as controls – to prevent unauthorised or accidental amendment or deletion of all or part of a spreadsheet.

(a) **Saving** and **back-up**. When working on a spreadsheet, save your file regularly, as often as every ten minutes. This will prevent too much work being lost in the advent of a system crash. Spreadsheet files should be included in standard back-up procedures.

(b) **Cell protection**. This prevents the user from inadvertently changing or erasing cells that should not be changed. Look up how to protect cells using Excel's Help facility. (Select Help from the main menu within Excel, then select Contents and Index, click on the Find tab and enter the words 'cell protection'.)

PART A   SPREADSHEETS

(c) **Passwords.** You can set a password for any spreadsheet that you create. In Excel, simply click on **Tools,** then on **Protection,** then on **Protect Sheet** or **Protect Workbook**, as appropriate.

9.3 Using spreadsheets with word processing software

There may be a situation where you wish to incorporate the contents of all or part of a spreadsheet into a **word processed report**. There are a number of options available to achieve this.

(a) The simplest, but least professional option, is to **print out** the spreadsheet and interleave the page or pages at the appropriate point in your word processed document.

(b) A neater option if you are just including a small table is to select and **copy** the relevant cells from the spreadsheet to the computer's clipboard by selecting the cells and choosing Edit, Copy. Then switch to the word processing document, and **paste** them in at the appropriate point.

(c) Office packages, such as Microsoft Office allow you to **link** spreadsheets and word processing files.

For example, a new, blank spreadsheet can be '**embedded**' in a document by selecting Insert, Object then, from within the Create New tab, selecting Microsoft Excel worksheet. The spreadsheet is then available to be worked upon, allowing the easy manipulation of numbers using all the facilities of the spreadsheet package. Clicking outside the spreadsheet will result in the spreadsheet being inserted in the document.

The contents of an existing spreadsheet may be inserted into a Word document by choosing Insert, Object and then activating the Create from File tab. Then click the Browse button and locate the spreadsheet file. Highlight the file, then click Insert, and then OK. You may then need to move and resize the object, by dragging its borders, to fit your document.

10 Three dimensional (multi-sheet) spreadsheets

10.1 Background

In early spreadsheet packages, a spreadsheet file consisted of a single worksheet. Excel provides the option of multi-sheet spreadsheets, consisting of a series of related sheets.

For example, suppose you were producing a profit forecast for two regions, and a combined forecast for the total of the regions. This situation would be suited to using separate worksheets for each region and another for the total. This approach is sometimes referred to as working in **three dimensions**, as you are able to flip between different sheets stacked in front or behind each other. Cells in one sheet may **refer** to cells in another sheet. So, in our example, the formulae in the cells in the total sheet would refer to the cells in the other sheets.

Excel has a series of 'tabs', one for each worksheet at the foot of the spreadsheet.

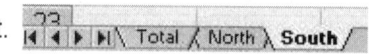

10.2 How many sheets?

Excel can be set up so that it always opens a fresh file with a certain number of worksheets ready and waiting for you. Click on **Tools ... Options** ... and then the **General** tab and set the number *Sheets in new workbook* option to the number you would like each new spreadsheet file to contain (sheets may be added or deleted later).

If you subsequently want to insert more sheets you just **right click** on the index tab after which you want the new sheet to be inserted and choose **Insert** ... and then **Worksheet**. By default sheets are called **Sheet 1, Sheet 2** etc. However, these may be changed. To **rename** a sheet in **Excel, right click** on its index tab and choose the rename option.

10.3 Pasting from one sheet to another

When building a spreadsheet that will contain a number of worksheets with identical structure, users often set up one sheet, then copy that sheet and amend the sheet contents. [To copy a worksheet in Excel, from within the worksheet you wish to copy, select Edit, Move or Copy sheet, and tick the Create a copy box.] A 'Total' sheet would use the same structure, but would contain formulae totalling the individual sheets.

10.4 Linking sheets with formulae

Formulae on one sheet may refer to data held on another sheet. The links within such a formula may be established using the following steps.

Step 1 In the cell that you want to refer to a cell from another sheet, type =.

Step 2 Click on the index tab for the sheet containing the cell you want to refer to and select the cell in question.

Step 3 Press Enter or Return.

Example: Formulae linking sheets

Start with a blank spreadsheet and ensure that it contains at least two sheets.

Type the number 1,746, 243 in cell A1 of the first sheet. Then select the tab for the second sheet and select A1 in that sheet (this is step 1 from the three steps above). Type =. Follow steps 2 and 3 above. The same number will display in cell A1 of both sheets. However, what is actually contained in cell A1 of the second sheet is the formula =**Sheet1!A1**

Cell A1 in the second sheet is now linked to cell A1 in the first sheet. This method may be used regardless of the cell addresses - the two cells **do not have to be in the same place** in their respective sheets. For instance cell Z658 of one sheet could refer to cell P24 of another. If you **move cells** or insert **extra rows** or columns on the sheet with the original numbers the cell references on the other sheet will **change automatically**.

10.5 Uses for multi-sheet spreadsheets

There are a wide range of situations suited to the multi-sheet approach. A variety of possible uses follow.

(a) A model could use one sheet for variables, a second for calculations, and a third for outputs.

(b) To enable quick and easy **consolidation** of similar sets of data, for example the financial results of two subsidiaries or the budgets of two departments.

(c) To provide **different views** of the same data. For instance you could have one sheet of data sorted in product code order and another sorted in product name order.

PART A SPREADSHEETS

Key learning points

- ☑ A **spreadsheet** is basically an electronic piece of paper divided into **rows** and **columns**. The intersection of a row and a column is known as a **cell**.
- ☑ Essential basic **skills** include how to **move around** within a spreadsheet, how to **enter** and **edit** data, how to **fill** cells, how to **insert** and **delete** columns and rows and how to improve the basic **layout** and **appearance** of a spreadsheet.
- ☑ **Relative** cell references (B3) change when you copy formulae to other locations or move data from one place to another. **Absolute** cell references ($B$3) stay the same.
- ☑ A wide range of **formulae** and functions are available within Excel. We looked at the use of conditional formulae that use an **IF** statement.
- ☑ A spreadsheet should be given a **title** which clearly defines its purpose. The contents of rows and columns should also be clearly **labelled**. **Formatting** should be used to make the data held in the spreadsheet easy to read and interpret.
- ☑ **Numbers** can be **formatted** in several ways, for instance with commas, as percentages, as currency or with a certain number of decimal places. **Rounding** differences may need to be dealt with.
- ☑ Excel includes the facility to produce a range of charts and graphs. The **Chart Wizard** provides a tool to simplify the process of chart construction.
- ☑ Spreadsheets can be **linked** to and exchange data with **word processing documents** - and vice versa.
- ☑ **Backing-up** is a key security measure. You can also use cell protection and **passwords** to prevent unauthorised access (these areas are covered in Unit 21).
- ☑ Spreadsheet packages permit the user to work with **multiple sheets** that refer to each other. This is sometimes referred to a three dimensional spreadsheet.
- ☑ Spreadsheets can be used in a variety of accounting contexts. You should practise using spreadsheets, **hands-on experience** is the key to spreadsheet proficiency.

Quick quiz

1. List three types of cell contents.
2. What do the F5 and F2 keys do in Excel?
3. What technique can you use to insert a logical series of data such as 1, 2 .... 10, or Jan, Feb, March etc?
4. How do you display formulae instead of the results of formulae in a spreadsheet?
5. List five possible changes that may improve the appearance of a spreadsheet.
6. What formula would be used in a worksheet named Calculations to refer to cell A5 in a sheet named Variables?
7. List three possible uses for a multi-sheet (3D) spreadsheet.

Answers to quick quiz

1. Text, values or formulae.
2. F5 opens a GoTo dialogue box which is useful for navigating around large spreadsheets. F2 puts the active cell into edit mode.
3. You can use the technique of 'filling' - selecting the first few items of a series and dragging the lower right corner of the selection in the appropriate direction.
4. Select Tools, Options, ensure the View tab is active then tick the Formulas box within the window options area.
5. Removing gridlines, adding shading, adding borders, using different fonts and font sizes, presenting numbers as percentages or currency or to a certain number of decimal places.
6. =Variables!A5 (you would not need to type this, you would enter = in the cell you wish the value to display, then navigate using the mouse to cell A5 in the sheet named Variables and hit Enter).
7. The construction of a spreadsheet model with separate Input, Calculation and Output sheets. They can help consolidate data from different sources. They can offer different views of the same data.

PART A SPREADSHEETS

Activity checklist

This checklist shows which knowledge and understanding point is covered by each activity in this chapter. Tick off each activity as you complete it.

Activity		
1.1	☐	Knowledge and Understanding: Methods of analysing information in spreadsheets
1.2	☐	Knowledge and Understanding: Methods of analysing information in spreadsheets
1.3	☐	Knowledge and Understanding: Methods of analysing information in spreadsheets
1.4	☐	Knowledge and Understanding: Methods of analysing information in spreadsheets

PART B

Using accounting software

chapter 2

Introducing the case study

Contents

1 Introduction
2 Using Sage
3 Loading the data for assignments
4 Account reference codes
5 The nominal ledger (or 'main ledger')
6 Using the Word and Excel files
7 Conclusion

Range statement
Relevant computerised records
Computerised records
Computerised ledgers

Knowledge and understanding
Operation of computerised accounting systems

PART B   USING ACCOUNTING SOFTWARE

1 Introduction

Sage is a 'user-friendly' software package and is designed to help you as much as possible. This first section describes some important features of the software.

2 Using Sage

2.1 Setting up and using Sage for the first time

To install Sage, follow the instructions Sage provide with the installation CD. When accessing the software for the first time, recent versions include an option to 'Restore a back-up'. You should select this option and restore 'Assignment 1' from the relevant folder on the CD that accompanies this book. Refer to Section 3 of this chapter.

When accessing older versions of Sage Line 50 or Sage Instant for the first time, choose the following options (these options may differ slightly depending upon the version):

- Create a **new** company or a new set of data files
- General Business – **Standard** chart of accounts
- If asked, enter the serial number and activation code sent to you by Sage with their software
- The **Company Details** you enter does not matter, as when you load one of the Assignments the correct Blitz company details and chart of accounts will overwrite existing data. But, for the record, the Blitz Company details are shown below.

  Blitz Limited
  25 Apple Road
  London
  N12 3PP

- **Financial Year** – starts in August 2000 (the case study is set in 2000 and 2001)
- If prompted to enter your **Serial Number** and **Activation Key** these are shown on the Invoice/Packing slip sent with your Sage software
- All other options can be ignored (ie by clicking on **Next** or on **Finish**)

Click on the Start button and search through the menus until you find Sage. Alternatively there may be an **icon** on the 'desktop'. If so, just **double-click** on it. The software *may* have been set up by your college so that you have to enter a password before you can get into the package. BPP **do not recommend this** for the Blitz case study.

If you will be using the case study data on a network, please consult the IT department of your organisation (the Sage data provided on CD may be copied to a network location and accessed from there). Check with your tutor how you are required to access Sage - the procedure may differ from that described above.

Activity 2.1

Make sure that you are aware of how to access the Sage software you will be using.

2: INTRODUCING THE CASE STUDY

Once you have gained access to the package, the **appearance** of the **Sage screen** you see **depends** on the **version** you are using and settings selected within the software. The first illustration below shows Line 50 **version 11**. If you are using an earlier version, the Task bar will not be available, and you may not see some of the icons shown, such as Period End and E-mail.

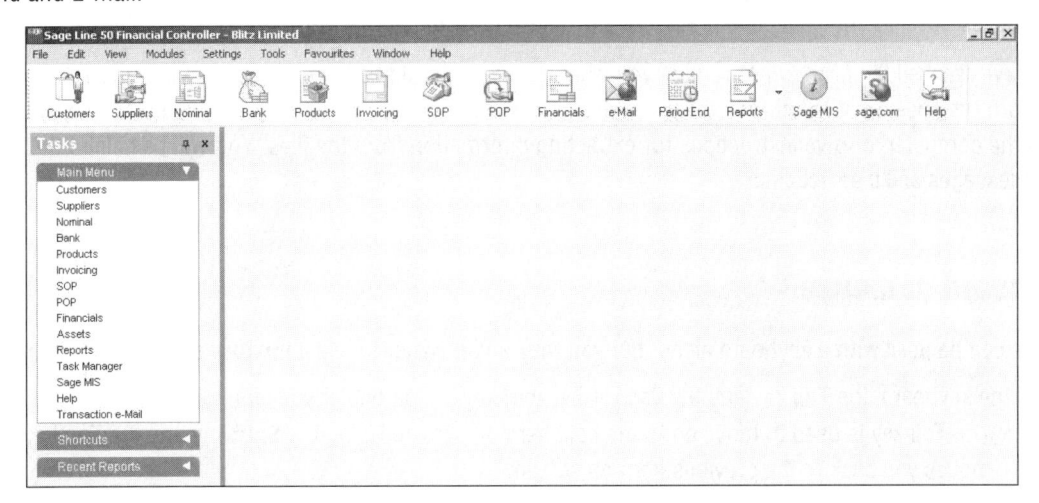

[Screenshot of Sage Line 50 Financial Controller - Blitz Limited, showing the main menu with Tasks panel on the left listing Customers, Suppliers, Nominal, Bank, Products, Invoicing, SOP, POP, Financials, Assets, Reports, Task Manager, Sage MIS, Help, Transaction e-Mail.]

Later versions have icons for **accessing different modules in the bottom left of the screen**. These also include the option to **Change View** (to a *Dashboard* or *Process* view).

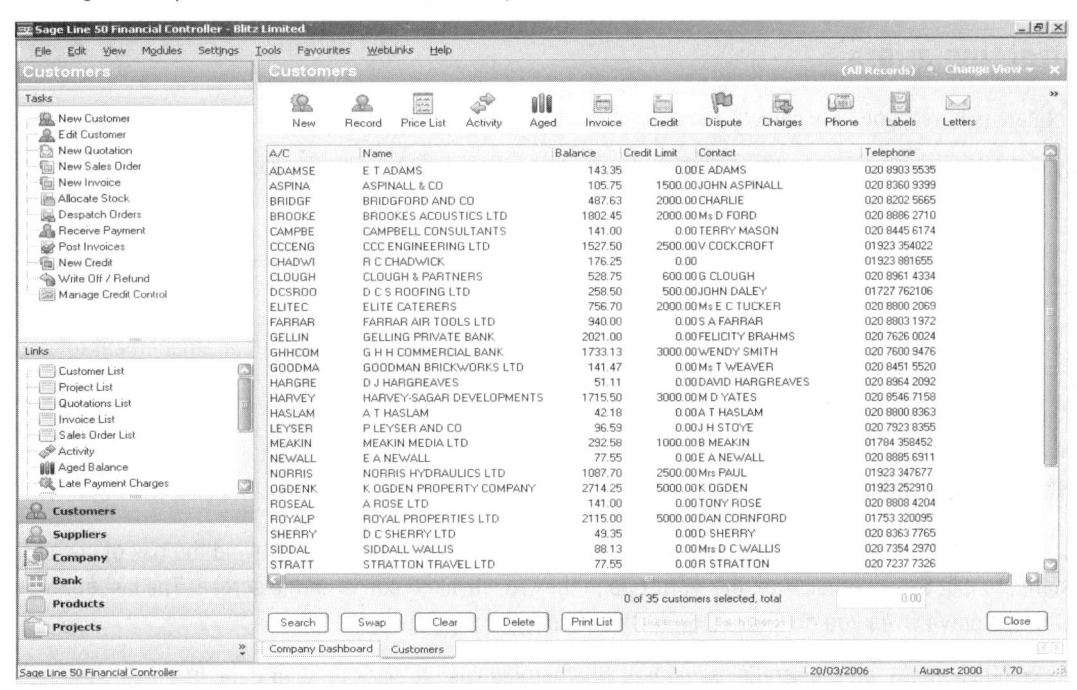

[Screenshot of Sage Line 50 Customers screen showing customer list with columns A/C, Name, Balance, Credit Limit, Contact, Telephone. Includes customers such as ADAMSE, ASPINA, BRIDGF, BROOKE, CAMPBE, CCCENG, CHADWI, CLOUGH, DCSROO, ELITEC, FARRAR, GELLIN, GHHCOM, GOODMA, HARGRE, HARVEY, HASLAM, LEYSER, MEAKIN, NEWALL, NORRIS, OGDENK, ROSEAL, ROYALP, SHERRY, SIDDAL, STRATT.]

The way you chose to view Sage and to access individual modules (Customers, Suppliers etc), and whether you use other options such as the Task bar, **does not really matter**. These different views and features simply provide different ways of accessing the functions available within Sage.

However, when using this book, to ensure you understand the illustrations provided we recommend you use the standard view rather than the *Dashboard* or *Process* views.

2.2 Buttons, icons and the task bar

To access the part of Sage required for a particular task you click on the appropriate 'button' or 'icon'. When you click on a button a further window will then appear, specifying more detailed areas of work within your initial selection. The selection process goes on until you have reached the program or 'routine' that you wish to use.

When you have reached the program or routine you want to use, it should be fairly clear, from instructions on the screen or from the position of the cursor, what you are expected to do next. You might, for example, enter transaction details into the computer, or give instructions for extracting information from the files. You will be helped throughout by on-screen messages and instructions.

2.3 Keyboard or mouse?

The package can be used with a keyboard alone, but you may find it easier to use a **mixture** of keyboard and mouse.

When using the keyboard, the **Tab** key and the **Esc** (or Escape) key are particularly useful.

(a) The **Tab** key is used to move on to the next item on screen. Using the **Shift** key and the **Tab** key together moves you back to the previous item on screen.

(b) The Escape key (**Esc**) can be used to close the current window and move back to the previous window.

2.4 Correcting errors

If incorrect data is keyed, you may correct it in a number of ways.

(a) If an error is spotted while still keying, wipe out the incorrect data using the **delete** key.

(b) If an error occurs whilst you are entering a transaction record, and you spot the mistake before the transaction is saved or posted, you can alter the details or cancel the transaction entirely and start again, using the **Discard** option.

(c) If errors are spotted much later, you will need to make an appropriate input or amendment to correct the error. This is covered in a later chapter.

2.5 Exiting from Sage

When you have finished working on Sage, you should exit from the system properly, to avoid the risk of corrupting data in the system. To exit Sage, you click on the word **File** in the top left-hand corner of the screen. The last option on the menu that drops down when you do this is **Exit**. Click on this word.

A message will then appear on the screen asking you whether you wish to back up your data. In a 'live' system, you would back data up at regular intervals – probably daily. In a training system, your course supervisor might instruct you to select No. If you choose No (by clicking on the No button or pressing N) you will exit from Sage, and you will be returned to the Windows desktop screen.

When you start doing the assignments in this book you may well want to make a copy of your work. Procedures for **backing up** and **restoring** data are described later in this chapter.

2.6 The Blitz case study

The assignments in this workbook are based on a case study of a fictional North London company, Blitz Limited. The **case study is set in late 2000 and early 2001**. Blitz Limited was established in August 2000 by two friends, Maria Green and Tim Nicholas. Each has put £20,000 into the company, and they are worker-directors.

The company provides cleaning services. Much of its business comes from office cleaning and other contract cleaning services (such as factory cleaning). However, the company also provides window cleaning services for businesses and domestic cleaning services for private individuals.

2.6.1 When does the case study begin?

The case study begins in October 2000. Blitz has had a fairly busy September, receiving 27 invoices from various suppliers and has issued 35 invoices to customers. Apart from payments of wages and salaries, there were no cash transactions in September, and all invoices are as yet unpaid.

At the beginning of October 2000, Blitz Limited has 27 supplier accounts on its purchase ledger and 35 customer accounts on its sales ledger.

3 Loading the data for assignments

In this section we explain how to use the Sage data contained on the CD that accompanies this Text. You **do not need to load the data while reading this section**. The instructions provided later in this book, at the start of each assignment, tell you when to load the data.

Blitz is the name of the fictional company on which the case study in this book is based. The CD contains data files to be used with either Sage Line 50 (now called Sage 50) or Sage Instant. To use this data **you need to have access to Sage software**.

The data is held on the CD in standard **Line 50** (now **Sage 50**) and **Instant** back-up files. Each back-up file is named in a way intended to identify the assignment it relates to.

> You will be asked to **load Assignment data while working through Chapters 2-8**. This serves two purposes; it gives you practice loading Assignment data and it enables us to explain Sage functions using 'real' data.
>
> **The Assignments themselves do not start until you reach Part C of this book**. When starting an Assignment you will be asked to load a fresh copy of the data so previous changes will not affect your performance in the Assignment.

PART B   USING ACCOUNTING SOFTWARE

3.1 Loading the Sage data

The latest version of Sage **Line 50** (at the time of publication) is version 14, which is also known as **Sage 50 2008**. The CD includes data in 2008 format. As many users are still using older versions, the CD also includes data in versions 10, 11, 12 and 13 (2007).

The latest version of Sage **Instant Accounts** (at the time of publication) is version 14 (2008). Previous versions were numbered 10, 11 and 12. The CD includes data in versions 10, 11, 12 and 14 (2008).

When working through the remainder of this book you will come across instructions such as 'load the data for Assignment 1'. Whenever you are instructed to load an Assignment in this book you should follow the following steps.

Step 1   Ensure the CD is in your CD-ROM drive (you will not see anything happen after inserting the CD – it is not designed to auto-run).

Step 2   Start Sage Line 50 or Sage Instant Accounts. If you do not know which version of Sage you have, start Sage then select Help, About from the Main Menu. The version number should then display – ignore any 'decimals' eg version 14.0.12.153 is version 14, which is also referred to as version 2008.

Step 3   From the Sage main menu select File, Restore. If you're using version 14 (2008), after answering *Yes* to the '*Do you wish to close all other windows*' question, you will be presented with a *Restore company* window. Click '*Browse*' and you will see the '*Open*' box shown below. If you're using an earlier version of Sage you will see a '*Restore*' box with similar options. Regardless of the version you are using, navigate to the CD contents by selecting the letter of your CD-ROM drive (eg drive D in the example below).

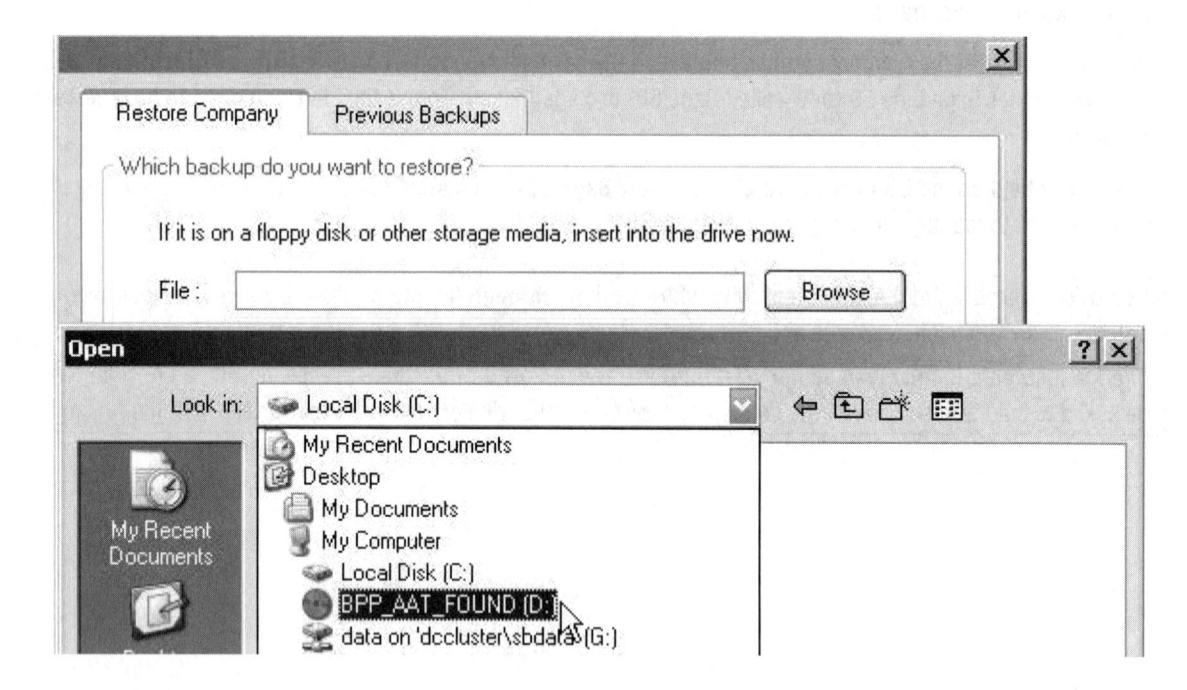

Step 4 After selecting your CD-ROM drive, you should see the contents of the CD, as shown below.

Double-click the folder that relates to the Sage software you are using. For example;

If you are using Instant Accounts version 12 double click **instantdata_ver12**

If you are using Instant Accounts version 14 double click **instantdata_ver14**

If you are using Line 50 version 13 (2007) double click **line50data_ver2007**

If you are using Line 50 version 14 (Sage 50 2008) double click **line50data_ver2008**

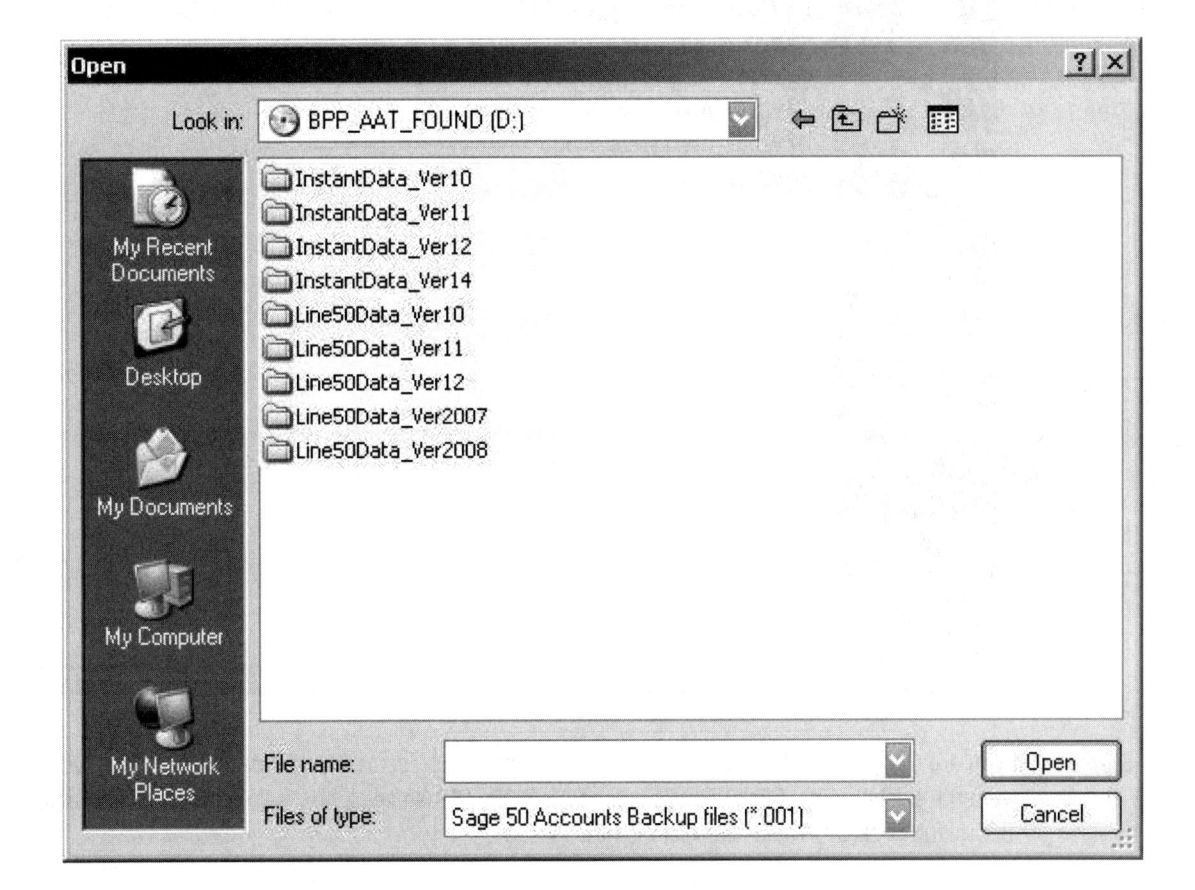

PART B USING ACCOUNTING SOFTWARE

Step 5 We now need to choose the Assignment to restore. The Assignment number is the number before the dot. For example, if we are using Line 50 version 2007 and we wish to load Assignment 3 we would click once on v2007_assignment_3.001 to highlight it, and then click on Open, and then on OK.

Step 6 If you are using a recent version of Sage, you will then be presented with a warning that the Restore will overwrite existing data. Click Yes to proceed. You should then see a box telling you the Restore has been successful. Click OK. The assignment is now loaded.

3.2 Overwriting Blitz data

Every time you restore an Assignment a fresh copy of the data is loaded. The program overwrites any data that was there previously, so you can, for example:

(a) Load Assignment 1 and make any entries you like, even if they are complete nonsense, and then load Assignment 1 again to get a fresh clean version. In other words you can *experiment with the data* as much as you like.

(b) Load Assignment 1, then load Assignment 2. Restoring Assignment 2 will overwrite the data for Assignment 1 and replace it with the data for Assignment 2.

3.3 Backing up and restoring data using Sage

As explained earlier, the data provided on the CD in effect provides a back-up of the data for each of the assignments. If you make changes to the data and wish to save these changes, you should use Sage's back-up facility to save the data to a convenient location (eg a memory stick).

3.3.1 Backing up

Whenever you Exit, Sage offers you the chance to back up your data onto an external storage device or to another folder. You can also do this at other times by selecting **File**, **Backup** from the main menu. For the Blitz case study, to save time and disk space, users of Line50 2007 may prefer to use the advanced options available within the back-up routine to select 'Data files' only. Back-up files may be saved to portable storage devices or the hard drive.

3.3.2 Restoring data

You restore data by clicking on **File** in the main window and choosing the **Restore** option. You should then be told the Restore has been successful.

3.3.3 Check files for errors

If when you enter Sage a window like the one shown below displays, choose Yes to check files, and then click on Check Data.

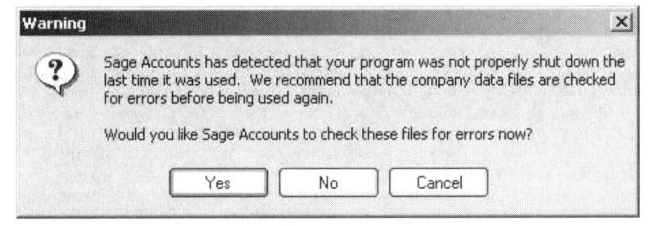

You should then be presented with one of the following two boxes.

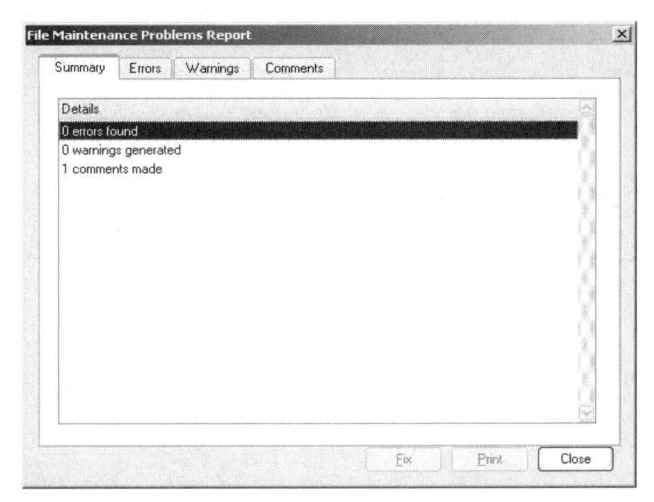

If you are presented with these options while using the data provided with this book, click OK and then Close, or on Close and then on Close again (appearance may differ slightly depending upon the version used).

PART B USING ACCOUNTING SOFTWARE

Activity 2.2

(a) Load the data for Assignment 1. Click on Suppliers. What is the code of the first supplier listed?

(b) Load the data for Assignment 2. Click on Suppliers. What is the code of the first supplier listed?

(c) Click on New and use the Supplier Record Wizard to create a new supplier record with the name and *Refn* 111111. (Leave all other details blank by clicking Next each time, then Finish.) What is the code of the first account listed now?

(d) Re-load the data for Assignment 2. Click on Suppliers. What is the code of the first supplier listed now?

3.4 Looking at the opening data

3.4.1 Suppliers ledger data

Re-load Assignment 1. Then, change the date within Sage to the timeframe when the Blitz Case study is set. To do this, from the main menu select **Settings**, **Change Program Date**. Enter 30/09/2000.

To view data in the suppliers ledger accounts, click on the **Suppliers** button in the main window or select Suppliers from the Modules option in the main menu. The following window will appear (or a similar window - depending upon the version of Sage you are using).

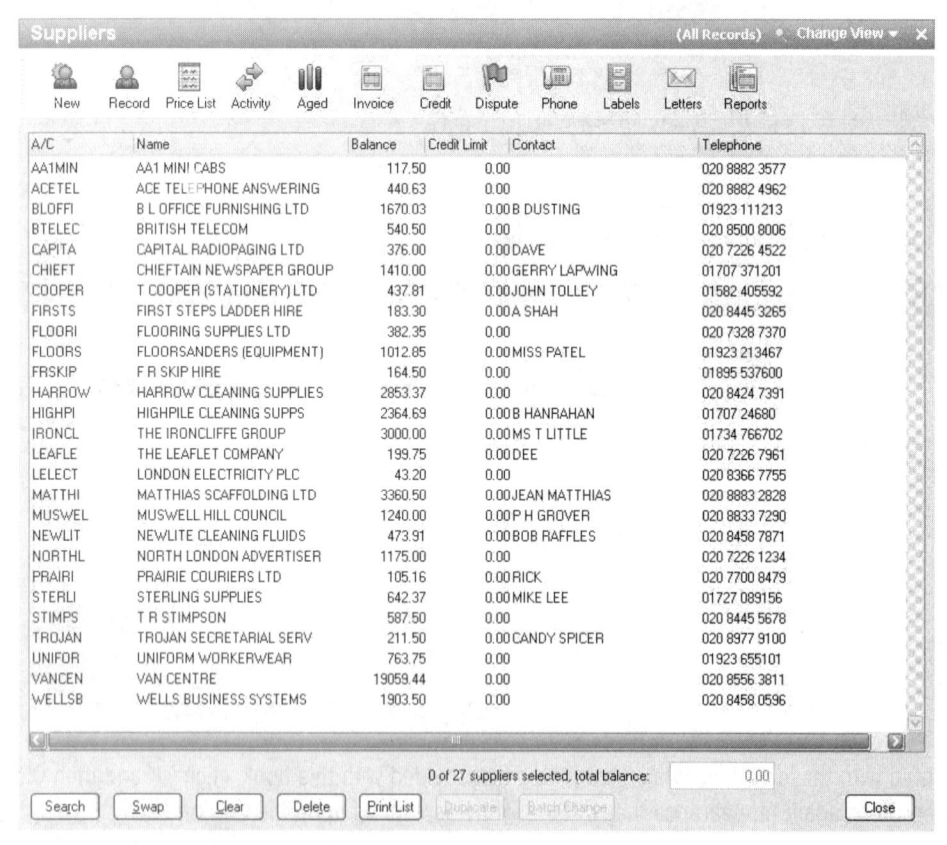

A/C	Name	Balance	Credit Limit	Contact	Telephone
AA1MIN	AA1 MINI CABS	117.50	0.00		020 8882 3577
ACETEL	ACE TELEPHONE ANSWERING	440.63	0.00		020 8882 4962
BLOFFI	B L OFFICE FURNISHING LTD	1670.03	0.00	B DUSTING	01923 111213
BTELEC	BRITISH TELECOM	540.50	0.00		020 8500 8006
CAPITA	CAPITAL RADIOPAGING LTD	376.00	0.00	DAVE	020 7226 4522
CHIEFT	CHIEFTAIN NEWSPAPER GROUP	1410.00	0.00	GERRY LAPWING	01707 371201
COOPER	T COOPER (STATIONERY) LTD	437.81	0.00	JOHN TOLLEY	01582 405592
FIRSTS	FIRST STEPS LADDER HIRE	183.30	0.00	A SHAH	020 8445 3265
FLOORI	FLOORING SUPPLIES LTD	382.35	0.00		020 7328 7370
FLOORS	FLOORSANDERS (EQUIPMENT)	1012.85	0.00	MISS PATEL	01923 213467
FRSKIP	F R SKIP HIRE	164.50	0.00		01895 537600
HARROW	HARROW CLEANING SUPPLIES	2853.37	0.00		020 8424 7391
HIGHPI	HIGHPILE CLEANING SUPPS	2364.69	0.00	B HANRAHAN	01707 24680
IRONCL	THE IRONCLIFFE GROUP	3000.00	0.00	MS T LITTLE	01734 766702
LEAFLE	THE LEAFLET COMPANY	199.75	0.00	DEE	020 7226 7961
LELECT	LONDON ELECTRICITY PLC	43.20	0.00		020 8366 7755
MATTHI	MATTHIAS SCAFFOLDING LTD	3360.50	0.00	JEAN MATTHIAS	020 8883 2828
MUSWEL	MUSWELL HILL COUNCIL	1240.00	0.00	P H GROVER	020 8833 7290
NEWLIT	NEWLITE CLEANING FLUIDS	473.91	0.00	BOB RAFFLES	020 8458 7871
NORTHL	NORTH LONDON ADVERTISER	1175.00	0.00		020 7226 1234
PRAIRI	PRAIRIE COURIERS LTD	105.16	0.00	RICK	020 7700 8479
STERLI	STERLING SUPPLIES	642.37	0.00	MIKE LEE	01727 089156
STIMPS	T R STIMPSON	587.50	0.00		020 8445 5678
TROJAN	TROJAN SECRETARIAL SERV	211.50	0.00	CANDY SPICER	020 8977 9100
UNIFOR	UNIFORM WORKERWEAR	763.75	0.00		01923 655101
VANCEN	VAN CENTRE	19059.44	0.00		020 8556 3811
WELLSB	WELLS BUSINESS SYSTEMS	1903.50	0.00		020 8458 0596

0 of 27 suppliers selected, total balance: 0.00

Still in the Suppliers window, now click on the **Aged** button. Enter 30/09/2000 in the Report date and Payments Up To boxes, and click OK. You should see the following data. Note again that the appearance of the illustrations used throughout this book may be slightly different to what you see on screen – depending upon the version of Sage you use. This does not matter – the data (account names, dates, totals etc) should be the same.

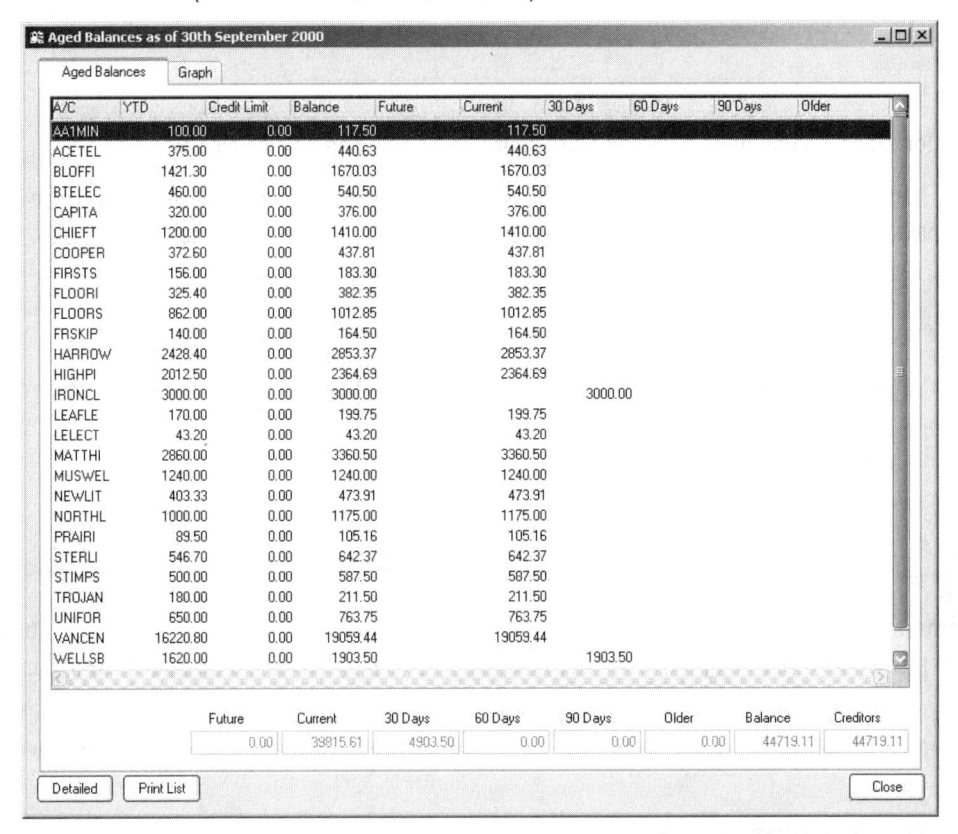

A/C	YTD	Credit Limit	Balance	Future	Current	30 Days	60 Days	90 Days	Older
AA1MIN	100.00	0.00	117.50		117.50				
ACETEL	375.00	0.00	440.63		440.63				
BLOFFI	1421.30	0.00	1670.03		1670.03				
BTELEC	460.00	0.00	540.50		540.50				
CAPITA	320.00	0.00	376.00		376.00				
CHIEFT	1200.00	0.00	1410.00		1410.00				
COOPER	372.60	0.00	437.81		437.81				
FIRSTS	156.00	0.00	183.30		183.30				
FLOORI	325.40	0.00	382.35		382.35				
FLOORS	862.00	0.00	1012.85		1012.85				
FRSKIP	140.00	0.00	164.50		164.50				
HARROW	2428.40	0.00	2853.37		2853.37				
HIGHPI	2012.50	0.00	2364.69		2364.69				
IRONCL	3000.00	0.00	3000.00				3000.00		
LEAFLE	170.00	0.00	199.75		199.75				
LELECT	43.20	0.00	43.20		43.20				
MATTHI	2860.00	0.00	3360.50		3360.50				
MUSWEL	1240.00	0.00	1240.00		1240.00				
NEWLIT	403.33	0.00	473.91		473.91				
NORTHL	1000.00	0.00	1175.00		1175.00				
PRAIRI	89.50	0.00	105.16		105.16				
STERLI	546.70	0.00	642.37		642.37				
STIMPS	500.00	0.00	587.50		587.50				
TROJAN	180.00	0.00	211.50		211.50				
UNIFOR	650.00	0.00	763.75		763.75				
VANCEN	16220.80	0.00	19059.44		19059.44				
WELLSB	1620.00	0.00	1903.50					1903.50	

	Future	Current	30 Days	60 Days	90 Days	Older	Balance	Creditors
	0.00	39815.61	4903.50	0.00	0.00	0.00	44719.11	44719.11

When you have had a look at this press the Esc key or click on **Close** to make this window disappear. Now click on the **Activity** button (next to the **Aged** button) and accept the defaults, except make the date range 01/09/2000 to 30/09/2000. Then click **OK**.

You may receive a warning stating 'Terms have not been agreed on this Account'. If you don't receive the warning carry on. If you do receive the warning just click OK – Blitz is a new company and has not yet finalised terms with suppliers.

The next screen you see shows you details of how the balance on an account is made up. To see details for another account click on the *button* at the right of the box labelled A/C. A list of all the supplier accounts will drop down. Just scroll around and *double-click* on any account name to see the activity for that account.

Alternatively, if you prefer not to use the mouse, press the function key F4. This will bring down the menu of accounts. You can use the up and down cursor keys to scroll from one account to another and press the **Enter** key when the account you want is highlighted.

3.4.2 Customers ledger data

Close the windows open within Sage by pressing the Escape key until you get back to the main window. When you get there, click on the **Customers** button.

PART B USING ACCOUNTING SOFTWARE

From the Customers window, you should then select the **Aged** button or **Activity** button and follow the same procedures as above for the Suppliers ledger. The first customer account on the file for Assignment 1, for example, is for E T ADAMS.

Alternatively, in either the Suppliers or Customers windows you can click on the Account you wish to view, then click Activity and accept the date range.

Activity 2.3

Click on the button labelled **Customers** and then on the new button that appears labelled **Record**.

Find the cursor: it should be in a box labelled A/C. Press **Tab** several times (slowly) and watch the cursor move from one box to the next. At some times it will highlight a button such as Save instead of appearing in a box.

Now experiment with the Shift + Tab combination and watch the cursor move in reverse order.

What happens if you place your mouse pointer in a particular white space on the screen and click?

Press **Esc** when you are happy that you understand the tools you have available for moving the cursor around the screen.

Activity 2.4

Click on **Customers**. If there are any customers listed note down the A/C code (eg ADAMSE) of the first one. Now click on **Record**, and type 000000 (six noughts) in the A/C box and press **Tab**. Now click on **Discard**. What happens? Then click on Close.

4 Account reference codes

The case study in this book (Blitz Limited) uses the first six significant letters (or numbers) in the supplier's or customer's name to create their code. For initials and surname, the first six significant letters are taken from the surname. If there are less than six characters in the name (and initials), the code is made up to 6 digits with Xs. Some examples follow.

Name	Account reference code
Matthias Scaffolding	MATTHI
Ace Telephone Answering	ACETEL
B L Office Supplies	BLOFFI
The Tomkinson Group	TOMKIN
R C Chadwick	CHADWI
A Wyche	WYCHEA
A Rose Ltd	ROSEAL
P Wood	WOODPX
C Fry	FRYCXX

If you select Customer or Supplier, then highlight an account and click on the Activity button you can view past transactions on an account – this is useful if a customer or supplier has an account query. Try the following Activity.

Activity 2.5

Load the data for Assignment 1, then start up Sage. A customer, Mr E A Newall, has telephoned Blitz to say he has not received an invoice for some domestic cleaning work. He would like to know how much the cost will be. Can you answer his query?

5 The nominal ledger (or 'main ledger')

Load the opening data for Assignment 1 now by following the instructions given earlier in this chapter.

IMPORTANT!

To ensure Sage is operating using the timeframe the case study is set in, you must change the program date. Close all Sage windows except the main window, then select **Settings**, **Change Program Date** from the pull-down menu. Insert the date 30/09/2000 and click OK.

Blitz Limited is using the 'default' nominal ledger account codes provided in the Sage software. The sales account codes 4000, 4001, 4002 and 4100 have been renamed. A list of the codes is given in Appendix 1 to this book.

5.1 Looking at the opening data

To produce a trial balance report showing the current Nominal ledger balances, click on the **Financials** button (or select **Financials** from within the **Modules main menu option**), then click on the **Trial** (Balance) button.

You will then be asked to choose the relevant Period and the output format for the report (the order in which these options are presented depends upon the version of Sage you are using. Choose the Period September 2000 and to preview the report on screen. Then click on **OK**. (Ensure you have changed the Program Date as explained above before running the report.)

The trial balance to the end of September follows (based on Assignment 1 data).

Date: 16/03/2004
Time: 11:28:47

Blitz Limited
Period Trial Balance

Page: 1

To Period: Month 2, September 2000

N/C	Name	Debit	Credit
0020	Plant and Machinery	5,734.50	
0030	Office Equipment	1,620.00	
0040	Furniture and Fixtures	1,421.30	
0050	Motor Vehicles	16,220.80	
1100	Debtors Control Account	22,620.43	
1200	Bank Current Account	33,946.07	
2100	Creditors Control Account		44,719.11
2200	Sales Tax Control Account		3,369.03
2201	Purchase Tax Control Account	6,022.38	
2210	P.A.Y.E.		1,370.00
3000	Ordinary Shares		40,000.00
4000	Sales Contract Cleaning		16,597.40
4001	Sales Window Cleaning		1,970.40
4002	Sales Domestic Services		683.60
5000	Materials Purchased	3,703.83	
6201	Advertising	2,200.00	
6203	P.R. (Literature & Brochures)	170.00	
7001	Directors Salaries	1,707.03	
7003	Staff Salaries	475.75	
7004	Wages - Regular	4,941.15	
7005	Wages - Casual	480.00	
7100	Rent	3,000.00	
7103	General Rates	1,240.00	
7200	Electricity	43.20	
7400	Travelling	100.00	
7500	Printing	500.00	
7501	Postage and Carriage	89.50	
7502	Telephone	1,155.00	
7504	Office Stationery	372.60	
7700	Equipment Hire	296.00	
8202	Clothing Costs	650.00	
	Totals:	**108,709.54**	**108,709.54**

Activity 2.6

Your supervisor has asked you for details of cash received into the bank account and paid from the bank account since the company was established. With assignment 1 loaded, can you provide this information using the Activity facility? The nominal ledger code for the bank account is 1200.

6 Using the Word and Excel files

The CD that accompanies this book includes a file called Word_&_Excel_exercises.exe. When you execute (run) this file, four Microsoft Word files and six Microsoft Excel files will be copied to your hard disk in a new folder called AATF. The files are used in exercises throughout this book.

To make use of the Word and Excel files you need:

- A CD-ROM drive
- Microsoft Windows (any version from 95 to Vista)
- Microsoft Excel 97 or above – to use the six spreadsheet files
- Microsoft Word 97 or above – to use the four Word documents

Microsoft Word 2007 and Microsoft Excel 2007 use a different menu structure to earlier versions. At the time of publication, Word 2007 and Excel 2007 were not widely used. For this reason, examples in this book refer to earlier versions.

The data from Word_&_Excel_exercises.exe needs to be installed on your computer's hard disk. Follow the instructions below.

6.1 Loading the Word and Excel files

To unload the files to a new folder on your hard disk (C:\AATF) follow these instructions.

6.1.1 First installation

View the CD-ROM in Windows Explorer and double-click on the Word_&_Excel_exercises.exe file. Then click on OK in the pop-up box. The files will then be extracted to your hard disk. If the screen then returns to Windows Explorer, the files have been installed on your hard disk in the folder C:\AATF.

6.1.2 File already exists

If you see a message like the one below, the data has already been installed on your computer.

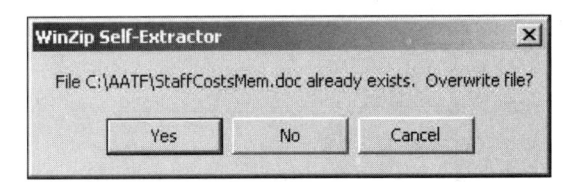

Click Yes to overwrite the file specified with a new version. Click No if you want to keep your current version of the file (for instance if you have made changes to it but saved it under its original name).

PART B USING ACCOUNTING SOFTWARE

6.1.3 What next?

If you have followed the instructions above the data has been copied into a folder on your hard drive called C:\AATF. (You may need to press the F5 key to refresh your screen before you can see this folder in Windows Explorer.)

When you view the contents of the folder C:\AATF you will see the files available for use in Word (the .doc files) or Excel (the .xls files) – as shown in the following illustration. You will be told when to use each file when working through this book.

Name	Size	Type
A2FAX.DOC	25 KB	Microsoft Word Document
A2INV.DOC	27 KB	Microsoft Word Document
A3SPRSHT.XLS	8 KB	Microsoft Excel Worksheet
A6AGED.XLS	24 KB	Microsoft Excel Worksheet
CashFcastFirstHalf2001.xls	18 KB	Microsoft Excel Worksheet
CashFcastFirstHalf2001Ans.xls	18 KB	Microsoft Excel Worksheet
DataEntryTests.xls	195 KB	Microsoft Excel Worksheet
StaffCosts.xls	16 KB	Microsoft Excel Worksheet
StaffCostsAns.doc	25 KB	Microsoft Word Document
StaffCostsMem.doc	21 KB	Microsoft Word Document

6.1.4 Using word processing software and spreadsheets

Further coverage of word processing software and spreadsheets may be found in BPP's study material for AAT Unit 4.

Introductory exercise: Using Excel and Word

Mr Tim Nicholas would like a memo giving details of total gross pay, total National Insurance, and total overall payroll cost for the month, and any differences from the previous months totals. A similar memo was prepared last month and saved in the file **StaffCostsMem.doc**.

On October 2 2000, Mr Nicholas handed you the following information and asked you to prepare the memo.

Month 2

	Total Gross	Employers Nat. Ins.
1 T. NICHOLAS	3,000.00	300.00
2 S. LYNCH	2,125.00	212.50
3 A. PATEL	1,650.00	165.20
4 J. ESCOTT	1,500.00	150.00
5 A. CROPPER	850.00	59.64
6 A. VAUGHAN	875.00	61.32
7 K. KNIGHT	900.00	63.00
8 L. LEROY	1,083.33	108.40
9 L. BROWN	1,100.00	110.00
10 M. KORETZ	1,083.33	108.40
11 N. PARKER	1,083.33	108.40
12 G. TURNER	0.00	0.00
13 M. KOTHARI	1,067.00	106.90
14 N. FAROUK	968.00	97.00
15 L. FARROW	927.00	86.73
16 E. PARKINSON	182.00	0.00
17 N. HAZELWOOD	1,350.00	135.20
18 C. STANLEY	1069.00	107.10
19 S. BABCOCK	983.33	63.28
20 D. COOMBES	1,150.00	60.48

Unload the Word and Excel exercises the folder AATF on your hard disk if you have not already done so.

Open the file **StaffCostsMem.doc** with your word processor and **StaffCosts.xls** with your spreadsheet package. Save each file with a different name (eg Staffcosts_Sep2000....).

(a) Using **StaffCosts.xls,** enter this month's figures and details in the appropriate columns. The totals will be calculated automatically.

(b) Copy the spreadsheet into the memo and make any other changes that you think are appropriate.

Hint: Highlight the relevant cells in the spreadsheet and click on **Edit**, **Copy**. Then switch to the memo in Word, place the cursor where you would like the figures to appear and click **Edit**, **Paste**.

(c) If possible, print out a copy of the memo.

Solution to introductory exercise

A suggested solution can be found in the file **StaffCostsAns.doc**.

7 Conclusion

7.1 You should now be able to do the following

(a) Use the BPP CD-ROM to load data for the Assignments.

(b) Refer to individual accounts in the Suppliers ledger, Customers ledger or Nominal ledger in order to answer queries about transactions in the account.

(c) Produce a Trial Balance.

(d) Key in data fairly quickly and (more importantly) accurately. If you require practice using the keyboard, try the exercises contained in the Excel file **DataEntryTests.xls** – if you have installed the Word and Excel files as instructed earlier in this chapter this file will be in the C:\AATF folder on your hard disk.

Key learning points

- ☑ We have looked at some important features associated with **modern accounting software** – we use Sage as an example.
- ☑ The assignments in this book are based on a **case study** of a fictional North London company called 'Blitz Limited'. The case study is set in late 2000 and early 2001.
- ☑ Every time you restore an Assignment from within Sage, using the data provided on the CD that accompanies this book, a **fresh copy of the ledger** as it exists before the Assignment begins is loaded. The program overwrites any data that was there previously.

Quick quiz

1. How do you exit from Sage?
2. What does the F4 key do within Sage?
3. What method does Blitz Limited use to devise customer and supplier account codes?
4. What range of accounts make up the Sales accounts in the Blitz nominal ledger?
5. How do you print a trial balance from Sage?

Answers to quick quiz

1. By selecting File (from in the top left-hand corner of the screen) and then selecting Exit.
2. If you are within a field that requires an entry from a list (eg an account number), the F4 key will show the list of possible entries (eg all existing account numbers).
3. Blitz Limited uses the first six significant letters (or numbers) in the supplier's or customer's name to create their code.
4. Blitz uses the nominal ledger account codes provided in the Sage software. Sales account codes start at 4000 and end at 4905 (a full list of the codes is given in Appendix 1 to this book).
5. By selecting the Financials button from the main menu, then the Trial (Balance) button. You then choose the appropriate accounting period.

PART B USING ACCOUNTING SOFTWARE

Activity checklist

This checklist shows which knowledge and understanding point is covered by each activity in this chapter. Tick off each activity as you complete it.

Activity

2.1	☐	Knowledge and Understanding: Operation of computerised accounting systems
2.2	☐	Knowledge and Understanding: Operation of computerised accounting systems
2.3	☐	Knowledge and Understanding: Operation of computerised accounting systems
2.5	☐	Knowledge and Understanding: Operation of computerised accounting systems
2.5	☐	Knowledge and Understanding: Operation of computerised accounting systems
2.6	☐	Knowledge and Understanding: Operation of computerised accounting systems

chapter 3

Supplier invoices and credit notes

Contents

1. Introduction
2. Suppliers
3. Supplier details
4. Entering details of invoices received
5. Entering details of credit notes received
6. Reports
7. Conclusion

Range statement

Relevant computerised records
Computerised records
Computerised ledgers

Knowledge and understanding

Operation of computerised accounting systems

PART B USING ACCOUNTING SOFTWARE

1 Introduction

We will now explain some of the most important options for dealing with suppliers. The Suppliers window is displayed on screen when you click on the **Suppliers** button, or by selecting **Modules**, **Suppliers** from the Main menu. (In Sage, this is how you access functions associated with the **Purchase ledger**.) The Suppliers window is shown below.

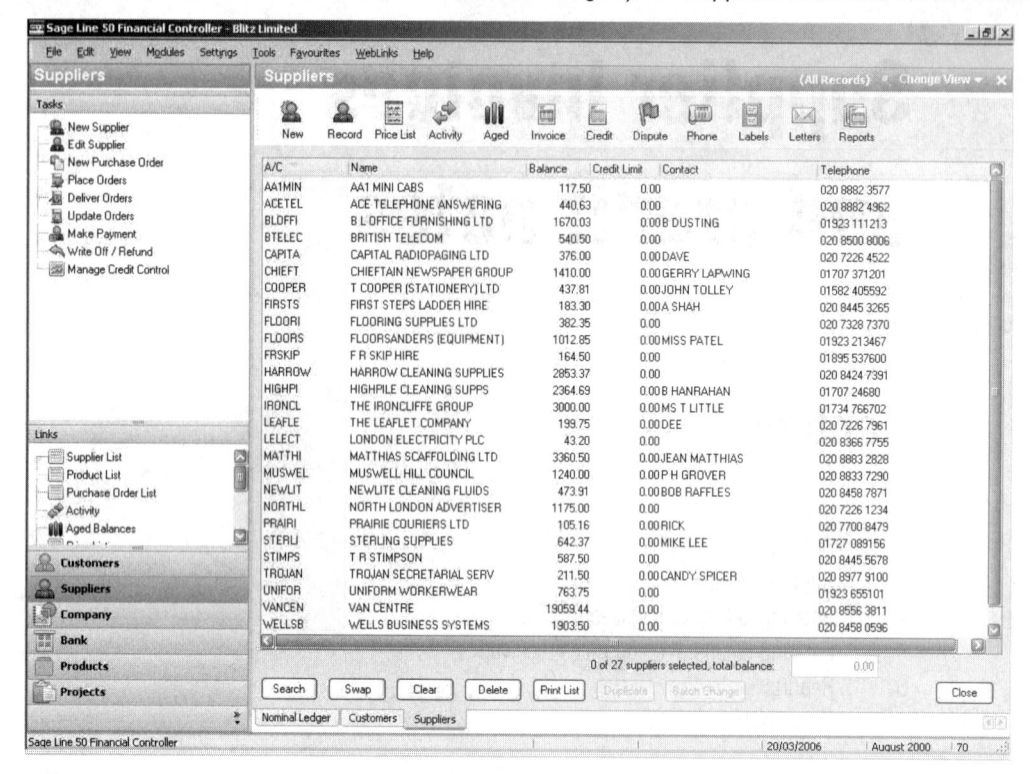

2 Suppliers

When an invoice is received from a new supplier, an account for the supplier must be set up. There are three ways of entering new supplier accounts.

(a) Using the Supplier **Record** button.
(b) Using the **Invoices** button.
(c) Using the **New** button from within Suppliers to access the Supplier Record Wizard.

The **Record** button method is described here. Experiment with the other two methods yourself.

3 Supplier details

To set up an account for a new supplier click on Suppliers. Then, ensure no existing supplier is highlighted (by clicking on Clear) and then click on the **Record** button. This option allows you to insert details of a new supplier (that is, create a new supplier account) or to amend details of an existing account, for example to change the supplier's address or telephone number.

3: SUPPLIER INVOICES AND CREDIT NOTES

Existing supplier accounts can also be deleted from the ledger in certain circumstances. When you click on the **Record** button, the following display will appear on screen. (There may be slight differences in layout depending upon the version of Sage you are using.) Note that different aspects of supplier details are depicted as index cards or tabs (Details, Defaults etc). You click on the index tab to activate the related options.

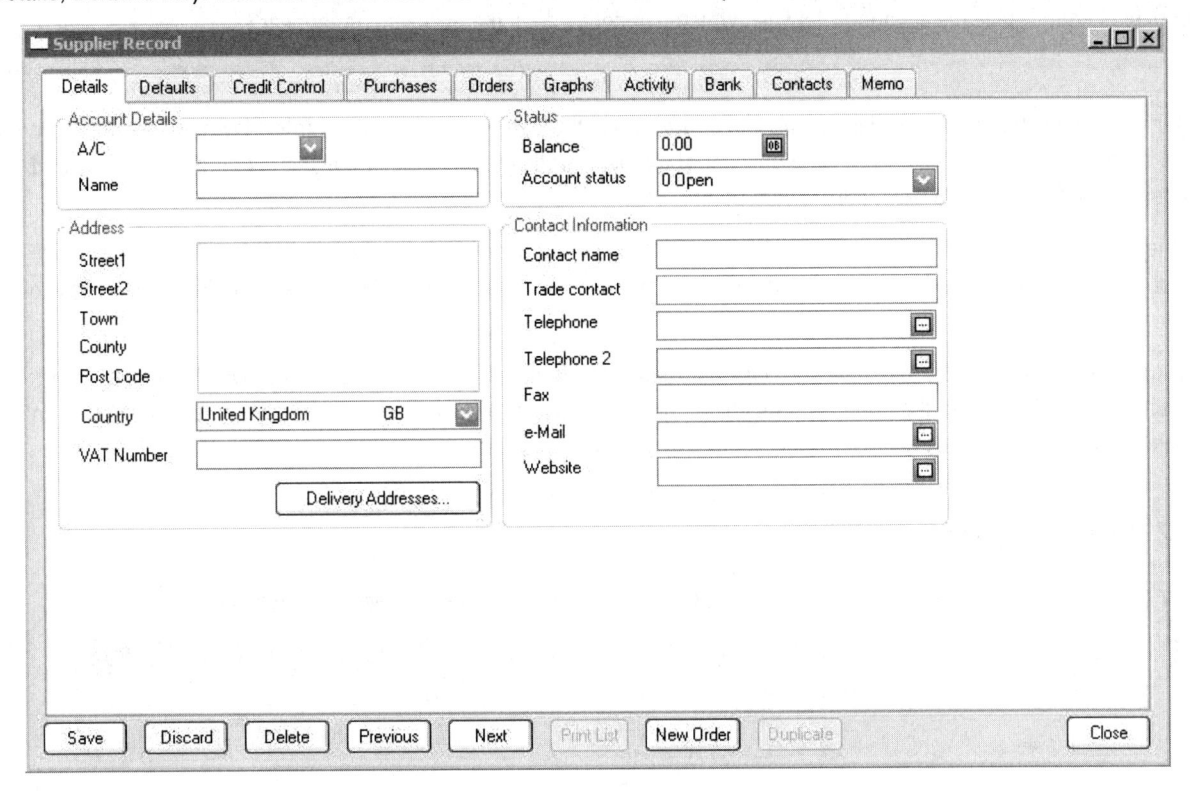

3.1 Details

The cursor starts at the **A/C box**. The supplier's reference code should be entered here. The maximum length for the code is eight digits. The coding system used by Blitz Limited uses six characters.

When you enter a code for a new supplier and press **Tab**, the words **New Account** will appear in the grey area next to the **A/C box**. The cursor will have moved down to the next line, ready for you to insert the supplier's name. Press **Tab** to move from the name line to the address section. Press the **Shift** key plus **Tab** to move *up* to the previous line. If you want to leave a line blank just press **Tab** again to move on to the next line. A typical entry is shown below.

Name	Lexington Supplies
Street 1	Billington House
Street 2	25-29 Dorchester Avenue
Town	London
County	
Postcode	W12 5TL

PART B USING ACCOUNTING SOFTWARE

Activity 3.1

Load up Assignment 6 and using the A/C code LEXING enter all of the details given in the previous paragraph as a new supplier account (save the account). Between which two codes does the new account appear?

After you have entered the supplier's name and address, use the **Tab** key to move the cursor down the screen, from one item to the next. A contact name (in case of account queries), trade contact, telephone and fax numbers, e-mail and website details can be entered in the relevant fields.

In the assignments in this book you will not be required to enter any details in the box for **Vat Reg No**. However, in practice these details would be entered in the box if required. You can just press **Tab** to leave the field blank and move on to the next field.

Click on the Delivery button to enter a **Delivery Address**. You would enter here the address to which the supplier in question normally delivers the goods you buy from him – a factory in Manchester, say. Blitz Limited has all its supplies delivered to its main address, so you will not need to enter anything here.

3.2 Credit control

Now click on the third index tab labelled **Credit Control**. This gives you a new screen – shown below.

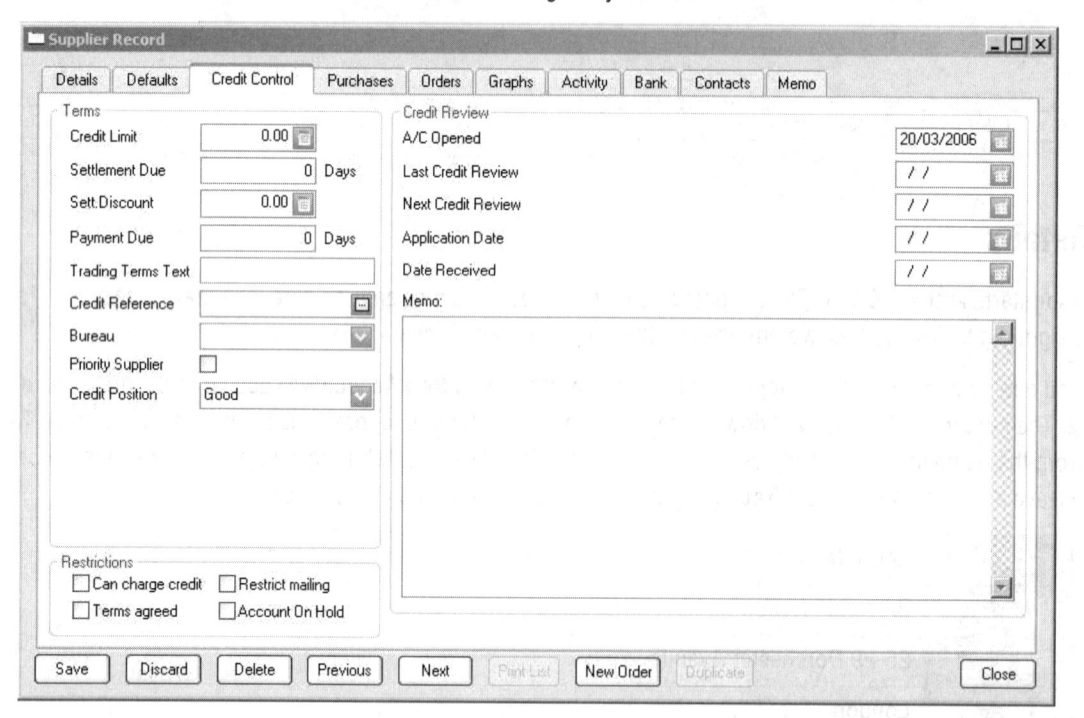

You would fill in the **Credit Limit** line if the supplier had allocated you an upper limit to the amount of credit you are allowed.

The **Sett Due Days** box refers to the terms of your account – how many days following the invoice date must payment (settlement) be made to qualify for any settlement discount. The amount of settlement discount, in percentage terms, is shown in the **Sett Discount** box. For example a supplier may offer you a 10% discount if you pay an invoice within, say, 7 days. In this case you would enter the number 7 in the **Sett Due Days** box and 10.00 in the **Sett Discount** box.

The entry in the **Pay Due Days** box is the number of *days* that you have to pay an invoice: typically a supplier might expect payment within 30 days. The **Terms** box is for a narrative description: 'Payment on delivery', or whatever is appropriate. When Terms have been agreed with a supplier the **small Terms agreed** box should be 'ticked'.

You need not be concerned with the **Credit Ref** and **Bureau** boxes (or other boxes that are available on later versions of the software). If you are interested, use the Sage on-line help facility to find out their purpose.

3.3 Defaults

The Defaults index tab allows you to specify certain details about how a transaction with the supplier will normally be posted. For example if one of your suppliers were Yorkshire Electricity you would probably be reasonably sure that all transactions on this account should be posted to the Electricity expense account in the nominal ledger.

If you make an entry in the **Def N/C** box when you first set up the Yorkshire Electricity account, then when you next have an invoice from Yorkshire Electricity the program will automatically suggest to you that it should be posted to the 'default' nominal account you specified when the account was set up. (You can, however, choose a different nominal code at the time when you are posting the transaction.)

Sage has a box for **Disc%**. This is for discounts other than settlement discounts. It is not used in the Blitz case study.

The **Def Tax Code** box will offer you a pull down list of possible VAT codes that apply to this supplier. In the assignments in the Blitz case study the default code is **T1 – 17.5%**, which is the standard rate of VAT at the time of preparation of this book.

Below the **Def Tax Code** box is a box labelled **Currency**. The default in the case study is '**1 Pound Sterling**'. If you click on this box and its downward pointing arrow you will be offered a number of other options such as French Francs or German Marks. The Blitz case study only uses UK currency, so you can just accept the default for this box.

In the assignments in this book *you will not be required* to enter any details in the boxes for **Analysis.** These are useful for management accounting purposes, but not part of the standards of competence at AAT Foundation level. In each case press **Tab** to leave the field blank and move on to the next field.

The other index tabs are not used in the assignments in this book, but you might find it interesting to have a look at them and see what happens when you click on various buttons. Don't be afraid of experimenting: you can always get a fresh copy of the data using the CD-ROM.

3.4 Checking and saving your work

When you have entered all the details that need to be entered you should *check* what you have on screen against the document you are working from (against the details given in this book in the case of the assignments).

(a) If you have made just one or two errors just press **Tab** until the entry is highlighted and type in the correct entry. If just one character is wrong it is quicker to click on the entry, and move the cursor using the cursor keys until it is in the appropriate place, delete the wrong character and insert the correct one.

PART B   USING ACCOUNTING SOFTWARE

(b) If you have made lots of mistakes, you can 'wipe the slate clean' and start again. To do so, click on the **Discard** button. The screen will be cleared and you can start again.

(c) If you are happy that all your entries are correct click on **Save**. The new supplier will be added to the Suppliers ledger.

(d) If you click on Save and only then realise you have made a mistake in posting the details you can call up the details you posted again by selecting the supplier code from the main Suppliers window, click on **Record** and edit out your mistakes. Alternatively you can call up the account and click on **Delete** to remove it entirely. However you can only delete a supplier in this way if no transactions have yet been posted to that account.

Activity 3.2

(a) What is the post-code for account AA1MIN?
(b) What is the contact name for account TROJAN?
(c) What is the full account name and telephone number of the account COOPER?

Activity 3.3

Set up a supplier account for the following supplier in the same way as details have been entered for existing Blitz supplier accounts. Refer to the paragraphs above if you don't know whether you need to put an entry in a particular box or how to make the entry.

Lineker Leisurewear Limited
Bernard House
647 Spenser Street,
Birmingham, BH1 2OD
Contact: Frederic Ferinella
Phone: 0161 123 6543
Credit limit: £1,500

4 Entering details of invoices received

When invoices are received from suppliers, the details of each invoice must be entered in the Suppliers Ledger, in the appropriate supplier's account.

4.1 The Invoices option

To enter supplier invoice details, you should click on the **Invoice** button in the **Suppliers** window. The following window (or similar) will be displayed.

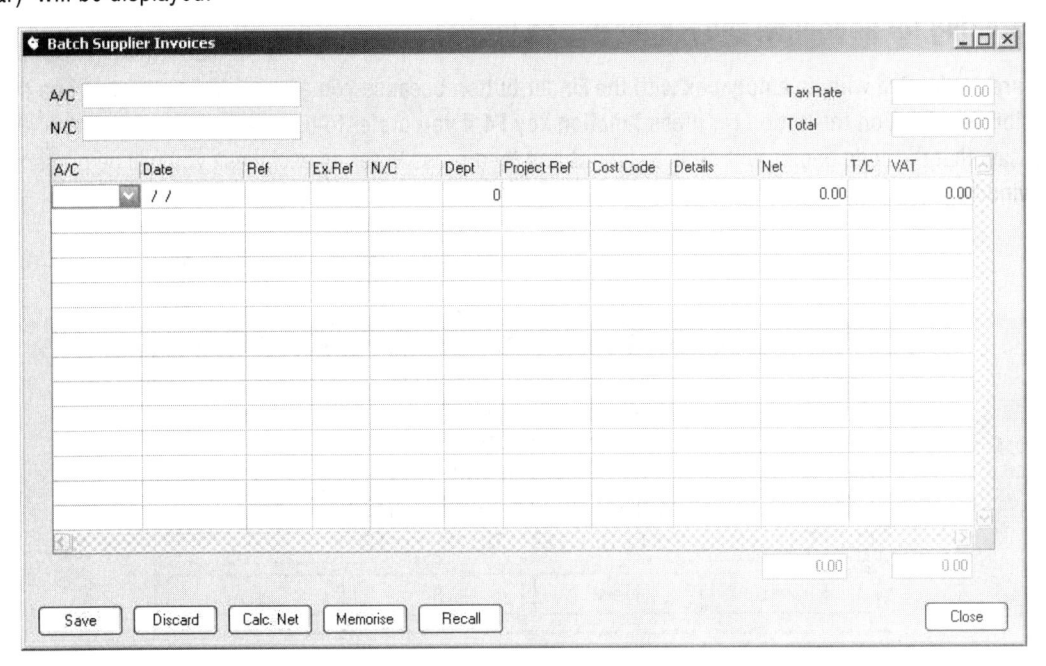

Suppose your company receives an invoice from a firm of public relations and marketing consultants as follows:

Invoice details	£	Nominal ledger item
Sales promotion expenses	2,000	Sales promotions
Advertising costs	1,500	Advertising
Public relations	600	PR
	4,100	

This invoice needs to be split into its three elements, £2,000 to charge to sales promotion expenses (nominal ledger account code 6200), £1,500 to advertising costs (N/C code 6201) and £600 to PR (N/C code 6203). You would enter three separate lines in the Supplier Invoices window.

You can enter as many lines as are necessary on each invoice. You can invoice *several different suppliers* on the same screen.

You can scroll back up and edit transactions if you realise you have made a mistake before you **Save** the invoice. If you want to delete an entire line, tab to it or click in it anywhere and then press function key F8. Other function keys are useful too. See Appendix 2 at the end of this book for a list.

Once you have finished entering the details of an invoice you click on **Save** and the screen is cleared ready for the next supplier's invoice.

4.2 A/C (account code)

Initially the cursor will be in the box labelled **A/C**. If you know the *code* for the supplier you can just type it in and press Tab. If you know some of the details for the supplier but you can't quite remember the code, Sage offers you a handy tool for finding out what you need to enter. At the right of the A/C box is a button. This is called the **Finder** button.

4.2.1 Searching for accounts: the Finder button (or F4)

When you are confronted with an empty box with the Finder button because you are required to choose one code from many possibilities. Click on the button (or press **function key F4** if you prefer to use the keyboard). Another alternative if you know, say, that the code begins with G, is to type G and then press Enter. In each case you will be presented with a selection window.

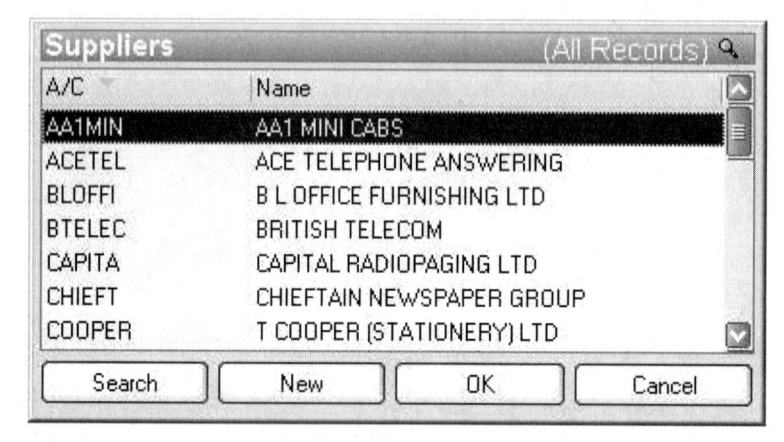

A/C	Name
AA1MIN	AA1 MINI CABS
ACETEL	ACE TELEPHONE ANSWERING
BLOFFI	B L OFFICE FURNISHING LTD
BTELEC	BRITISH TELECOM
CAPITA	CAPITAL RADIOPAGING LTD
CHIEFT	CHIEFTAIN NEWSPAPER GROUP
COOPER	T COOPER (STATIONERY) LTD

If you can see the account you want in the list immediately just click on it to highlight it and then click on OK or press Enter. If not, use the scroll bar or the cursor keys to scroll up or down until you see the name you want, then click on it and click OK.

Activity 3.4

Click the relevant buttons until you reach the Supplier Invoices window and then press F4. What appears in the A/C *Name* box at the *top* of the window when you select the account code BLOFFI and click on OK or press Enter? What if you type in the code MUSWEL?

4.2.2 Searching for accounts: the Search button

The **Search** button at the foot of the Finder window offers you a means of searching for accounts that fulfil certain conditions. Let's say, for the sake of argument, that you are in charge of the purchase ledger for accounts of suppliers who come from Watford. Click on the Search button and you will see the following screen.

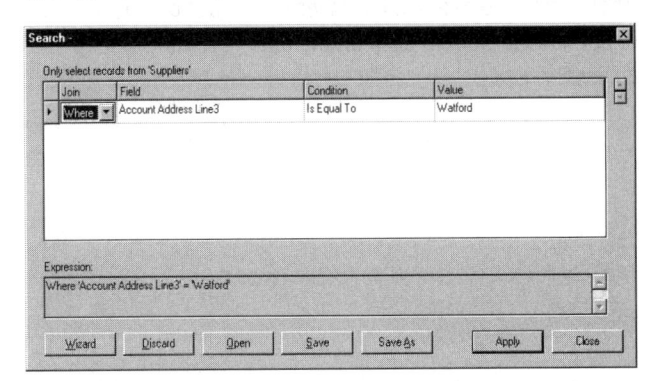

Click the down arrow to the right of the Join heading and select **Where**. Tab to the white square below the heading Field. From the drop down menu select **Account Address Line 3**. Tab through the condition field, ensuring it is set to 'Is Equal To'. In the Value field type *Watford*. Click on **Apply**, then click on **Close**. You will be returned to a window which shows only the names of those suppliers whose records indicate that they are located in Watford. If you are trying this out using Blitz data there will be now be only three account names: BLOFFI, FLOORS and UNIFOR.

You can search on more than one criteria. For example, from within the Suppliers finder window click on **Search** again, the criteria entered previously will show. Press **Tab** four times and you will be on a new line. Using the drop down menus under each heading select **And** (hit Tab), **Balance** (Tab), **Is Greater Than** (Tab), and type in 1000.00. Click **Apply** and **Close**. The suppliers in Watford with balances over £1,000.00 will be displayed.

Wherever you see the **Search** button within Sage the same principles for searching and selecting records apply.

When you close the Suppliers Record window you will notice that the 'filter' you designed still applies. Therefore, only those records that meet the criteria appear in the Suppliers window. To view all records click on the magnifying glass button.

There are symbols that may help you with searches. For example, if you wish to find all accounts with a post code that begins with W a search on W in the postcode line would not find any records. You can, however, search using W* – the asterisk is a 'wildcard', standing for **any other character** or characters. Try it.

The magnifying glass symbol in the suppliers window has the effect of switching between all suppliers record and just those records that meet the Search Criteria. Try the button out.

Activity 3.5

Try out the techniques described in the previous paragraphs.

4.3 Date

When the right account code is entered the supplier's full name will be shown in the A/C Name box. Pressing Tab will highlight the **Date** box. The date you enter should be the date *on the supplier's invoice*.

Sage has a delightful feature for entering dates. When the cursor enters the date field another Finder button appears. If you click on this or press F4 a little calendar appears and you just have to *double-click* on the date you want. Use the arrows at the top to scroll through the months and years if necessary.

The calendar is fun, but it is probably quicker to type in the date using the numeric keypad. This is a matter of personal preference.

4.4 Ref

Press Tab again and you are taken to a box headed **Ref**. You can leave this blank but it is best to use it for the supplier's invoice number for reference purposes. There is also an extra reference box **Ex Ref** for an additional reference if required.

4.5 Entering the invoice details

Pressing Tab once more takes you to the parts of the invoicing screen that do what you would think of as the double entry in a manual system. The entries you make are as follows.

(a) The nominal ledger code (**N/C**). This is the account in the nominal ledger to which the purchase or expense relates. You can use the search facilities described above to find the nominal code you want.

A good shortcut here, if you have an approximate idea of the nominal account code, is to type in the approximate number and then press Enter, or function key F4, or click on the Finder button. This brings up the Nominal Accounts list starting from the number you typed. So, for example, if you know an invoice is an overhead and that overhead account codes are in the range 7000 to 7999 you can type in 7 and press F4.

(b) The **Dept** box can be used to analyse the information further. This is not used in the Blitz case study, so just press Tab again.

(c) In the **Details box** you type details of the goods or service supplied. Try typing a long sentence and see how the text scrolls across as you reach the end of the box.

(d) In the **Net** box key in the amount of the invoice item *excluding value added tax* (the net amount). Just key in figures, with a decimal point between the pounds and the pence. Don't try to key in a £ sign. You don't need to key in zeros for pence at the end of a round figure amount.

- Keying 123 gives you 123.00
- Keying 123.4 gives you 123.40
- Keying 1230 gives you 1230.00

(e) The code for the VAT rate (**T/c**) will automatically show T1, though you can alter this if necessary. The VAT codes used in the Blitz case study are:

- T0 Zero-rated items (VAT = 0%)
- T1 Standard-rated items (VAT currently = 17.5%)
- T9 Transactions to which VAT does not apply

You will be told what code to use at AAT Foundation level.

(f) The **Tax** is calculated automatically from the net amount of the invoice already entered and the VAT tax code.

4.5.1 The Calculate Net button

If you prefer, instead of entering the net amount of the invoice in the **Net** box, you can enter the total amount, *including VAT*. *Before* pressing Tab, click on the **Calculate Net** button or press function key F9. The program will now deduct VAT *at the standard rate* from the invoice amount you have keyed in, and display the VAT automatically in the **Tax** column.

When the VAT has been calculated and you have entered all the invoice details, press Tab again, and the cursor will move down to the next line of the screen. Details of another invoice item can then be entered on this line.

Note that running totals of your entries are shown at the foot of the Net column and the VAT column. You can compare the totals with the total shown on the invoice once you have posted all the items. If the totals are not the same there is a mistake somewhere. If it is your mistake you can scroll back up or tab to the error and correct it.

Remember that a whole line can be deleted by clicking on it or tabbing to it and pressing function key F8. Only use the **Discard** button if you wish to scrap *all* the details you have just entered on the screen.

PART B USING ACCOUNTING SOFTWARE

Activity 3.6

With **Assignment 6** still loaded (we loaded it for Activity 3.1), enter the following invoice details, following the instructions given earlier in this chapter. Use the features of the Sage package to calculate the correct figures for you.

A/C	Date	Refn	N/C	Details	Net	T/C	VAT
NEWLIT	01/10/2000	SW369	5000	Materials	100.00	T1	??.??
IRONCL	04/10/2000	214876	7701	Repairs	???.??	T1	??.??

The gross amount of the second invoice is £240.

Task

Find out the total amount of VAT for the two transactions, and what the N/C codes 5000 and 7701 stand for.

Save the details, once you have checked the answer.

4.6 Posting the invoice details

When you have entered details for all the items on the invoice(s) you are processing and you are satisfied that they are correct, click on the **Save** button. **Saving the transaction posts the invoice**.

When you post the details of an invoice, the **program**:

(a) Updates the individual account of the supplier in the Suppliers Ledger;

(b) Updates the appropriate accounts in the Nominal Ledger. The accounts that are updated are the Creditors Control Account, the VAT Control account and the various purchases, expense or fixed asset accounts to which the invoices relate (as specified in the transaction details by your choice of N/C codes). The double entry posting to the nominal ledger will be:

Debit   Nominal Ledger Account selected

Debit   Purchase Tax Control, code 2202

Credit   Creditors Control Account, code 2100

Note that the standard chart of accounts in Sage has two VAT control accounts, one for VAT on purchases (debits), the other for VAT on sales (credits).

Activity 3.7

When you have done Activity 3.6 find out the debit or credit balances on the Nominal Ledger accounts 2100, 2202, 5000 and 7701 and the Suppliers ledger accounts NEWLIT and IRONCL and make a note of them.

Now reload a fresh copy of Assignment 6. How do the balances on the accounts differ? Explain each of the differences.

5 Entering details of credit notes received

When a credit note is received from a supplier, the supplier is acknowledging that, for one reason or another, he has charged too much. Credit notes can be issued when goods are returned to the supplier as faulty or unwanted, or when there is a dispute about an invoice and the supplier agrees to reduce the bill.

Details of credit notes received from suppliers must be entered in the Suppliers Ledger, in the account of the appropriate supplier. The procedures are very similar to those for entering details of purchase invoices.

- (a) Click on the **Credit** button in the Suppliers window.
- (b) The screen will display a new window just like the Supplier Invoice window, except that the details of the credit note appear in red as you enter them.

The procedure is the same as that already described for entering details of purchase invoices. You must make sure, however, that:

- (a) The nominal ledger code you select (N/C) is the same as the code that was chosen for the original purchase invoice details.
- (b) The VAT code (T/C) is also the same as for the original purchase invoice.

Some other points should also be noted.

- (a) Enter the **Date** on the credit note, not 'today's date'.
- (b) The **Ref** item is for the credit note number, which you can copy from the credit note itself.
- (c) The **Details** item can be used for recording brief details of the reason for receiving the credit note.

After you have entered the details of your credit note(s) click on **Save** as before. When you Save a credit note, the program:

- (a) Updates the account(s) of the individual supplier(s) in the purchase ledger.
- (b) Updates the Creditors Control Account and the other relevant accounts in the nominal ledger.

PART B   USING ACCOUNTING SOFTWARE

Activity 3.8

With Assignment 6 data loaded (from Activity 3.7) post the invoice for £240 to supplier IRONCL again and check the balance on the IRONCL account and on the nominal ledger accounts.

Then post a credit note for the same amount to the IRONCL account and check that the balances have reverted to their previous amounts.

6 Reports

6.1 Supplier reports

When you have entered a day's batch of invoices you can print a list of the details, with totals. These listings are sometimes called 'Day Books'.

A wide range of supplier reports are available from within Sage. The procedure for printing these reports differs slightly between earlier and later versions of Sage. If you click on the Reports button from within the Suppliers window, you will see the screen shown below (or similar, depending upon the version of Sage you are using).

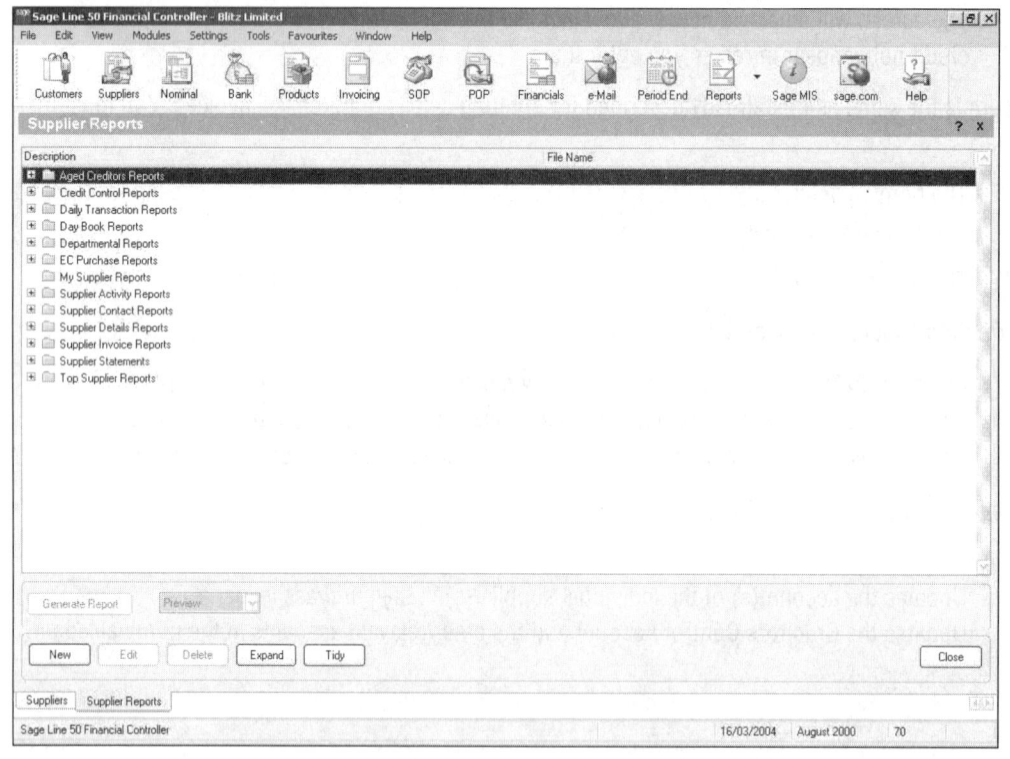

You double click on the appropriate folder, such as Day-Book Reports and then highlight the report you wish to run (for example Day Books: Supplier Invoices (detailed)).

3: SUPPLIER INVOICES AND CREDIT NOTES

In **older versions** of Sage you would reach this point by simply clicking on the Reports button in the Suppliers window. You will then see the following screen, from where you can choose the report you require.

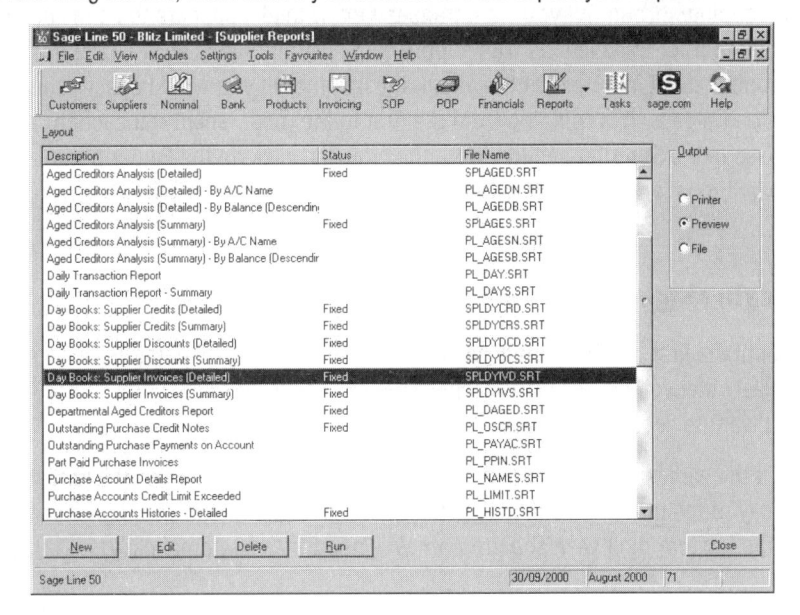

6.2 Output

In later versions, you select the type of output by using the drop down list to the right of the Generate Report button. Later versions also include the option of **e-mailing** the report (this option is not used in this book). In older versions, choose your output type by clicking in the white circle next to the appropriate label in the Output section of the screen.

(a) **Printer**. This sends your report straight to a printer to be printed out. The usual Windows Print window will appear, allowing you to choose what part of the document you want printed, what printer you want to send it to and so on. Printing things using Windows applications is explained in Chapter 2.

(b) **Preview**. This option brings up a screen display of the information that you can edit to some extent for printing purposes. For example you might want to change the font style or the width of the margins.

(c) **File**. This option allows you to save a copy of the report on disk. The usual Windows **Save As** window will appear and you will have to choose a name for report and specify the directory in which you want it to be saved. Again, see Chapter 2 if you have forgotten how to use the Save As window.

When you have selected the Report and output type you require, click on **Run** (older versions) or **Generate Report**.

6.3 Criteria

You must now choose what transactions you want to appear in your listing. There are five main criteria for doing this.

(a) By specifying a supplier range (the accounts you wish to be included).
(b) By specifying a date range (the date or dates of the transactions you wish to list).
(c) By specifying a transaction range (the range of transaction numbers for which you require a listing).
(d) By specifying a department range.
(e) By specifying a nominal account range.

6.3.1 Supplier range

Accept the defaults (by 'Tabbing' through) if you want transactions with all suppliers to be included in the report. However, you may want a report of transactions with suppliers in a certain range eg A – D. If, for example, you had a query from a specific supplier about invoices sent to you in the last month you would specify the appropriate date range, leave the transaction range as it is (ranging from the first to the most recent transaction) and then enter the supplier code in *both* boxes in the **Supplier** section. Note that you can click on the Finder button (or press F4 when the cursor is in the appropriate box) if you are not sure of the account code.

6.3.2 Specifying a date range

Press Tab if necessary until the first box in the date section is highlighted. As a default this may show the date 01/01/1980, but it is unlikely that you will want to accept this. The second box may show a date like 31/12/2019. Again it is unlikely that you will want to accept this.

Instead you should key in the earliest date for transactions you wish to list and then the latest date. Key in each date using *two digits* for the day of the month, two digits for the month of the year and two digits for the year (there is no need to type slashes or the full four digit year, the program will insert these automatically).

Examples	Enter
6th April 2000	060400
15th May 2000	150500
2nd November 2000	021100

Suppose today is 5 October and you have just entered invoices received from suppliers with various dates from 30 September to 2 October. In the first Date Range box enter 30092000 then press Tab. In the second box type 02102000. You can use the calendar button if you prefer.

You are now ready to produce your report. Just Click on **OK** and wait for the report to be output in the way you specified earlier.

6.3.3 Specifying a transaction range

Choosing the date range for a listing of purchase invoices or supplier credit notes can be a problem because the invoices or credit notes will have different dates. When an invoice has a date that is now several weeks old, it could be very difficult to be sure of including it in a report by specifying the date range, without listing other invoices you have already processed in the past.

You can specify the invoices (or credit notes) you wish to list by specifying their transaction numbers. These are unique numbers, automatically allocated to each entry into the system by the program. To specify a transaction range, you should remember to *take a note* of the first transaction number for the invoices and the credit notes when you start to process them. The second box in the Transaction section shows the total number of transactions entered so far on the system (purchase ledger, sales ledger and nominal ledger). Your next transaction will be the next number in the sequence. For example, if the box shows that 70 transactions have been processed (number of entries = 70) your next entry will be transaction 71.

You can find the last transaction number by clicking on **Financials** in the main window and jumping to the end of the list that appears.

3: SUPPLIER INVOICES AND CREDIT NOTES

The Transaction boxes on screen will display a transaction range from 1 to 9999999 (or to the most recent transaction number). You should alter the range, to specify the transactions you wish to list.

Don't worry about mixing purchase invoices and credit note transaction numbers. The report will contain only one type of transaction or the other (ie invoices only or credit notes only), depending on the type of report you have selected.

You are now ready to produce a report of transaction within the range specified. Just Click on **OK** and wait for the report to be output in the way you specified earlier. (Blitz does not operate with more than one Department so you can tab through this option.)

6.3.4 Nominal account range

The procedure is the same if you wanted to know about all transactions posted, say, to nominal account codes 7000 to 7999, or code 1200 to 1200 (ie account 1200 only).

Again when you have specified the range you want you are ready to produce your report as before.

Activity 3.9

Load a fresh copy of Assignment 6 data. Run the report Day Books: Supplier Invoices (Detailed). Make sure that the data range covers the period from 1 August 2000 to 30 October 2000.

What are the totals shown and what is the number of the last transaction listed.

If you use the Preview option for Output, Sage will open a Report or 'File View' window for the report. You can switch between the report and the program itself by clicking on the word **Window** at the top of the screen and then clicking on whichever window you want.

6.4 Closing a Report or File View window

Buttons at the bottom of the screen give you a variety of options for moving about in the report, viewing it in different ways, saving it, printing it, or just closing the report window.

7 Conclusion

Experiment ...

This is an important chapter because it introduces many of the widely used features of the Sage package. Spend some time going over what you have read, ideally while sitting at a computer. Try calling up windows and making entries in the way we describe. You won't break the software by experimenting with its features and you can always call up a 'clean' copy of Blitz case study data.

... and try an Assignment!

If you think you can follow the instructions in this chapter, **you should now be able to attempt Assignment 1** at the end of this Workbook. If you haven't yet attempted the **Activities** in this and the previous chapter, you should do these first.

3: SUPPLIER INVOICES AND CREDIT NOTES

Key learning points

- ☑ In Sage, you access functions associated with the **Purchase ledger** through the **Suppliers** button. Sage calls the '**Purchase ledger control account**' the '**Creditors control account**'.

- ☑ We have looked at some important features associated with **processing supplier invoices and credit notes**. Suppliers button in the main window.

- ☑ Supplier records include basic **details** such as Company Name, Address and contact details as well as **accounting data** such as payment terms and any agreed credit limit.

- ☑ Invoices are entered into Sage from the options accessed by selecting the **Suppliers** icon from the main menu and then clicking on the **Invoice** button.

- ☑ Credit Notes are entered into Sage from the options accessed by selecting the **Suppliers** icon from the main menu and then clicking on the **Credit** button.

- ☑ Modern accounting systems offer various **reports** and **enquiry** facilities to enable information regarding transactions to be extracted from the system easily.

Quick quiz

1. List three possible methods of setting up a new supplier account.
2. What is the purpose of the Defaults tab in the Supplier Record?
3. What is the Search button within the Finder window used for?
4. Give one reason why a credit note may be issued.
5. List three alternatives for outputting a report from Sage.

Answers to quick quiz

1. Through the options provided using the Supplier Record button; Using the Invoices button; Using the New button from within Suppliers to access the Supplier Record Wizard.

2. The Defaults index tab allows you to specify certain details about how a transaction with the supplier will normally be posted. These details are used as default values when inputting transactions – this saves time.

3. The Search button within the Finder window enables a search to be made for accounts that meet the criteria you specify.

4. Credit notes can be issued if a mistake was made in the initial invoice, or if goods are returned as faulty or unwanted, or if a dispute arises and the supplier agrees to reduce the bill.

5. The report could be output to a printer, to the screen or to a computer file. A fourth alternative is to use Sage's facility to automatically e-mail the report – but the system must be set-up to allow this.

PART B USING ACCOUNTING SOFTWARE

Activity checklist

This checklist shows which knowledge and understanding point is covered by each activity in this chapter. Tick off each activity as you complete it.

Activity		
3.1		Knowledge and Understanding: Operation of computerised accounting systems
3.2		Knowledge and Understanding: Operation of computerised accounting systems
3.3		Knowledge and Understanding: Operation of computerised accounting systems
3.4		Knowledge and Understanding: Operation of computerised accounting systems
3.5		Knowledge and Understanding: Operation of computerised accounting systems
3.6		Knowledge and Understanding: Operation of computerised accounting systems
3.7		Knowledge and Understanding: Operation of computerised accounting systems
3.8		Knowledge and Understanding: Operation of computerised accounting systems
3.9		Knowledge and Understanding: Operation of computerised accounting systems

chapter 4

Customer invoices and credit notes

Contents

1. Introduction
2. Customers
3. Producing invoices
4. Invoicing for services
5. Invoicing for the sale of products
6. Producing credit notes
7. Printing invoices and credit notes
8. Updating the ledgers
9. Updating the ledgers without producing invoices
10. Reports
11. Customer queries
12. Conclusion

Range statement

Relevant computerised records
Computerised records
Computerised ledgers

Knowledge and understanding

Operation of computerised accounting systems

PART B   USING ACCOUNTING SOFTWARE

1 Introduction

The **Customers** button (or the *Customers* option under *Modules* in the main menu) is used to access functions associated with the **Sales ledger**. The options available under *Customers* are shown below. Earlier versions of Sage don't include some options (eg Price Lists). These options aren't required to complete the exercises in this book.

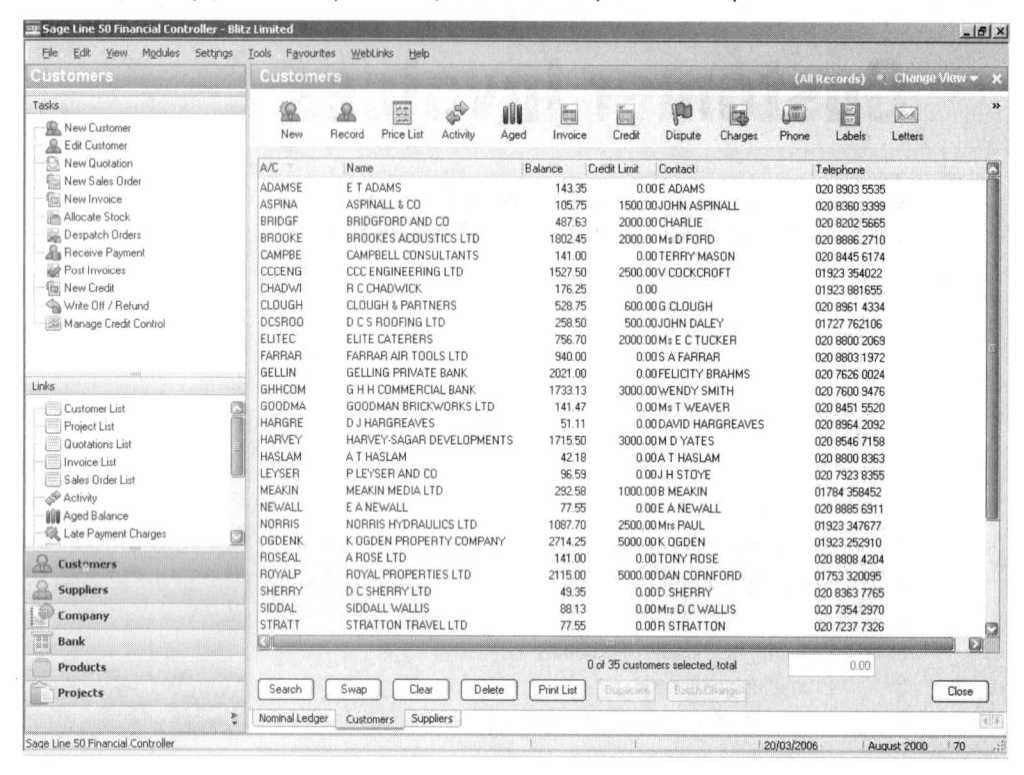

2 Customers

When an invoice has to be produced for sending to a new customer (ie a customer who has not been invoiced before by your company), an account for the customer must be set up in the customers ledger. There are four ways of entering new customer accounts in the ledger:

(a) Using the **Record** button in the Customers window.
(b) Using the **Invoices** button in the Customers window.
(c) Using one of the buttons in the **Invoicing** window.
(d) Using the **New** button from within Customers to access the Customer Record Wizard.

The **Record** button option and the Wizard option are similar to the options for entering details of new supplier accounts in the purchase ledger described in the previous chapter.

The option to set up new customer accounts from the **Invoices** button in the *Customers* window also works in a similar way to the method described in the context of the *Suppliers* window in Chapter 3.

4: CUSTOMER INVOICES AND CREDIT NOTES

Note that the **Invoices** option from within the Suppliers window would only be used if the actual invoices were not going to be printed from Sage. In the Blitz case study we will be producing Invoices and Credit Notes using Sage, therefore we will be using the **Invoicing** option from the **main** window.

Activity 4.1

If you have forgotten what a 'record' looks like, or what details are needed, load up any Assignment you like, click on **Customers** then on **Record** and select any account to remind yourself.

2.1 Credit limits

For the purpose of the case study and Assignment 2 you will be required to enter an amount for the maximum credit that will be allowed to the customer (ie the maximum value of goods or services that will be supplied on credit at any time). This amount should be entered as the 'Credit Limit' in the appropriate box.

How you enter new customer accounts from within the **Invoicing** window is described later in this chapter.

3 Producing invoices

If you select the **Invoicing** module under Modules from the main menu (or the Invoicing button from the **main** window in earlier versions of Sage), one of two boxes will appear, depending on the version of Sage you are using.

3.1 Older versions of Sage

If you are using an older version of Sage you will be presented with the following window.

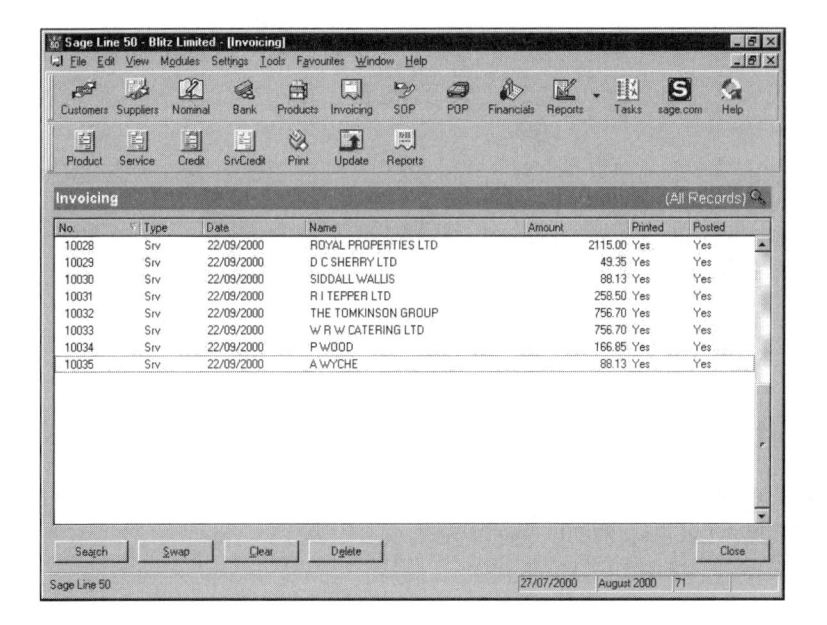

PART B USING ACCOUNTING SOFTWARE

In older versions of Sage the following options are available in the Invoicing window.

Icon	Use
Product	To invoice for the sale of goods or a product
Service	To invoice for the supply of services
Credit	To produce a credit note for goods
Service Credit	To produce a credit note for services
Print	To print invoices or credit notes
Update	To post invoices and credit notes to the ledgers
Reports	To produce lists of invoices in various stages of production

As you process invoices the blank space in this window will gradually be filled up with key details of each invoice, providing a handy numerical index of all invoices in the system. The **Swap** and **Clear** buttons affect which items are selected (highlighted) in the main part of the screen. Test these functions for yourself. The **Search** button will be explained later in this chapter.

3.2 Later versions of Sage

In later versions of Sage the Invoicing window will be the same or similar to the one shown below. To produce an Invoice or a Credit Note for a product or service, you would select New/Edit. Unlike earlier versions, you specify whether you are producing an Invoice or a Credit Note, and whether this related to a product or service, later in the process.

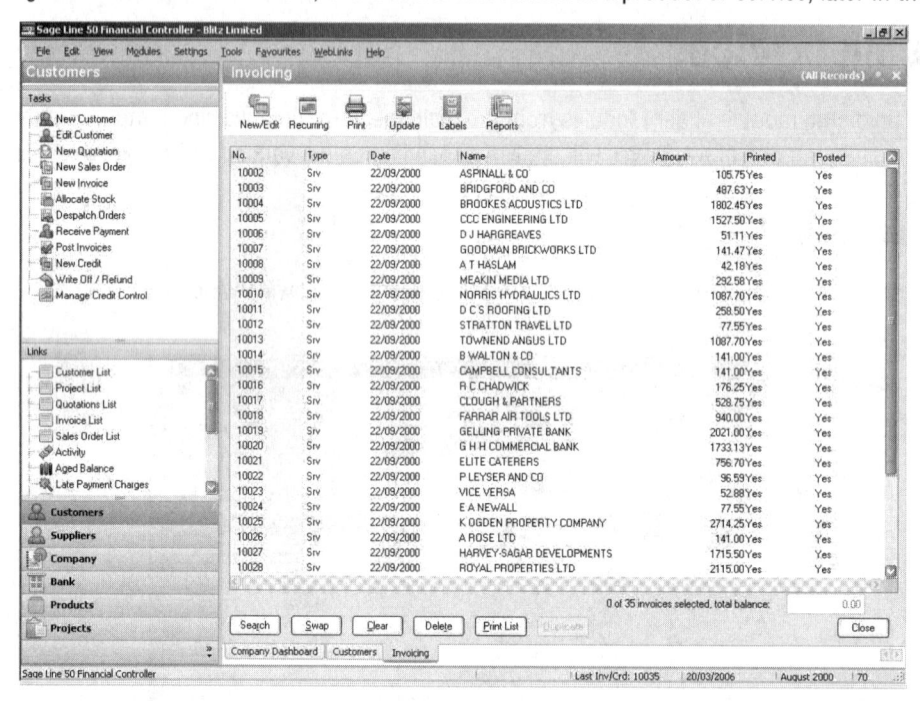

3.3 Invoice and credit note numbering

Invoices should be numbered sequentially. The program therefore allocates a number to each invoice automatically as you work, by adding 1 to the number of the previous invoice.

Activity 4.2

Familiarise yourself with the above by clicking on **Invoicing** in the main window and seeing what happens when you click on the various buttons and options available. Press **Esc** to get back to the initial Invoicing screen whenever you like.

4 Invoicing for services

In **older versions** of Sage, invoices for services can be produced using the **Service** button in the Invoicing window. In **later versions**, service invoices are produced by selecting **New/ Edit** from the **Invoicing** window. The fact that it is a Service Invoice is entered from within the 'Format' option when entering the Invoice details.

This window is used to enter the details for one invoice. Each invoice is for the sale of one or more services or items. There is a separate line for the details of each item, in the main (central) part of the screen.

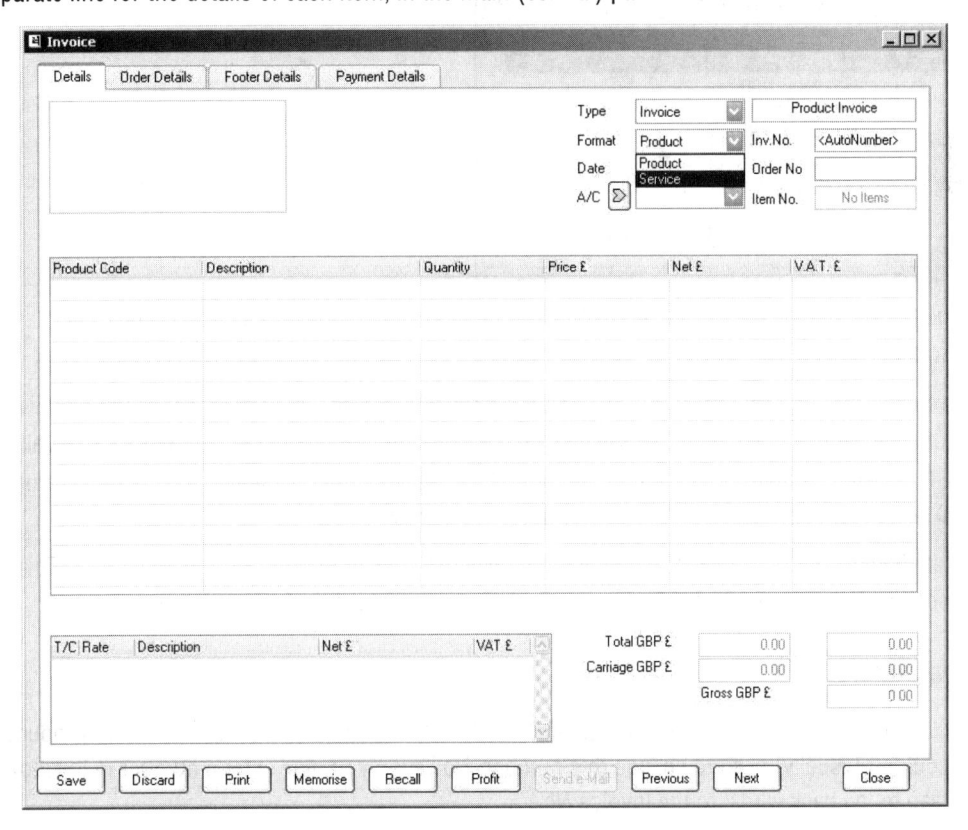

4.1 Details

Whether you are using an older version of Sage or a newer version, you will be presented with a series of options for your invoice. The Details Tab contains basic Invoice details as explained in the following paragraphs.

4.1.1 Type

Select whether you are producing an Invoice or a Credit Note. For the purposes of the case study in this book, you may ignore the other options.

4.1.2 Format

It is here, in newer versions of Sage, that you specify whether the Invoice or Credit Note refers to a Product or to a Service.

4.1.3 A/C (account)

In this box you enter the customer's account code. You can type in the code directly if you know it, or just type *part* of the code and press Tab, a list of Customer Accounts will appear with the nearest code to the one you entered highlighted. If this is correct, click on OK or press Enter to accept the code. If not you will have to scroll up or down the list in the usual way to find the customer you want. Alternately, you may bring up the list of all existing customers by clicking the 'Finder' button to the right of the A/C box.

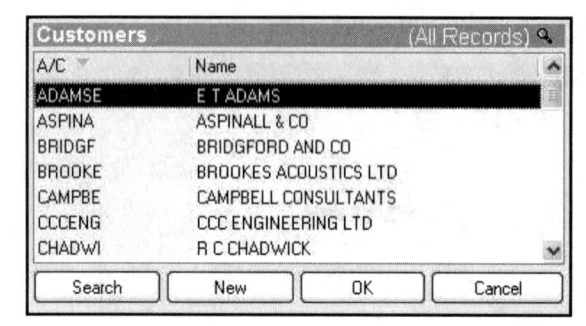

A/C	Name
ADAMSE	E T ADAMS
ASPINA	ASPINALL & CO
BRIDGF	BRIDGFORD AND CO
BROOKE	BROOKES ACOUSTICS LTD
CAMPBE	CAMPBELL CONSULTANTS
CCCENG	CCC ENGINEERING LTD
CHADWI	R C CHADWICK

You may use the **Search** button if you don't know the Customer account code. We explained the principles of using the Search button in the previous chapter.

If the invoice is to be sent to a new customer, click on the **New** button at the bottom of the Finder window. A screen will appear that is just like the one you met in the previous chapter for entering new Supplier records. Enter all the details for the new account and click on **Save**. You will then be returned to the customer accounts list and the account that you have just set up will be highlighted. Press Enter or click on OK to accept this.

Once you are satisfied that you have the correct customer account code in the A/C Ref box press Tab. This will take you to the **Details** section of the screen, but before we proceed there are a couple of things to check.

4.1.4 Invoice number

The invoice will be automatically entered as the next number in sequence after the previous invoice produced by the system. You shouldn't (usually) need to change this number. However, you may enter a number in this box if required. (Use Shift and Tab to 'go backwards' to the Invoice No.)

4.1.5 Invoice Date

The screen will display today's date (ie the date in the computer system). To accept this date, press Tab. Another invoice date can be entered, if required. As the Assignments in this book are set back in the Year 2000, you will need to enter an appropriate date for every invoice. (Note: If you are going to enter many invoices with the same date, use the

4: CUSTOMER INVOICES AND CREDIT NOTES

Change Program Date function under the **Settings** menu option from the main menu before you start entering invoices.)

Activity 4.3

Load up the data for **Assignment 1** and then enter these details in a service invoice, following the instructions above.

A/C Ref:	WRWCAT
Invoice number:	20000
Date:	25 November 2000
Details:	Contract cleaning
Amount:	£100.00 plus VAT

What is the name and address details of the customer concerned?

4.1.6 The Details box

Having entered the Account, press Tab until you get to the main part of the screen. In the details box enter a description of the service that has been delivered. In the Blitz case study this will be something like 'Window Cleaning' or 'Domestic Services'.

4.1.7 Edit item line

Before tabbing on from the Details box to the Amount box you should activate the Edit Line Box to enable you to enter details such as the appropriate Nominal ledger code. To do this either press the function key F3, or click on the little button in the right corner of the Details box. You will then be presented with the following (the appearance of this box may differ slightly depending on the version of Sage you are using).

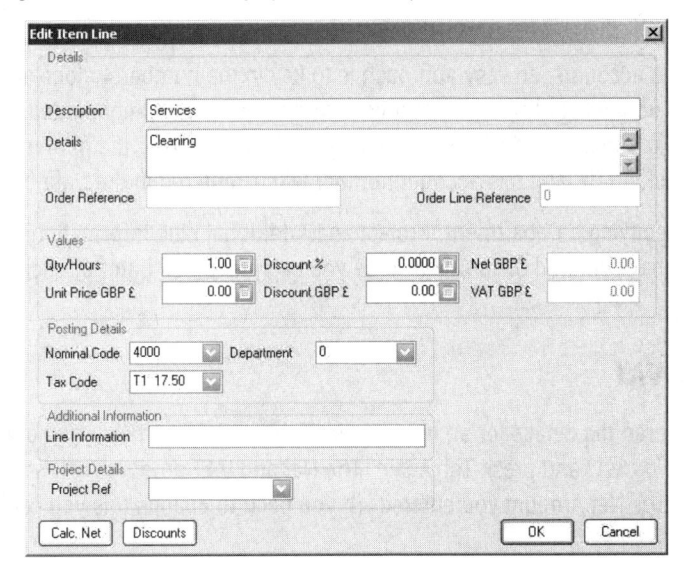

This window shows the text you entered in the details box in the main Service Invoice window. This is how the text will appear on the invoice. You can change this text if required. You may change other details such as the Tax Code if required.

You can also enter any Discount details (*not* settlement discount, which is handled elsewhere). In later versions of Sage, you may enter Discount as either a percentage or as an amount. If you click on the buttons beside these boxes (or press F4) a little drop-down calculator appears.

This can be operated by using the *numeric keypad* on the keyboard.

In fact you can bring up a calculator window at *any* time, just by pressing F2. To enter the result of a calculation into a field in a Sage screen you can press Ctrl + C, to copy the value from the calculator, then click on the field in question and press Ctrl + V.

The **Nominal code box** is where you specify the nominal code for the invoice. Each item on the invoice can have a different nominal ledger code if appropriate (in other words different items on the same invoice can be given different nominal ledger sales account codes). For each item (each line of Details you enter in the main Service invoice window) the code for the appropriate nominal ledger sales account should be entered using the Service Item Line screen.

In the Blitz Limited case study, the nominal ledger codes that are used are:

Code	Nominal ledger account
4000	Sales – Contract Cleaning
4001	Sales – Window Cleaning
4002	Sales – Domestic Services
4100	Sales – Materials

Rather than memorising these accounts, an easy approach is to key in the number 4 alone and then press Tab (or use function key F4). This brings up the list of Nominal Accounts with number 4000 highlighted. If Contract Cleaning is not the account you want then just scroll to find Window Cleaning or whatever. Once the nominal account you want is highlighted press Enter or click on OK and this account number will be entered in the right box.

There are also options for specifying a Department, Project and Additional Line Information. These are not used in the Blitz case study so once you have entered the nominal code you can just press Enter or click on OK to be returned to the main Invoice window.

4.1.8 Amount, Net and VAT

Press Tab once you have entered the details for an item and hit Tab, you will be taken to the **Amount** box. Enter the amount of the invoice *excluding VAT* and press Tab again. The Net and VAT amounts will be calculated automatically. By default VAT will be 17.5% of the Net Amount you entered. (If you need to change this you can return to the Edit Item Line window and do so.)

Later versions of Sage provide the option to use Hourly Rates within Service Invoicing. If you use this function, you would enter Details such as '2 hours heavy duty cleaning' then, within the Edit Item Line box, enter 2 in Hours and the price per hour in Unit Price. You can follow the same procedure to enter a second invoice line and a third, and so on.

Activity 4.4

Load up the data for **Assignment 6** and change the date within Sage to 25/11/2000 (use Settings, Change program data). Prepare the following service invoices (you have to find out the Nominal code yourself). Click on **Save** when you have entered the details for each invoice.

No.	Date	A/C	Details	N/C	Price
10065	25/11/2000	ADAMSE	Window cleaning	?	£100
10066	25/11/2000	GARDEN	Contract cleaning	?	£100

When you have finished press **Esc** (or click on **Close**) to return to the initial Invoicing screen. Scroll down to the bottom and make a note of the amount of each of the invoices you entered. Explain the results.

4.2 Order details

Occasionally, you might want to include extra details about the order on the invoice, for example:

(a) To specify a delivery address when this differs from the invoice address.
(b) To specify payment terms (eg 'PAYMENT REQUIRED WITHIN 30 DAYS OF INVOICE DATE').

To add these details, you should click on the **Order Details** index tab and enter the details in this window.

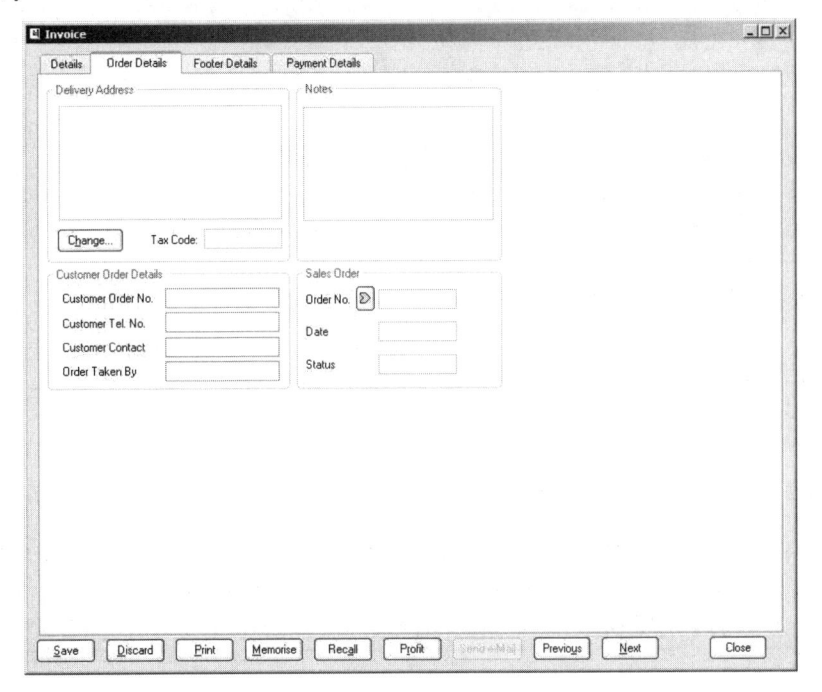

4.2.1 Customer Order No

This is where any customer reference number for this order would be entered.

4.2.2 Customer Tel. No./Contact

The customer's telephone number and contact name will be displayed automatically (from their account details).

4.2.3 Delivery Address

The delivery name and address can be entered here, when this is different from the name and address on the invoice (and in the records in the customer's account in the customers ledger).

4.2.4 Notes

Notes can be added, to appear on the invoice. These can be used, if required, to bring special information to the customer's attention; for example '5% DISCOUNT FOR SETTLEMENT WITHIN 7 DAYS OF INVOICE DATE'.

4.3 Footer Details

If you wish, you can also add details to the invoice for the following:

(a) Charging for the delivery of goods (Carriage).
(b) Providing details of any discounts offered to the customer for early payment (Settlement Terms).
(c) Giving every item on the invoice the same tax code, nominal ledger code or department code (Global).

Only (a) is relevant to the Blitz case study in this book. If you click on the **Footer Details** index tab, a new window will appear, as shown below (or a similar window if you use a previous version of Sage).

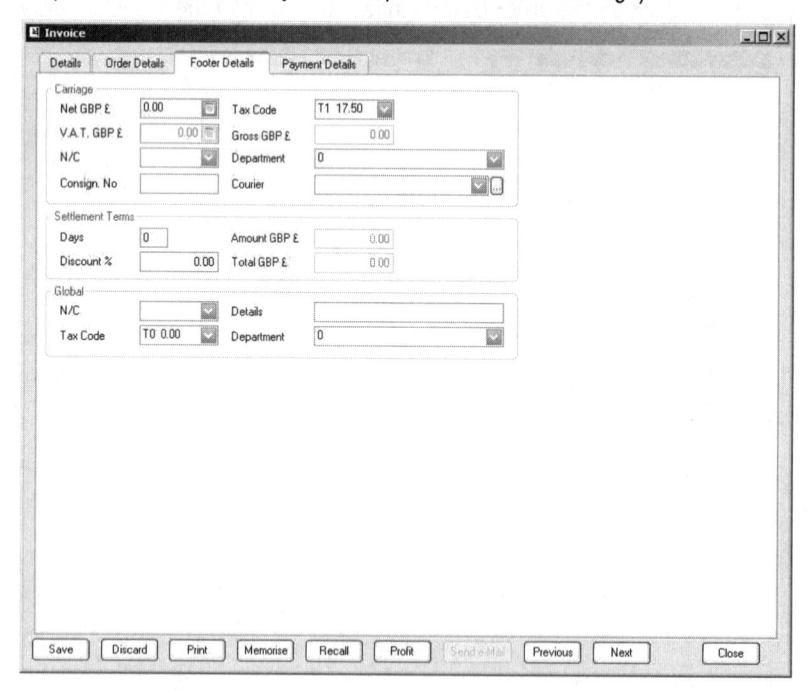

4.3.1 Carriage

The amount of charges for carriage outwards can be entered in the Net box at the top of the window. The charge for carriage, *excluding VAT*, should be keyed in.

4.3.2 Tax code (T/c)

Unless told otherwise use the same tax code for VAT as for the main invoice. It should usually be T1, meaning that VAT is chargeable at the standard rate of 17.5%.

4.3.3 Nominal code

Enter the nominal ledger code for the Carriage Outwards account in the nominal ledger. In the Blitz Limited system, this code is 4905. Otherwise you may need to click on the Finder button beside this box to find the right code.

Activity 4.5

Re-load the data for Assignment 6. Enter the following details, referring back to the previous paragraphs for instructions if necessary.

No.	Date	A/C	Details	N/C	Price
10065	31/12/2000	OWENLO	Sundry	4101	£100

Delivery address: 14 Woodgate Street, Barnet, N16 3BB
Order no.: 14879
Telephone number: 020-7734 2843
Customer contact: Jennifer
Carriage: £5
Settlement discount: 5% if settled within 30 days

What is the total amount of the invoice as shown on screen? Did any discrepancies arise as you were doing this activity, and if so what should you do about them?

4.4 Saving the invoice details

When you have entered all the details of the invoice (which might or might not include footer details) click on the **Save** button. This adds the main details of the invoice to the index shown in the main Invoicing window. The Service Invoice window will be cleared and you can start entering details for a new invoice. However:

(a) The invoice you have saved is *not yet posted* to the customers ledger and nominal ledger.
(b) An invoice is not printed.

This feature of the Sage package very sensibly recognises that in practice you might realise that you want to change the details to be posted and printed at a later stage.

We shall see how to print and post invoices later in this chapter.

4.5 Discard

As an alternative to Saving the details you have entered, the **Discard** button allows you to cancel all the details of the invoice you have just entered. It is sometimes easier and safer to start again than trying to edit an incorrect set of entries.

4.6 Editing saved entries

You can change any of the entries you have made so far, so long as you haven't posted them (updated the ledgers). Click on the relevant invoice (which you will now see listed in the main Invoicing window) and then click on the **Service** button again. Alternatively, just double-click the invoice you wish to edit.

Activity 4.6

Firstly, re-load the data for Assignment 6, and find out the balance on the Customer account WOODPX.

Then enter the following service invoice details (accept the invoice number offered by Sage and find out the nominal code for yourself). Then click on **Close** and respond **Yes** to the question 'do you want to save changes?'

Date	A/C	Details	Price
31/12/2000	WOODPX	Domestic services	£600

What is the balance on customer account WOODPX now?

5 Invoicing for the sale of products

5.1 Invoices in the case study

In the Blitz case study all invoices and credit notes are processed as Service Invoices or Service Credits. The reason for this is that, as a cleaning company, Blitz is essentially a service provider.

The few sales of materials Blitz does make are processed on 'Service' invoices for simplicity and consistency. For example, a customer can then be invoiced for cleaning services and purchases of cleaning materials on the same invoice.

However, it is perfectly acceptable to invoice these sales using the Product Invoice option. The important thing, from an accounting point of view, is to ensure sales of products are **posted to the correct nominal account** – in Blitz's case account 4100 – Sales Materials.

5.2 Product invoices in recent versions

In later versions of Sage, the procedure for Invoicing for the sale of products is very similar to the process of invoicing for services explained in the previous section. This involves selecting Invoicing from the main menu, then the New/ Edit option, and then choosing the product format from within the Invoice Details.

5.3 Product invoices in older versions

If you use an older version of Sage to produce an invoice for the sale of products, you use the **Product** button in the Invoicing window. When you click on this button, the screen will display windows similar to those that appear when you select the **Service** invoice option.

5.4 Product code

The main difference between a Service Invoice and a Product Invoice is the use of Product codes. On each line of the Invoice you enter the relevant Product code for items to be included in the Invoice.

If you don't know the code for the product you can use the Finder button beside the Product Code heading. A window will appear with a list of items and their codes. There is also the facility to set up a new Product if you wish. This is much like setting up a new customer or supplier account. When the item you want is highlighted, press Enter or click on the OK button and this code will be shown in the Product Code field in the main screen, together with its description.

A company might not use product codes in its Sage system, perhaps because, like Blitz Ltd in the case study, selling materials is just a sideline, or because stock is set up on a different system. There may also be times when an item sold is 'non-standard' and does not have a stock code because it is not usually carried in stock. In this case you can make one of four entries in the Product Code field (earlier versions of Sage may not have all four options available).

M		This simply allows you to type a message in the Description box. You might want to type something like '*Thank you for ordering the following items*' before listing out the items ordered with their prices.
S1		This code is used for a non-stock product item to which VAT applies.
S2		This code is used for a non-stock product item to which VAT does not apply.
S3		This code is used for a non-stock service item to which VAT applies.

You will only use the **S1** code in the Blitz case study. Type in S1 and press Tab. A window headed Edit Item Line will appear. This is very similar to the Edit Item Line that we explained when we explained Service Invoices in the previous section.

5.5 Edit item line

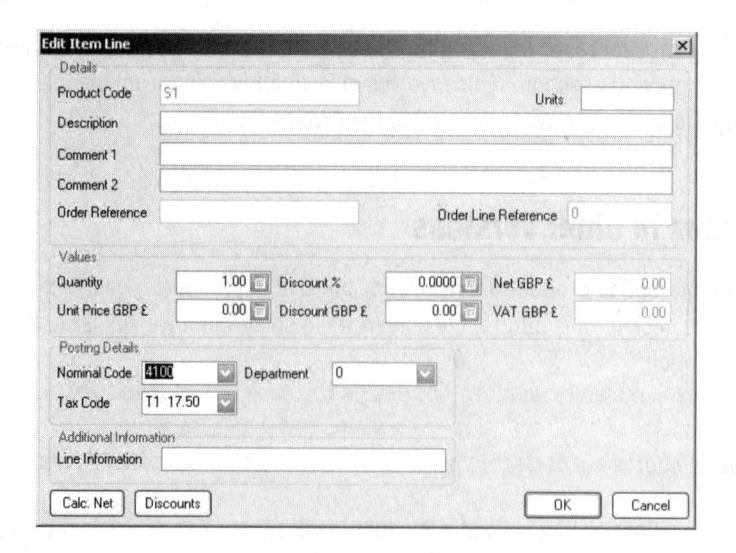

The entries to make are as follows.

(a) *Description.* One line's worth of description can be entered. You can follow this with two lines of *Comments* which might describe the item further, or make it clear that it is a non-stock item, or explain how the item is packaged ('box of 12'), or whatever else you like.

(b) Once you have entered your description and comments, Tab down to the *Quantity* box and key in the number of items you are selling. Note that if the item is sold and priced in, say, boxes of twelve you should key in the number of *boxes*, not the number of individual items.

(c) Pressing Tab takes you to the *Unit Price*. This is the price of one unit of sale (eg a box), not of an individual item.

Suppose for example an item's price is £2 per can and cans are sold in boxes of 12. If you were selling somebody 36 cans you could enter this in two ways.

Method 1		Method 2	
Quantity	36	Quantity	3
Unit Price	2	Unit Price	24

Method 2 is generally preferable. To make things crystal clear on the invoice you might include the words 'box of 12 cans' in your description or comments.

(d) *Discount %.* This is zero, unless the customer is entitled to a trade discount on the net price; for example, a discount for bulk purchasing. You can simply Tab on to the next item when there is no trade discount. If you do offer a discount of, say, 2%, key in 2.

(e) *Nominal Code.* This is the nominal ledger code for the sales account to which the sales item relates. In the Blitz system, this will be the code for the Sales – Materials account, which is code 4100.

(f) *Department.* This can be used to enter a code for the department which has made the sale. In the Blitz system, department codes are *not used*, and you should leave this item blank simply by pressing Tab.

(g) The same *Tax Codes* apply as described previously. In the Blitz system, these are as follows.
- T0 for zero-rated items
- T1 for standard-rated items (with VAT currently at 17.5%)
- T9 for items to which VAT does not apply

(h) *Net, Discount and VAT*. The total net amount payable for the item (Quantity × Unit Price), the amount of discount and the VAT payable are displayed automatically.

Once you have completed all the details you want to enter in this window click on OK. If the Quantity, the Tax Code or the Nominal account are blank you will get a message telling you so. Click on OK in the message box or press Enter to clear the message, type in the entry required, then click on OK.

This will take you back to the main Invoice window. The details you have just specified will now be shown in the relevant boxes. The cursor will be flashing in the Description box and you add whatever details you like. Once you have done this and you are satisfied that the figures are correct (change them if not), press Tab until you reach the next line of the invoice.

The main invoice screen also gives you options for Order Details and Footer Details. These features were described in the previous section of this chapter.

When the invoice is complete and correct Save it by clicking on the **Save** button and the screen will be cleared ready for the next invoice. If you have entered details of all the invoices you have to process click on Close or press Esc to get back to the main Invoicing window.

Activity 4.7

On 21 October 2000 a customer R I Tepper Ltd purchased 4 cases of Gleamo. One case contains 12 tins and costs £10.68.

Re-load Assignment 6 and enter this transaction as a **Product** invoice number 10065, following the instructions given in the preceding paragraphs (use Product Code 51).

What is the total amount of the invoice? Which nominal code should be used?

6 Producing Credit Notes

6.1 Older versions

In older versions of Sage Credit Notes are entered using the **Credit** or **SRV Credit** button from the Invoicing window.

6.2 Later versions

In later versions Credit Notes are entered exactly the same way as Invoices, that is, by using the New/Edit button from within the Invoicing window. You are then able to select **Credit** in the **Type** field, and **Product** or **Service** in the **Format** field.

7 Printing invoices and credit notes

To print invoices and credit notes you have two main options.

(a) At any time during the preparation of an invoice you can print out a hard copy,

To print out a copy of the invoice while you are preparing it click on the **Print** button at the bottom of the invoice window. Further windows will appear as explained below.

(b) You Save each invoice or credit note before leaving the input screen. A list of invoices and credit notes will be shown in the main Invoicing window and from this you can select invoices to print.

7.1 The Print button (on the main Invoicing screen)

If you are going to use the **Print** button you must first select which invoices you want to print out. One way of doing this is simply to highlight the invoice(s) concerned in the index list in the main Invoicing window by clicking on them. This is the easiest option if you only want to print one or two invoices.

If you want to highlight *all* the invoices in an index list quickly, first use the **Clear** button at the bottom of the main invoicing window (this takes away any odd highlighting there might be) and then click on the **Swap** button (this will now highlight *all* the invoices). Every time the **Swap** button is clicked it changes highlighted invoices into unhighlighted invoices and vice versa.

7.1.1 The Search button

You may want only to print or look at some invoices and credit notes rather than all of them. To cope with this problem you can use the **Search** button at the bottom of the main Invoicing screen. Click on this and the following window will appear.

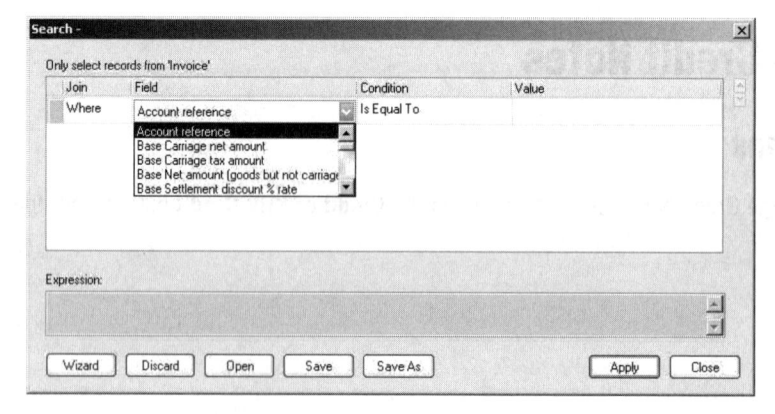

4: CUSTOMER INVOICES AND CREDIT NOTES

The search button appears in many places throughout Sage and always works in the same way. Re-read section 4.2.2 of Chapter 3 now, then attempt Activity 4.8.

Activity 4.8

Load **Assignment 5** and click on the Invoicing button. Use the Search button to produce the following lists in the Invoicing window.

(a) A list of Service invoices with an Invoice Total greater than £1,500.00, with an invoice number less than 10040.
(b) A list of invoices or credit notes that have not been posted.
(c) A list devised by you using the wildcard symbol (*).
(d) A full list of all invoices and credit notes on the system.

7.2 Printing

After clicking the Print button in the main Invoicing window (and answering Yes if asked if you wish to continue), another window will appear. If you are using a recent version of Sage, the window will appear as shown below.

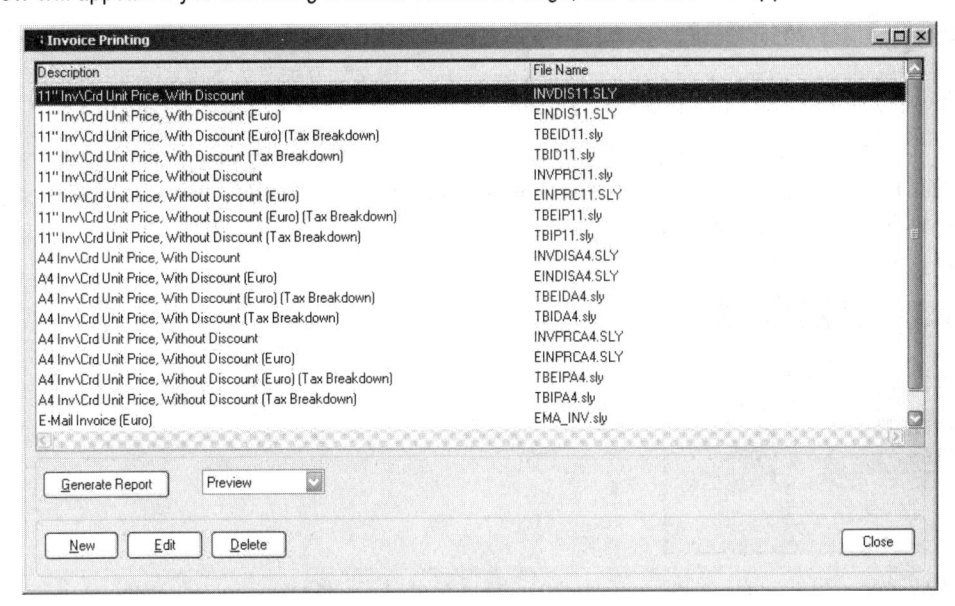

Description	File Name
11" Inv\Crd Unit Price, With Discount	INVDIS11.SLY
11" Inv\Crd Unit Price, With Discount (Euro)	EINDIS11.SLY
11" Inv\Crd Unit Price, With Discount (Euro) (Tax Breakdown)	TBEID11.sly
11" Inv\Crd Unit Price, With Discount (Tax Breakdown)	TBID11.sly
11" Inv\Crd Unit Price, Without Discount	INVPRC11.sly
11" Inv\Crd Unit Price, Without Discount (Euro)	EINPRC11.SLY
11" Inv\Crd Unit Price, Without Discount (Euro) (Tax Breakdown)	TBEIP11.sly
11" Inv\Crd Unit Price, Without Discount (Tax Breakdown)	TBIP11.sly
A4 Inv\Crd Unit Price, With Discount	INVDISA4.SLY
A4 Inv\Crd Unit Price, With Discount (Euro)	EINDISA4.SLY
A4 Inv\Crd Unit Price, With Discount (Euro) (Tax Breakdown)	TBEIDA4.sly
A4 Inv\Crd Unit Price, With Discount (Tax Breakdown)	TBIDA4.sly
A4 Inv\Crd Unit Price, Without Discount	INVPRCA4.SLY
A4 Inv\Crd Unit Price, Without Discount (Euro)	EINPRCA4.SLY
A4 Inv\Crd Unit Price, Without Discount (Euro) (Tax Breakdown)	TBEIPA4.sly
A4 Inv\Crd Unit Price, Without Discount (Tax Breakdown)	TBIPA4.sly
E-Mail Invoice (Euro)	EMA_INV.sly

In older versions, you will see a similar window, but the options are laid out slightly differently and a **Run** button is used instead of **Generate Report**.

You are given the options of sending the invoice(s) straight to the Printer, seeing a Preview on screen, creating a computer File copy or sending a copy via E-mail (if Sage has been set-up appropriately).

You get a list of possible layouts for your invoice in the Description box. We suggest you use the layout INVDIS. You have two of each of these – one set for 11" paper and one set for A4 paper. Alternatively your tutor might tell you to use a special layout designed by your college.

When you have selected your layout, click in the **Preview** circle and then click on **Run** (or in later versions ensure Preview is selected and click on **Generate Report**). A screen display of your invoice will shortly appear. Click on **Zoom** and then Page Width to get a decent view of your invoice. If you are happy with what you see click on **Print**.

7.3 Extra copies

Once you have printed an invoice or credit note a Yes will appear in the Print column in the main Invoicing window. This is a useful check if you are not sure whether or not an invoice has been printed, but *you can still print out a duplicate copy* of the invoice if you want to. An invoice might get lost in the post or damaged before it is sent, for example. To print another copy just select the invoice in the main Invoicing window, click on the **Print Invoices** button and proceed as usual.

Activity 4.9

Load Assignment 6 and print out a copy of Invoice No. 10042.

8 Updating the ledgers

When you click on the **Save** button after processing an invoice or credit note, the details are *not* posted to the customers ledger or nominal ledger.

To post the details to the ledgers, you must click on the **Update** button in the Invoicing window. Just like printing, you can post many invoices (or credit notes) all at the same time, or you can select individual ones for posting. After you have made your selection and clicked Update, you will see the following window.

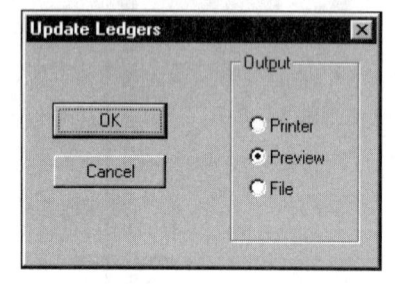

This procedure will generate a report telling you what has been posted. Decide whether you want a printed report or just a screen display or preview, or if you want a file copy of the report. Then click on OK or press Enter.

The Update Ledgers report is a list of the invoices or credit notes you have just posted to the ledger, showing details of each item posted. The listing shows:

- Invoice number or credit note number
- Invoice date
- Customer's account code
- Transaction number given to the entry by the accounts
- Product code, if any

- Nominal ledger code for each transaction
- Department code (if any) for the transaction
- Description of the goods or services sold (and quantity)
- Net amount of the invoice (or credit note)
- Tax code for the VAT
- Amount of the VAT
- Total of each invoice and a grand total for all invoices posted

Activity 4.10

Re-load up Assignment 5 and confirm the balances on the following accounts.

GOODMA	0.00
HASLAM	0.00
Sales – Window cleaning (4001)	2,634.40

Now enter the following details exactly as shown and **Save** each invoice.

Invoice.	Date	A/C	Details	Nominal code	Amount (net)
10053	25/10/2000	GOODMA	Window cleaning	4001	£100.00
10054	25/10/2000	HASLAM	Window cleaning	4001	£100.00

(a) What is the balance on the three accounts now?

(b) In the Invoicing window click on **Clear** at the bottom of the screen and then on the option **Update** at the top of the screen. Say **Yes** to the message that appears and choose whether you want a print-out or just a screen preview.

What is the balance on the three accounts now?

9 Updating the ledgers without producing invoices

In some companies, invoices could be produced manually or on a different system. When this situation occurs, the accounting system is used to post invoice and credit note details to the customers ledger and nominal ledger, but not to produce invoices.

To update the ledgers without producing invoices, you should click on the **Customers** button in the main Sage window and then on the **Invoices** button in the Customers window. Entering and posting invoice and credit note details can then be done in the same way as entering and posting details of invoices and credit notes from suppliers. These procedures have already been described in Chapter 3.

10 Reports

When you have entered a batch of invoices or credit notes (or several batches of invoices or credit notes) you can print a list of the details, with totals. This is often called a day book listing. In Sage these reports can be generated by clicking on the **Reports** button in the *Customers* window, then selecting the report required eg Day Books: Customer Invoices (Detailed).

You can choose between detailed and summary reports, and specify a particular Date Range, Transaction Range, Customer Account Range or Nominal Account Range. You should look through the various options available.

11 Customer queries

Customers often telephone the accounts department of a company with queries about invoices or credit notes. These queries can often be answered by looking up the invoice details on the system. Typical queries could be:

(a) I haven't received the credit note you promised. Have you sent it yet?
(b) I haven't had an invoice from you yet. Can you tell me how much will it be?
(c) I haven't received your invoice yet. It might be lost in the post. Can you send me a duplicate copy?

11.1 Invoice or credit note details

You can look up the details of an invoice or credit note, to find out:

(a) Whether it is on the system.
(b) Whether the invoice or credit note has been printed (and presumably sent).

You can also obtain details of the invoice or credit note. To look up these details, you can use **Invoicing** button to display a complete list of all invoices then use the **Search** button to specify the customer's account code as your condition (for example you would set your criterion as, say, Where Account Reference Is Equal to ADAMSE). You can narrow the field further by specifying additional criteria, such as a date range.

11.1.1 Example

You receive a telephone enquiry from David Hargreaves, asking about an invoice that had been expected but not yet received. You might know the customer's account reference number already. In the case study of Blitz Limited, the customer's code would start with the first letters of the surname. There are two ways of finding the details you want.

(a) Call up the Invoicing window, set your Search criteria as Account Reference Is Equal to HAR* and click on **Apply** and then on **Close**. All accounts with codes beginning with the letters HAR will be shown. Highlight the account and click on the **Service** button. You will probably get a warning telling you that the invoice has been posted and that amendments will not be saved. You only want to *look* at the details, so just click on OK and the invoice window that you used to prepare the invoice will be displayed once more.

(b) Alternatively click on the **Customers** button in the main Sage window. This too has a **Search** button and you might find it quicker to use this than to scroll right through the list. Once you find the account code for D Hargreaves click on it to highlight it, click on **Activity** and on **OK**. You will see on screen details of the account. However this will not tell you whether the invoice has been printed yet. Take a note of the number and use the Invoicing window to find this information.

11.1.2 Duplicate invoices

We saw how to print extra copies of invoices in section 7.3 of this chapter.

12 Conclusion

If you can follow the instructions in this chapter, you should be ready to attempt **Assignment 2**.

Key learning points

- ☑ In Sage, you access functions associated with the **Sales ledger** through the **Customers** button. Sage calls the '**Sales ledger control account**' the '**Debtors control account**'.

- ☑ Customers who deal regularly with an organisation should have an account in the **customers ledger** (or sales ledger).

- ☑ In Sage, there are four ways of entering **new customer accounts** in the ledger:
  - Using the Record button in the Customers window
  - Using the Invoices button in the Customers window
  - Using one of the buttons in the Invoicing window
  - Using the New button from within Customers to access the Customer Record Wizard

- ☑ Customers who purchase products or services can be **invoiced** through the Invoicing window in Sage.

- ☑ **Invoices** (and **credit notes**) are built up in sections, and the appropriate details must be entered in each section.

- ☑ If you use Sage software, you click on the **Save** button after processing an invoice or credit note. This saves the details entered, but **does not post the transaction** to the customers' ledger or nominal ledger.

- ☑ To post the details to the ledgers, you must click on the **Update** button in the Invoicing window.

Quick quiz

1   List four methods for setting up a new customer account.
2   Are you able to change the default invoice number allocated by Sage if required?
3   You have just entered all the details of a new invoice to Sage, and clicked on the Save button. The new Invoice appears within the list of invoices shown in the main Invoicing window. Has details of this Invoice been posted to the customers ledger and nominal ledger?
4   If an organisation uses Sage, but elects to produce their Invoices using a different system, should invoice and credit note details be entered through the Invoicing option?
5   How would you print a Sales Ledger day book listing?

Answers to quick quiz

1   Using the Record button in the Customers window; Using the Invoices button in the Customers window; Using one of the buttons in the Invoicing window; Using the New button from within Customers to access the Customer Record Wizard.
2   Yes, the number can be altered if required simply by typing in a new number. (Use Shift and Tab to 'go backwards' to the Invoice No.)
3   No, to post the details to the ledgers, you must click on the Update button in the Invoicing window.
4   No, in this situation it would make more sense to update the ledgers without producing invoices. This can be done by selecting the Customers button in the main Sage window, and then selecting the Invoices button from within the Customers window. The processing of invoice and credit note details can be done from here.
5   These can be generated by clicking on the Reports button in the Customers window, then selecting the report required eg Day Books: Customer Invoices (Detailed).

PART B USING ACCOUNTING SOFTWARE

Activity checklist

This checklist shows which knowledge and understanding point is covered by each activity in this chapter. Tick off each activity as you complete it.

Activity		
4.1	☐	Knowledge and Understanding: Operation of computerised accounting systems
4.2	☐	Knowledge and Understanding: Operation of computerised accounting systems
4.3	☐	Knowledge and Understanding: Operation of computerised accounting systems
4.4	☐	Knowledge and Understanding: Operation of computerised accounting systems
4.5	☐	Knowledge and Understanding: Operation of computerised accounting systems
4.6	☐	Knowledge and Understanding: Operation of computerised accounting systems
4.7	☐	Knowledge and Understanding: Operation of computerised accounting systems
4.8	☐	Knowledge and Understanding: Operation of computerised accounting systems
4.9	☐	Knowledge and Understanding: Operation of computerised accounting systems
4.10	☐	Knowledge and Understanding: Operation of computerised accounting systems

chapter 5

Payments to suppliers

Contents

1. Introduction
2. Source documents
3. Identifying invoices for payment – Aged analysis
4. Posting payments
5. Discounts
6. Credit notes
7. Payments on account
8. 'One-off' payments: cheque requisitions
9. Producing cheques
10. Reports
11. Queries about payments to suppliers
12. Conclusion

Range statement

Relevant computerised records
Computerised records
Computerised ledgers

Knowledge and understanding

Operation of computerised accounting systems

PART B   USING ACCOUNTING SOFTWARE

1 Introduction

Suppliers who have provided goods or services, and have invoiced us for these goods or services, require payment. In this chapter, we look at how payments to suppliers are processed.

2 Source documents

Cheques for payments may be produced manually or printed from within Sage. Regardless of which method is used, the payment must be correctly authorised. Therefore, those signing the cheques may need to see the source documents which may include:

(a)   The *invoice* or *invoices* for payment, and possibly a statement from the supplier listing all invoices still outstanding and unpaid;

(b)   Any *credit note* or *credit notes* from the supplier; and

(c)   Possibly *goods received note*, to confirm receipt of the goods that are being paid for.

The invoice must be signed or initialled by an *authorised* person, giving authority for the invoice to be paid. This signature could be written on the invoice itself, and dated. If any invoice has not been properly authorised, it should be referred to your supervisor.

A payment could be made for which there is an authorised *cheque requisition* form, instead of an invoice from regular supplier with an account in the Suppliers Ledger. The procedures for recording such transactions in the accounts are different, and are explained later.

3 Identifying invoices for payment – Aged analysis

If your supervisor tells you, say, to pay all invoices that have been outstanding for over one month, your first task would be to find the relevant source documents.

(a)   If your department keeps unpaid invoices in date order in a separate file, this is usually a simple manual task. You can take the invoices for payment out of the file.

(b)   Alternatively, you can identify which suppliers to pay by checking the records in the Suppliers Ledger. The most efficient way of doing this is to use an Aged Analysis.

3.1 Aged Analysis

An aged analysis is a listing of all accounts or selected accounts with the invoices analysed according to how long they have been outstanding. Start by clicking on **Suppliers** and then on **Aged.** You should see the following dialogue box.

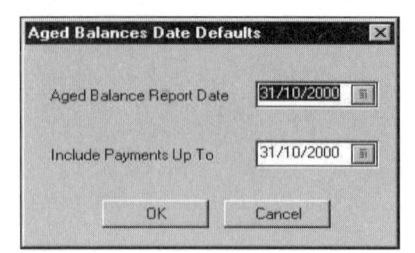

5: PAYMENTS TO SUPPLIERS

(a) *Aged Balances Report Date.* This will show the Program Date which will be today's date unless you have changed it (under Settings, Change Program Date).

You should enter the date you want to use to calculate the aged balances: the program will count back 30 days, 60 days, 90 days and so on from this date and analyse the balances accordingly. For example, if you enter 31/10/2000 you will get balances that were 30, 60, 90 etc days old as at 31/10/2000.

(b) *Include Payments Up To.* You might have paid lots of invoices in early November but this might not be relevant to your report on the state of affairs at the end of October. You might only wish to include payments made up to 31/10/2000 (or another date): if so specify this here.

Click on **OK** and the following report will appear – the figures shown below were obtained using Assignment 1 data.

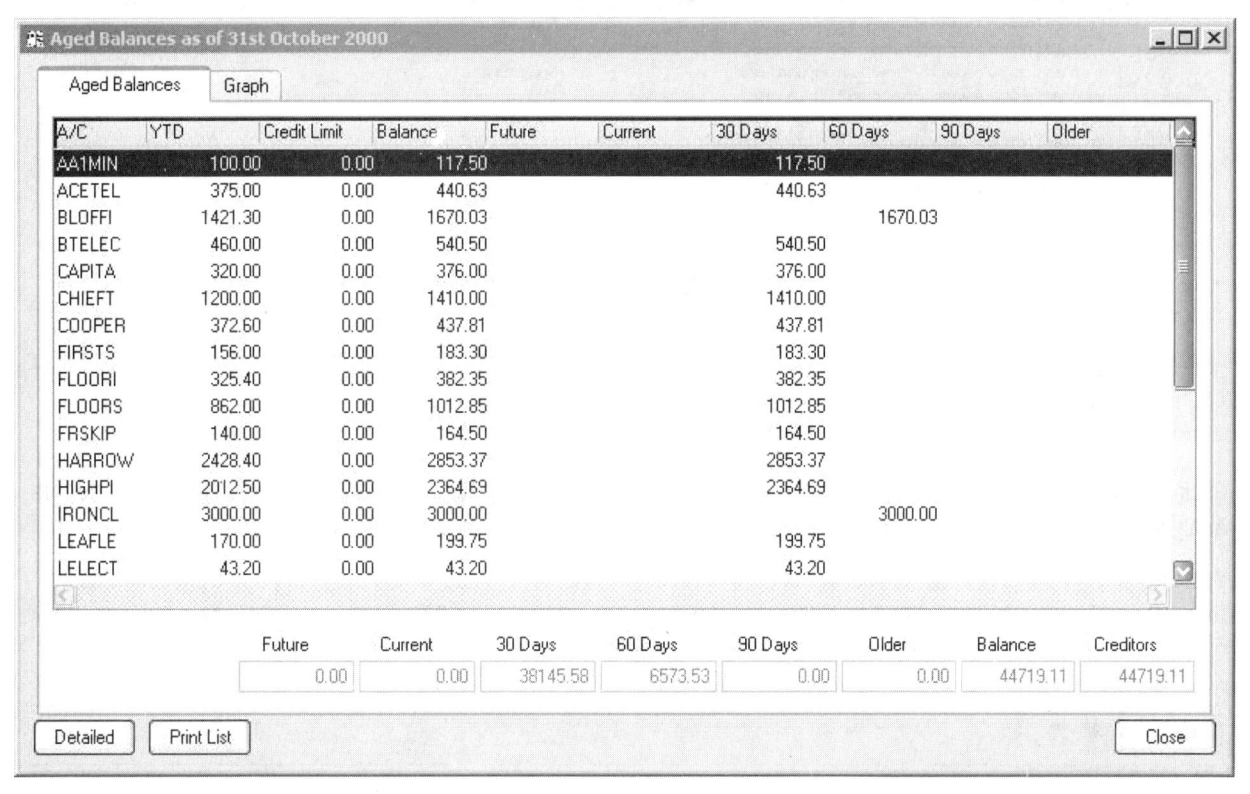

A/C	YTD	Credit Limit	Balance	Future	Current	30 Days	60 Days	90 Days	Older
AA1MIN	100.00	0.00	117.50			117.50			
ACETEL	375.00	0.00	440.63			440.63			
BLOFFI	1421.30	0.00	1670.03				1670.03		
BTELEC	460.00	0.00	540.50			540.50			
CAPITA	320.00	0.00	376.00			376.00			
CHIEFT	1200.00	0.00	1410.00			1410.00			
COOPER	372.60	0.00	437.81			437.81			
FIRSTS	156.00	0.00	183.30			183.30			
FLOORI	325.40	0.00	382.35			382.35			
FLOORS	862.00	0.00	1012.85			1012.85			
FRSKIP	140.00	0.00	164.50			164.50			
HARROW	2428.40	0.00	2853.37			2853.37			
HIGHPI	2012.50	0.00	2364.69			2364.69			
IRONCL	3000.00	0.00	3000.00					3000.00	
LEAFLE	170.00	0.00	199.75			199.75			
LELECT	43.20	0.00	43.20			43.20			

	Future	Current	30 Days	60 Days	90 Days	Older	Balance	Creditors
	0.00	0.00	38145.58	6573.53	0.00	0.00	44719.11	44719.11

You can see at a glance how long each amount making up the current balance on each account has been outstanding.

3.1.1 Future

If you are using dates for your reports that are prior to the actual date, the report will show the value of transactions that have been posted between the report date and the actual date in the **Future** column. For example, if you received and posted £5,000 of new invoices on 1 November, but ran a report on that day for 31 October the report would show an amount of £5,000 in the Future column.

3.2 Aged analysis report

In the later version of Sage, the on-screen aged analysis can be printed using the Print List button that displays when the analysis is on-screen.

PART B USING ACCOUNTING SOFTWARE

A more detailed report, that includes contact names and phone numbers may be produced. Such a report can be obtained by using the **Reports** button in the Suppliers window. Close the Aged analysis window - you should now be back in the Suppliers window. Click on the **Report** button, then double-click on the **Aged Creditors Reports** folder.

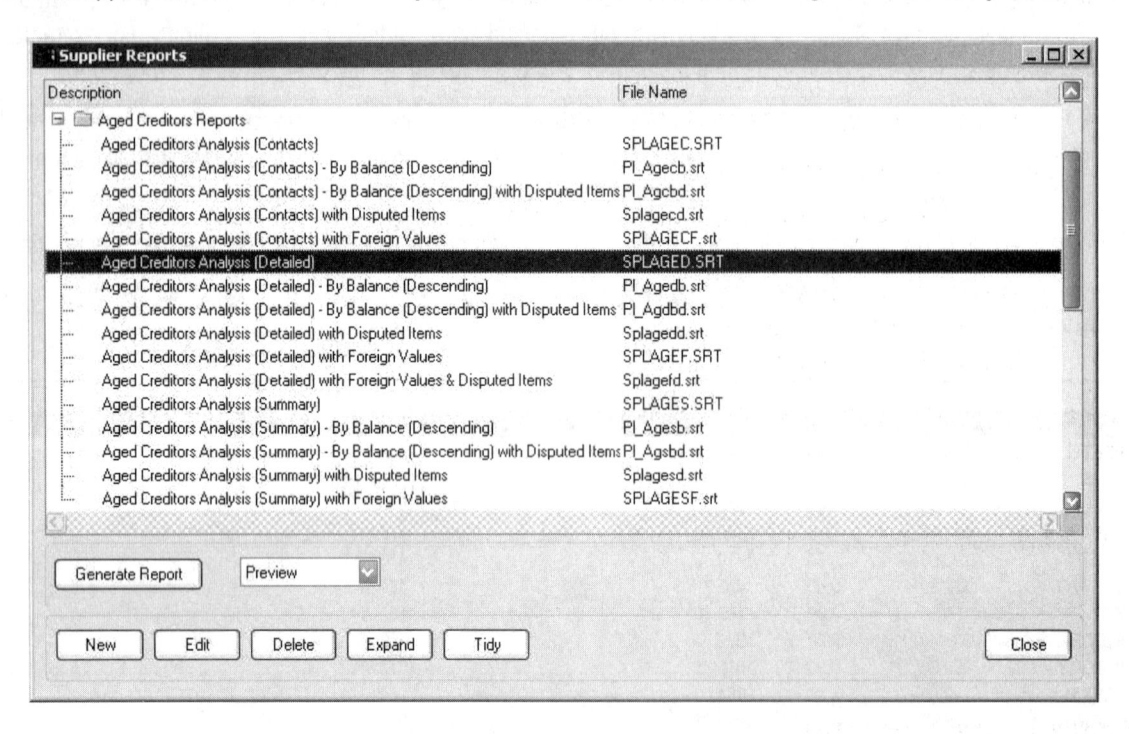

```
Supplier Reports                                                          _ □ ×
Description                                                      File Name
□ 📁 Aged Creditors Reports
    Aged Creditors Analysis (Contacts)                           SPLAGEC.SRT
    Aged Creditors Analysis (Contacts) - By Balance (Descending) Pl_Agecb.srt
    Aged Creditors Analysis (Contacts) - By Balance (Descending) with Disputed Items Pl_Agcbd.srt
    Aged Creditors Analysis (Contacts) with Disputed Items       Splagecd.srt
    Aged Creditors Analysis (Contacts) with Foreign Values       SPLAGECF.srt
    Aged Creditors Analysis (Detailed)                           SPLAGED.SRT
    Aged Creditors Analysis (Detailed) - By Balance (Descending) Pl_Agedb.srt
    Aged Creditors Analysis (Detailed) - By Balance (Descending) with Disputed Items Pl_Agdbd.srt
    Aged Creditors Analysis (Detailed) with Disputed Items       Splagedd.srt
    Aged Creditors Analysis (Detailed) with Foreign Values       SPLAGEF.SRT
    Aged Creditors Analysis (Detailed) with Foreign Values & Disputed Items Splagefd.srt
    Aged Creditors Analysis (Summary)                            SPLAGES.SRT
    Aged Creditors Analysis (Summary) - By Balance (Descending)  Pl_Agesb.srt
    Aged Creditors Analysis (Summary) - By Balance (Descending) with Disputed Items Pl_Agsbd.srt
    Aged Creditors Analysis (Summary) with Disputed Items        Splagesd.srt
    Aged Creditors Analysis (Summary) with Foreign Values        SPLAGESF.srt

[ Generate Report ]  [ Preview ▼ ]

[ New ] [ Edit ] [ Delete ] [ Expand ] [ Tidy ]                     [ Close ]
```

Click on Aged Creditors Analysis (Detailed) if you wish to see the invoices that make up the balance, or Aged Creditors Analysis (Summary) if you just wish to see the Aged Balances. Then click on the **Generate Report** button.

You then have the opportunity to select a range of suppliers (accept the defaults to include all) and transaction dates (ensure the 'To' date is 31/10/2000 to continue our previous example). Click **OK** and the report will be produced.

Activity 5.1

The Search button was explained in the previous chapter in relation to customers, but can also be used in the Suppliers Window. To practice using the Search button, load up the data for Assignment 2 and try getting listings of Suppliers' accounts according to a variety of criteria: all those with codes in the alphabetical range P to S, say, or all those with a balance over or under a certain amount, all those that do not have an address in London, or anything else you think of.

4 Posting payments

When payments are processed to suppliers accounts entries are made to:

- The suppliers' individual accounts in the Suppliers Ledger
- The creditors control account in the Nominal Ledger (debit)
- The bank account in the Nominal Ledger (credit)

To post a payment, you should have the following data:

(a) The nominal ledger code for the bank account. In the Blitz case study, this is code 1200.
(b) The supplier's account reference code.
(c) The date of the payment.
(d) If possible, the cheque number.
(e) Usually, the cheque amount.

If you want to check the previous transaction details on a supplier's account before recording the payment, you can use the **Activity** button.

4.1 Allocation of payments to invoices

Normally, a payment is made to pay off one or more outstanding invoices. Instead of just recording a payment in the supplier's account, the payment should be allocated to the invoice or invoices to which it relates.

4.2 How to post payments

If you Click on the **Bank** button in the main Sage window a bank accounts window will appear with a number of buttons and a list of all the company's bank accounts. Highlight the Account the payments will be made from - in this case the Bank Current Account.

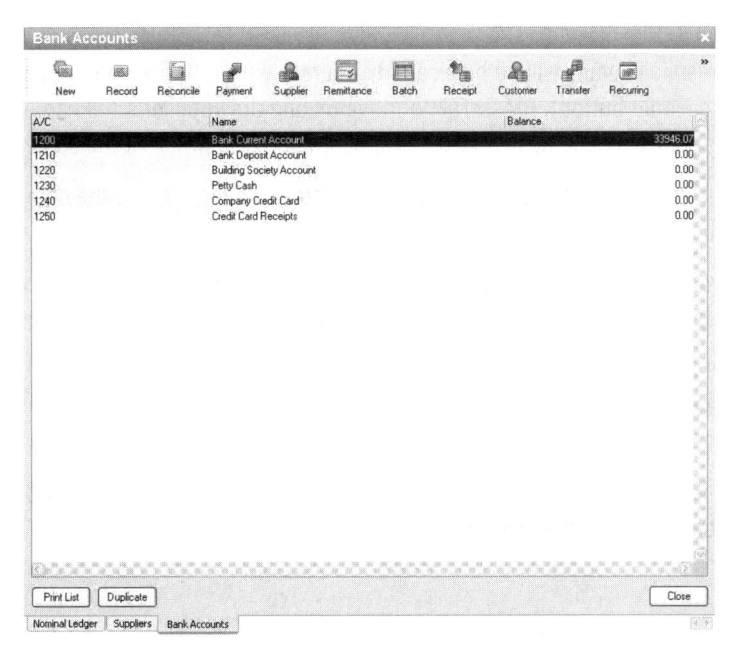

Click on the **Supplier** button and you will get a new window the top of which looks very much like a cheque book and the lower half of which tells you about outstanding invoices on a supplier's account. The following illustration assumes the data for Assignment 2 is currently loaded.

No.	Type	A/c	Date	Ref	Details	T/C	Amount £	Disputed?	Payment £	Discount £
17	PI	NEWLIT	12/09/2000	26115	Cleaning materia	n/a	473.91		0.00	0.00
72	PI	NEWLIT	01/10/2000	26187	Cleaning materia	n/a	198.22		0.00	0.00

Bank Balance: 33946.07   Analysis Total: 0.00

Most of the headings are self-explanatory. The **Type** column in the lower half of the screen identifies the type of transaction as a purchase invoice (PI), a purchase credit note (PC), or a purchase payment on account (PA).

When you first see this screen, all details will be blank and the cursor will be flashing in the **Payee** box. Here you enter the supplier's code (use the Finder button). Press Tab to move on and the supplier's full name will appear alongside the Payee box and the details of any outstanding invoices will appear in the lower half of the screen.

By default the **Date** box will show today's date (or the program date) – change this to the date of the payment. If you do change it, the new date you enter will become the default date until you click on Close to shut down the window.

When the date is the one you want, press Tab again and in the **Chq No.** box enter the number of the cheque you are posting. You must enter a unique cheque number for *every* payment. This is an important control and a useful reference.

Press Tab again and you are taken into a box with a pound sign. What you do next depends upon the instructions you have regarding payment.

    (a)   If you know that the cheque you are entering is to be for, say, £500, *type in* 500 and press Tab.
    (b)   If you have been told to pay certain invoices, type nothing: just press Tab.

On the previous illustration relating to Newlite Cleaning Fluids two outstanding invoices are shown, one for £473.91 and another for £198.22 - a total of £672.13. The information and instructions you might have could be as follows.

(a) A cheque for £473.91 is to be sent to Newlite Cleaning Fluids. **OR**
(b) Any invoices received from Newlite Cleaning Fluids in September 2000 should be paid. **OR**
(c) The balance on the Newlite Cleaning Fluids account should be paid in full.

4.3 Predetermined cheque amount

If you have been told the amount of the cheque, type it into the box with the pound sign. Press Tab and two things will happen.

(a) The amount that you typed in figures (eg '473.91') will appear in words ('Four hundred seventy-three Pounds and 91p'), just like on a real cheque.

(b) You will be taken to the first **Payment** box in the lower half of the screen. The amount shown (highlighted) in this box will at this point be 0.00. Look also at the Analysis Total box at the bottom of the window, which also shows 0.00 at this point.

Now click on the **Pay in Full** button at the bottom of the screen. The amount in the first Payment box (next to the invoice Amount box) will change to £473.91. The amount in the Analysis Total box will also change to £473.91. This is the total amount of the invoice you are paying.

The cursor, meanwhile will have moved down a line to the next Payment box and 0.00 will be highlighted. If you click on the Pay in Full button nothing will happen. This is because there is no difference between the amount in the £ sign box (the amount of the cheque) and the amount in the Analysis Total box match: the cheque total has already been allocated.

4.4 Posting payments

You can now click on the **Save** button. The payment is then posted and the screen is cleared for the next payment. Payments will only be posted if the amount in the analysis total box equals the amount of the cheque.

Activity 5.2

(a) Load the data for Assignment 3. Change the program date to 31/10/2000 (from the main menu choose Settings, Change program Date). What is the balance on the Supplier account NEWLIT and the Bank account (1200)?

(b) Enter the details for a cheque to NEWLIT for £473.91 dated 10 October 2000, cheque number 010203. Print out a remittance advice, then save your entry.

(c) What is the balance on the account NEWLIT and the bank account now?

PART B   USING ACCOUNTING SOFTWARE

4.5 Paying specific invoices

Our second scenario suggested that you had been told to pay invoices with a September 2000 date only. If you look back to the Newlite illustration you will see that the only invoice that fits into this category is the one for £473.91. You proceed as follows.

(a) When you reach the box with the pound sign, just press Tab, leaving the box blank.

(b) The cursor will move to the September 2000 invoice's Payment box with an amount 0.00 highlighted.

(c) Click on the Pay in Full button. The amount in the first Payment box will change to £473.91, and so will the amount in the cheque amount box, and the amount in the Analysis Total box.

(d) The cursor will move to the next Payment box, beside the outstanding invoice amount of £198.22.

(e) You *do not* want to pay this second invoice because it is not a September 2000 invoice. Therefore (unless you first want to print a remittance advice note) just click on the **Save** button. The payment is posted and the screen will clear for the next entry.

Activity 5.3

Load Assignment 3 again. Change the program date to 31/10/2000. Following the above, pay any invoices received from Newlite Cleaning Supplies in September 2000. Cheque number is 010203. Also pay any received from British Telecom in September 2000. Cheque number is 010204.

4.6 Paying off the balance

The final scenario suggested that you were told to pay off the balance on the account. The procedure is exactly the same as the procedure for paying specific invoices, except that instead of Saving at step (e) you click on Pay in Full. You continue to do this for each invoice listed until all the invoice Amount boxes on screen have an equivalent amount in the Payment box. The cheque amount and the amount in the Analysis Total box will increase by the amount of each invoice that you Pay in Full. When all the invoices shown are paid, print a remittance advice if you want to and then click on the **Save** button.

To finish processing payments click on the **Close** button or press Esc.

4.7 Part payments

If you had been instructed, say, to pay Newlite Cleaning Fluids an amount of only £150 (perhaps because of a dispute), you would enter a 'part payment'. The procedure is exactly as for any other predetermined cheque amount. Enter the amount of the cheque, then press Tab until you reach the Payment box of the invoice you want to part pay. In this example you would enter £150 here. When you save the payment the outstanding amount will be reduced by £150.

If you want to pay the whole of some invoices but only part of others, use the Pay in Full button on those invoices you wish to pay all of, but enter the amount you wish to part pay when in the Payment box of an invoice you are part paying.

Activity 5.4

Load Assignment 3 again. Change the program date to 31/10/2000.

Pay off the balance on the Newlite Cleaning Fluids account. Cheque number is 914785.

Pay Prairie Couriers Ltd £50.

What is the balance on these two accounts, now?

4.8 Remittance advices

A remittance advice can be sent with a payment to a supplier, indicating the invoices that are being paid, together with discounts taken and credit notes being used. It is, quite simply, a statement to show what the payment is for.

To produce and print a remittance advice, **after you have entered the details of a payment** and returned to the Bank window, click on the **Remittance** button. In later versions of Sage you will be presented with a list of payments available for Remittance Advice printing. Clicking on the Print button will bring up the following window.

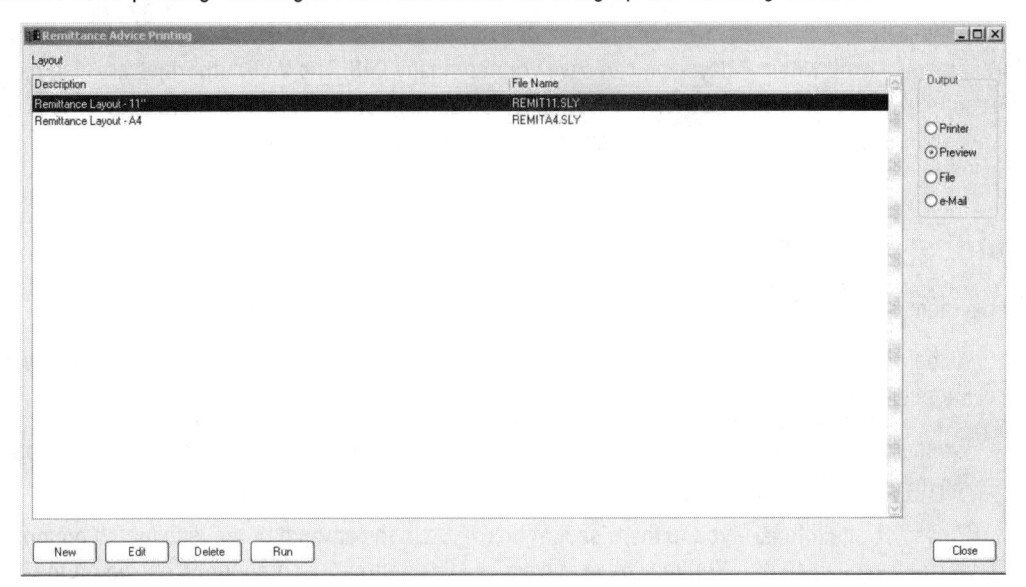

Pick one of the default layouts, REMIT11 or REMITA4, depending on your printer's paper size. Choose what sort of Output you want – printed, preview, file or e-mail – and then click on Print.

Activity 5.5

Load Assignment 3. Change the program date to 31/10/2000.

Pay Newlite Cleaning Fluids £198.22. Cheque number is 246264. Then, print a remittance advice.

5 Discounts

5.1 Settlement discount

As mentioned in Chapter 3, some suppliers offer a discount for early payment of an invoice. For example, payment terms of '30 days net, 3% discount 7 days' means that the invoice should be paid in full within 30 days, but a discount of 3% is available if payment is made within 7 days of the invoice date.

When such a discount (a 'settlement discount') is taken, you will need to calculate the amount of the discount. VAT rules stipulate that VAT should be charged on the discounted *net* amount (whether or not the discount is taken). Check that you can do the calculation accurately. For example, suppose that a supplier offers a 3% settlement discount for the following invoice.

	Taking the discount £	Not taking the discount £
Net amount	1,600.00	1,600.00
Discount (3%)	(48.00)	
VAT-able amount	1,552.00	
VAT at 17.5%	271.60	271.60
Total payable	1,823.60	1,871.60

In other words, if you pay up within 7 days you can save your company £48. The VAT authorities are also happy, because your supplier's accounts show a VAT *output* (sales) tax amount of £271.60 and yours show a VAT *input* (purchases) tax amount of £271.60, whether you take the discount or not.

5.2 Recording settlement discount

To record a payment when a settlement discount is being taken the procedure is as follows.

(a) As before, click on **Bank** in the main window and then **Supplier** in the Bank Accounts window. Enter the supplier code, date and cheque number.

(b) When you get to the box with the pound sign in it leave it blank by pressing Tab to take you on the Payment box. Make no entry here.

(c) Press Tab again to take you to the Discount box. Type in the amount of the discount in pounds (for example type in 48.00). You may have to calculate this yourself, or it might be shown on the invoice already.

(d) Press Tab. The amount in the Payment box will automatically be calculated as the amount of the invoice minus the discount. The cursor will move to the next payment line.

(e) **Save** the payment as usual.

Activity 5.6

Load Assignment 3. Change the program date to 31/10/2000.

Pay off the full balance on the account SAMURA, taking a discount of 5% on the total amount owing. The cheque number is 222354

How much do you actually pay? What is the VAT element?

6 Credit notes

6.1 Offsetting credit notes

When a credit note has been posted to a supplier's account, this can be offset against an invoice that is being paid. For example, if a supplier has submitted an invoice for £100 and there is a credit note for £25, only £75 has to be paid to settle the account. Credit notes that have been posted to suppliers' accounts will appear with invoices in the list on the cheque screen.

To use a credit note, enter the details on the cheque in the usual way, leaving the cheque amount box with the pound sign blank by Tabbing through it. Press tab until you reach the *credit note's* Payment box. Click on the **Pay in Full** button. You will see the amount in the Payment box change to the amount of the credit note – in the example given it would be £25.

Now Tab up or down to the Payment box of the invoice you want to pay. Click on **Pay in Full**. The amount in the invoice's Payment box will now be equal to the amount of the invoice (£100, say), but the Analysis Total box and the cheque amount box will show the amount of the invoice less the amount of the credit note: £75 in our example.

If the amount of the credit note is greater than the amount of any outstanding invoice, proceed as follows. Without entering a cheque amount, Tab down to the Payment boxes of the invoices in question and click on Pay in Full. Then Tab to the Payment box of the credit note and *type in* the amount shown in the Analysis Total box. Press Tab.

The cheque amount will then be nil – in other words no cheque needs to be sent. This will be relatively rare, but if it happens Tab back up to the cheque number box and clear any number you typed there by pressing Delete. When you click on **Save** this has the effect of clearing off the invoices that have been offset against the credit note, and reducing the amount of the credit note outstanding.

Activity 5.7

Load up Assignment 3. Change the program date to 31/10/2000.

Pay Trojan Secretarial Services £141. Cheque number is 147853.

PART B   USING ACCOUNTING SOFTWARE

7 Payments on account

7.1 What is a payment on account?

Occasionally, a payment might be made to a supplier 'on account', before an invoice is received.

7.2 Making a payment on account

To make a payment on account, enter the supplier, date, cheque number details and the amount to pay. When the total cheque amount is entered Tab down to the Payment box and click on **Pay in Full** for each invoice. When you have finished, click on **Save**. If the payment is for an amount greater than the total of the invoices, a message like the one shown below will appear. Click on Yes (or key in Y or press Enter) to accept this.

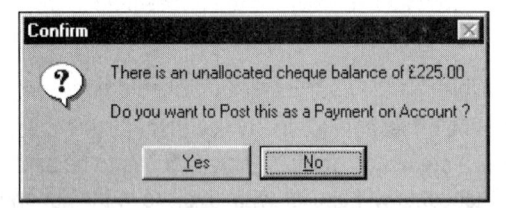

> **Confirm**
> There is an unallocated cheque balance of £225.00
> Do you want to Post this as a Payment on Account ?
> Yes   No

If you want to send a remittance advice, use the **Remittance** button as explained earlier.

7.3 Offsetting payments on account against invoices

Later, when invoices have been received, the payment on account should be offset against them. This is done in the same way as using a credit note. Without entering a cheque amount, Tab down to the Payment boxes of the invoices in question and click on Pay in Full. Then Tab to the payment on account item, and *type in* the *smaller* of:

- The total of the payment on account.
- The amount now shown in the Analysis Total box.

If the payment on account is not large enough to cover the newly-received invoices there will now be an amount shown on the cheque to make up the difference.

If the amount of the payment on account still exceeds the amount of any invoices received the cheque amount will be nil – in other words no cheque will be sent. Again, this will be relatively rare, but if it happens Tab back up to the cheque number box and clear it by pressing Delete. If you click on **Save** this has the effect of clearing off the invoices that have been offset against the payment on account, and reducing the amount of the outstanding payment on account.

Activity 5.8

Load up Assignment 6. Change the program date to 31/10/2000.

Pay the Leaflet Company £500 (cheque number 278400), part of which is a payment on account. Note down how much.

Post an invoice for leaflets dated 5 November 2000 (number WE4582) received from The Leaflet Company for £700 (gross). The Nominal account is the Printing account.

Change the program date to 15/11/2000 and clear the balance on this supplier's account (cheque number 278487).

5: PAYMENTS TO SUPPLIERS

Tasks

(a) How much was the payment on account?
(b) What is the amount of the cheque needed to clear the balance?

8 'One-off' payments: cheque requisitions

Payments are sometimes made against a cheque requisition.

(a) If an invoice from a supplier will be received in due course, the payment can be entered as a payment on account, as described above.

(b) If the supplier does not have or need an account, there won't be an entry for the transaction in the suppliers ledger.

A cheque payment for a bank transaction that will not be processed through the suppliers ledger should be recorded directly to the nominal ledger accounts. The payment should be processed as follows.

(a) Click on the **Bank** button in the main window.

(b) If different bank accounts are used for nominal ledger payments and Supplier payments, make sure the correct one is highlighted. (Only one account is used in the Blitz case study.)

(c) Click on the **Payment** button in the Bank Accounts window.

The following box, or a similar box if using an earlier version, will appear.

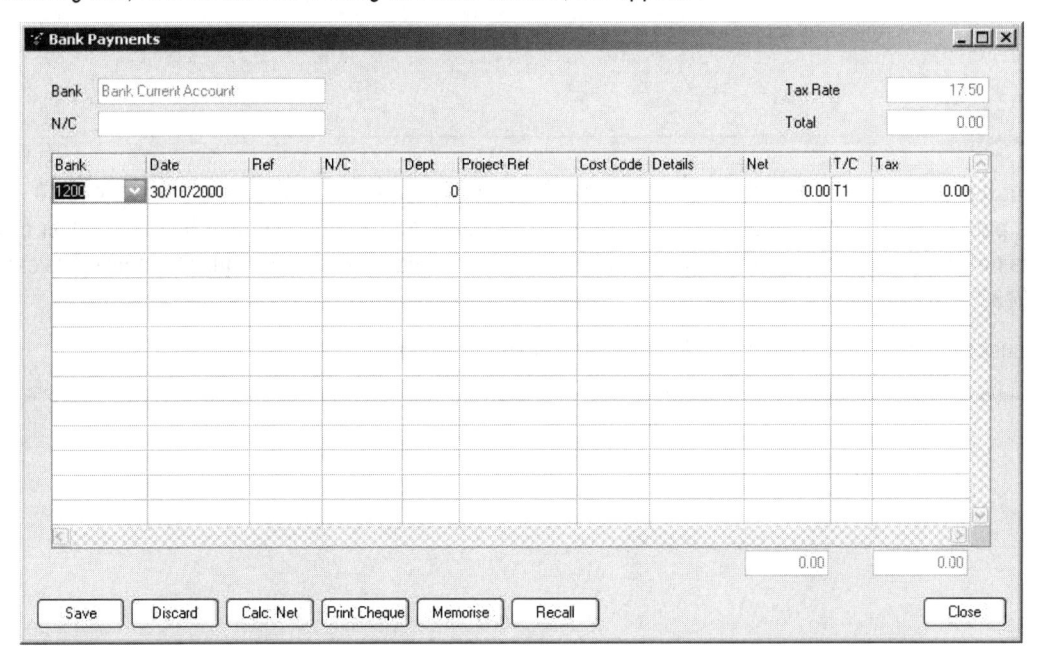

The cursor begins in the Bank column with the usual finder button. This is because many businesses make use of a number of bank accounts, although this does not apply in the case of Blitz, where you would simply choose A/C 1200 as usual.

PART B USING ACCOUNTING SOFTWARE

Enter the **Date** in the usual way. The **Ref** should be the cheque number.

Press Tab again to take you to the **N/C** box. Here you enter the nominal ledger account code for the account to which the payment refers. For example, a cheque payment for the hire of a motor car should be allocated to nominal account code 7401 in the standard Sage chart of accounts (the account code for Car Hire expenses). As usual, a list of codes can be displayed on screen by clicking on the Finder button or pressing the F4 function key.

In the Blitz case study you can Tab straight through any other options until you reach **Details**, where you should type in an appropriate brief description of what the payment is for.

In the **Net** box you have two options.

(a) Enter the *net amount of the payment (excluding VAT)* and press Tab. The cursor will move to the **T/c** (Tax code) box. The default code T1 for standard rate VAT will already be shown and the **Tax** box will already show VAT calculated at this rate. You can, however alter the tax code (usually to T0 for zero rated items). If you do this and press Tab the VAT will automatically be recalculated at the appropriate rate.

(b) Alternatively you can enter the *total payment inclusive of VAT* in the **Net** box. Before pressing Tab click on the **Calc Net** button at the foot of the window. This will automatically calculate VAT at the standard rate and divide the total amount that you entered into net and VAT amounts. The tax code T1 will be shown in the **T/c** box. You can change this to another rate (in which case the figures will be recalculated) if necessary.

When you click on **Save** the transactions will be automatically posted to the appropriate nominal ledger accounts:

Credit: Bank Account (probably code 1200)

Debit: Nominal ledger account specified in the N/C field for the transaction.

Activity 5.9

Your supervisor has asked you, on 5 October 2000, to record a cheque payment to Goodtime Ltd for £1,410.00 (£1,200.00 net plus £210.00 for VAT at the standard rate.) The cheque is for UK Entertainment (nominal ledger code 7403). There is no invoice, and the request for payment has been submitted on a cheque requisition form. The cheque number is 345432.

Record this transaction. (It does not matter which Assignment you have loaded.)

9 Producing cheques

The option to print cheques using Sage is only available in Sage Line 50 (ie this option is not available in Sage Instant Accounts). To print cheques using Sage, follow these steps.

Step 1   The date of your printed cheques are retrieved from the computer system date. To create post-dated cheques, change your computer's system date.

Step 2   From the main Sage screen, choose the Bank option.

Step 3   In Bank Accounts window, ensure the account that you want to make the payments from is highlighted (for Blitz this would be **1200**).

Step 4   Click on the Cheques button (if it's not showing click on the small >> symbol in the upper right of the screen to reveal other buttons). The Print Cheques window appears listing all remittances for all purchase invoices), purchase credit notes and purchase payments on account that have not been printed before and have blank references. Remittances for bank payments that selected to print the cheque during processing are also shown.

Step 5   To restrict the transactions that appear to a certain date range, select the Date Range checkbox and enter the range you require.

Step 6   If you want to include cheques that have already been printed, select the Show Printed Items checkbox. If you have already printed a cheque it appears in a different colour in the Print Cheques window and a 'Y' appears in the Printed column.

Step 7   The starting cheque number is automatically entered for you. You can change this number if required.

Step 8   Select the transactions you want to print cheques for.

Step 9   Print the cheques you have selected by clicking on the Print cheques button. If you have not selected any transactions cheques will be printed for all listed transactions.

Step 10   Select the layout you require and click Run. The cheques are printed and you are asked to confirm that they have all printed correctly. If your cheques have printed correctly, each cheque is given a reference number.

10 Reports

To see on screen a list of all the *transactions* on the bank account, click on **Nominal,** highlight account number 1200 and click on **Activity**, and then on OK.

To get an equivalent print-out, click on **Nominal**, then on **Reports,** and choose **Nominal Activity** from the options you are offered. You will need to specify the relevant date range and account range (eg 1200 to 1200).

To get reports on *payments* click on **Bank** in the main window, ensure the account you want is highlighted (A/c 1200 in the Blitz case study), and then click on **Reports**. The options you are then presented with depends upon the version of Sage you are using. Experiment with the reports available on-screen.

11 Queries about payments to suppliers

You might be asked to deal with a query from a supplier who wants to know when you are going to pay an outstanding invoice.

Simply highlight the account in the main supplier window and click on Activity. To see all transactions relating to that supplier accept the defaults by clicking **OK**.

12 Conclusion

If you were able to follow the instructions in this chapter, you should now be ready to attempt Assignment 3.

5: PAYMENTS TO SUPPLIERS

Key learning points

- ☑ **Cheques** for payments may be produced manually or printed from within an accounting software package such as Sage. Regardless of which method is used, payments must be correctly **authorised**.
- ☑ An **aged analysis** is a listing of all accounts or selected accounts with the invoices analysed according to how long they have been outstanding.
- ☑ Payments can be posted in Sage from the **Bank** button in the main Sage window. The user selects the bank account the payments will be made from (usually the Bank Current Account) and then clicks on the **Supplier** button.
- ☑ Details of the payment are **entered on-screen** into a form that looks very much like a cheque.
- ☑ Modern accounting software packages also include the option of printing **Remittance Advices** to be sent with cheques detailing the invoices paid.
- ☑ Sage and other similar packages can also handle '**payments on account**' and automate **discount** calculations.

Quick quiz

1. List three possible source documents that may be required to be viewed before payment is made to a supplier.
2. What is an Aged Analysis report?
3. To post a payment to Sage, you will need certain information. List three pieces of information you will need.
4. What is a remittance advice?
5. What is a 'payment on account'?

Answers to quick quiz

1. Source documents may include: The invoice or invoices for payment; Possibly a statement from the supplier listing all invoices still outstanding and unpaid; Any credit notes offset from the invoice totals; and possibly a goods received note.
2. An aged analysis report is a listing of all accounts or selected accounts with the invoices analysed according to how long they have been outstanding.
3. Any three of the following: The nominal ledger code for the bank account; the supplier's name or account code, the date of the payment; possibly the cheque number, the cheque amount or invoices to be paid.
4. A remittance advice is a document showing the invoices that are being paid by a cheque, together with discounts taken and credit notes being used. It's purpose is to show exactly what the payment is for.
5. A 'payment on account is a payment made to a supplier 'on account', before an invoice has been received.

PART B USING ACCOUNTING SOFTWARE

Activity checklist

This checklist shows which knowledge and understanding point is covered by each activity in this chapter. Tick off each activity as you complete it.

Activity		
5.1	☐	Knowledge and Understanding: Operation of computerised accounting systems
5.2	☐	Knowledge and Understanding: Operation of computerised accounting systems
5.3	☐	Knowledge and Understanding: Operation of computerised accounting systems
5.4	☐	Knowledge and Understanding: Operation of computerised accounting systems
5.5	☐	Knowledge and Understanding: Operation of computerised accounting systems
5.6	☐	Knowledge and Understanding: Operation of computerised accounting systems
5.7	☐	Knowledge and Understanding: Operation of computerised accounting systems
5.8	☐	Knowledge and Understanding: Operation of computerised accounting systems
5.9	☐	Knowledge and Understanding: Operation of computerised accounting systems

chapter 6

Receipts from customers

Contents

1. Introduction
2. Receipts
3. Credit notes and customer receipts
4. Discounts
5. Returned cheques
6. Refunding paid invoices
7. Account balances
8. Payments with order (bank receipts)
9. Reports
10. Conclusion

Range statement

Relevant computerised records
Computerised records
Computerised ledgers

Knowledge and understanding

Operation of computerised accounting systems

PART B   USING ACCOUNTING SOFTWARE

1 Introduction

In this chapter we explain the process of recording payments sent to us from customers.

2 Receipts

2.1 Recording customer receipts

The information required to process the payment to the customer's Sales ledger account includes:

- (a) The nominal ledger code of the bank account (1200 in the Blitz case study).
- (b) The name of the customer and the customer's account reference code.
- (c) The date of the receipt.
- (d) The customer's cheque number (although this is not essential).
- (e) The cheque amount.
- (f) The amount of early settlement discount taken, if any.

You should also receive information showing which invoice (or invoices) the customer is paying, such as a remittance advice. This should also identify any credit notes that are being used.

Click on the **Bank** button in the main Sage window. As you learned in the previous chapter this gives a list of all the company's bank accounts. If there is more than one, highlight the one to which customer receipts are posted (probably account 1200, as in the Blitz case study) and then click on the **Customer** button. The following window, or a similar one depending upon the version of Sage you are using, will appear.

The cursor will be positioned the A/C box. Here you enter the customer account code. You can use the Finder button on the right of the A/C box to find the code. When you enter a code and press Tab the full name of the customer appears in the Name box and details of any outstanding transactions on the account appear in the lower half of the screen.

The Type column shows the type of transaction on each line:

- (a) SI means sales invoice.
- (b) SC means sales credit note.
- (c) SA means sales payment on account.

Enter the Date of payment. By default this field will show today's date, as recorded in the computer system, but you can alter this. If you do so the new date will appear each time you start a fresh receipt until you close the window, so there is no need to change it every time.

Pressing Tab takes you to the Ref box. Here you can enter something like the customer's cheque number or the number of the customer's remittance advice or the number of the invoice being paid, or some other identifying reference. *Do not* leave this field blank: enter a unique reference of some kind.

2.2 Allocating receipts

When you reach the Amount box you have two options.

- (a) If you can see at a glance that the amount of the cheque that you have received is the same as the amount of the outstanding invoice(s) shown in the lower half of the screen, leave the Amount box empty: just press Tab.
- (b) If you are not sure what invoices are being paid it is safer to key in the amount of the cheque in the Amount box and press Tab. (A £ sign is not required.)

You must now allocate the receipt of the customer's payment to the outstanding invoice or invoices in the account, to indicate which invoice or invoices have been paid. The procedure is just like the procedure for allocating payments, as described in the previous chapter.

When you press Tab you will be taken to the **Receipt** box and an amount of 0.00 will be highlighted. If you click on the **Pay in Full** button this will change to the full amount of the invoice.

- (a) If you left the Amount box blank this will also change to the amount of the invoice, as will the amount in the Analysis Total box. Press Tab again to move to the next line and repeat the procedure until the amount in the Amount box and the Analysis Total box equal the amount of your receipt. Click on **Save** and the screen will clear.
- (b) If you did key in the amount of the receipt in the Amount box there are three possibilities.
    - (i) If the amount you entered was *less than* the amount of any invoice, it is a part payment by the customer. When you click on the **Pay in Full** button the amount you keyed in will appear in the Receipt box and in the Analysis Total box. There is no more money to allocate so you can just click on **Save**.
    - (ii) If the amount you keyed in was exactly the *same as* the amount of an invoice (or the same as the total of several invoices), then clicking on the **Pay in Full** button for the invoice or invoices will make an amount equal to the amount of the invoice(s) appear in the Receipt box and the Analysis Total box. Click on **Save** when there is no more money to allocate.

PART B USING ACCOUNTING SOFTWARE

(iii) If the amount you keyed in was *greater than* the total of all the outstanding invoices you have received a payment on account. Click on the **Pay in Full** button each time you Tab to the next Receipt box until any outstanding invoices are paid. The total will accumulate in the Analysis Total box, but when you have finished the Amount box will still show a greater total than the Analysis Total box. Click on **Save** and you will get a message telling you that there is an unallocated cheque balance of £X, and asking if you want to post it as a payment on account. Assuming that this is what you want, click on Yes.

This might sound complicated, but it is not really when you start using the system. The following table summarises what we have said so far.

Amount received	Amount(s) outstanding	Action
£254.31	£254.31	Leave the Amount box blank and Tab to the Receipt box beside the invoice amount £254.31. Click on Pay in Full then Save.
£500	£200 £300	You can see at a glance that what you have received is the same as the amount outstanding. Proceed as in the previous example for the two invoice amounts.
£193.46	£247.82 £193.46	The customer is clearly paying the second of the two invoices. Leave the Amount box blank and Tab to the Receipt box beside the amount £193.46. Click on Pay in Full and then Save.
£752.57	£466.18 £286.39	Key in the amount £752.57 in the Amount box and press Tab. Click on Pay in Full for each of the two invoices. The total in the Analysis Box will show £466.18 the first time you do this and increase to £752.57 the second time. The two invoices have been paid in full. Click on Save.
£200 (Part payment)	£350	Key in the amount £200 in the Amount box and press Tab. Click on Pay in Full. The amount in the Receipt box will show £200, as will the total in the Analysis Box. Click on Save. When you next call up the account it will show that £150 is still outstanding.
£500 (Payment on account)	£350	Key in the amount £500 in the Amount box and press Tab. Click on Pay in Full. The amount in the Receipt box will show £350, as will the total in the Analysis Box. However the Amount box will still show £500. Click on Save and respond Yes when you get a message asking if you want to post a payment on account of £150.

Activity 6.1

Load Assignment 6 and find out the balances on the bank account and the debtors ledger control account.

Post the following receipts from customers, all dated 15/11/2000, following the procedures described above. Use the number of the first invoice that is being paid as your reference number.

ASPINA £211.50

BRADLE £500.00

DCSROO £200.00

ELITEC £941.11

ROSEAL £146.00

What are the balances on the bank account and the debtors ledger control account now?

Print out a report of the activity on the ELITEC account.

3 Credit notes and customer receipts

Customers will generally pay the balance due – which is the total of Invoices due less the total of any Credit Notes relating to those invoices.

The best way of recording a receipt in the customer's account where a credit note is being used is to include the credit note in the allocations as follows.

(a) Enter the *actual cheque amount* in the Amount box.

(b) Tab down to the Receipt box of the credit note transaction and click on **Pay in Full**.

(c) Tab to the Receipt box of the other outstanding invoice or invoices being paid and click on **Pay in Full** until the total amount of the cheque is used up.

Activity 6.2

Load up Assignment 3.

You have received a cheque for £1,762.50 from Royal Properties Ltd. Post this receipt as you think appropriate.

PART B   USING ACCOUNTING SOFTWARE

4 Discounts

A customer might take advantage of an early settlement discount, when this is offered. When a customer takes a discount, you will need to be informed of the amount of discount that has been taken. (You might also be asked to check that the customer has calculated the discount correctly. You can do this with the calculator buttons if you like.)

Recording a receipt net of discount is similar to recording a payment to a supplier net of discount.

   (a)   In the Discount box type in the amount of the discount in pounds. Press Tab.
   (b)   The Receipt box will automatically show the reduced balanced due.

Activity 6.3

Load up Assignment 3.

You have decided to offer Harvey-Sagar Developments a settlement discount of 2% on all future invoices.

(a)   Amend the record of this customer accordingly.

(b)   Post an invoice to Harvey-Sagar Developments dated 15 November 2000 for £850 (net) for Office Cleaning. (Accept the default invoice number offered by Sage.)

(c)   Post a receipt dated 20 November 2000 from Harvey-Sagar Developments for £2,694.28, following the instructions above.

5 Returned cheques

Occasionally, a cheque received from a customer might be returned by the bank ('bounced') marked 'Refer to Drawer'. The customer's bank is refusing to pay the cheque, possibly because there are insufficient funds in the customer's bank account.

When a cheque bounces, the receipt will already have been recorded in the customer's account. This must now be corrected.

The following instructions apply to Sage Line 50 and Sage Instant Accounts Plus only. 'Standard' Sage Instant Accounts Solutions users should read through these sections, but will not be able to perform the operations on-screen as this 'Wizard' is not included in the software. (In the 'real-world', users of software without a 'Wizard' would key-in the entries required to record the returned cheque.)

In version 12 and version 2007, the 'Wizard' used to record returned cheques is accessed via the **Write Off / Refund** option within the Tasks listing on the left of the Customers screen. You should then see the box shown on the following page.

In older versions, this is accessed by clicking on **Tools** at the top of the main window, then on the option **Write Off, Refund, Return**. Ensure the **Sales ledger** option is selected and click Next. You should then see the box shown on the following page.

6: RECEIPTS FROM CUSTOMERS

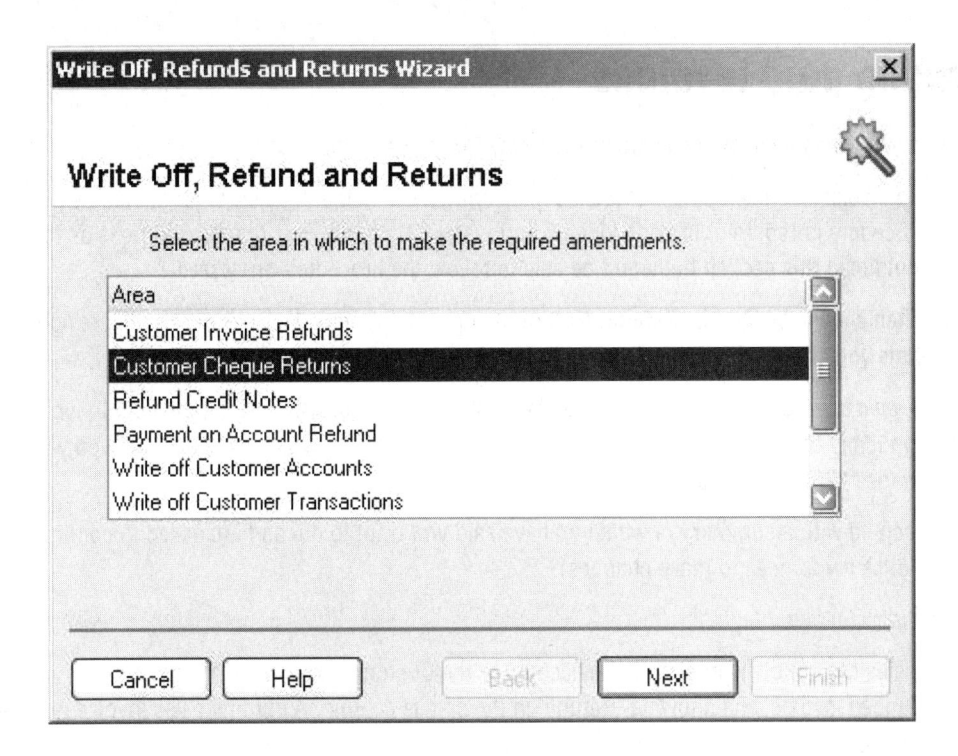

[Screenshot: Write Off, Refunds and Returns Wizard dialog box showing options: Customer Invoice Refunds, Customer Cheque Returns (highlighted), Refund Credit Notes, Payment on Account Refund, Write off Customer Accounts, Write off Customer Transactions. Buttons: Cancel, Help, Back, Next, Finish.]

The list of options includes the item **Customer Cheque Returns**. Highlight this and click on the **Next** button. A list of customer accounts will appear. Highlight the one you require and click on Next.

Next, select the cheque that has 'bounced', then click on Next. Enter the date of the transaction, which would usually be the date the cheque was dishonoured, and click Next.

You're then presented with a summary of what you have requested. If you are happy with this, click on **Finish** to post the transaction. If not there is a **Back** option, allowing you to go back through these steps and make changes as necessary.

Activity 6.4

Load Assignment 6.

It is 31 October 2000. A cheque from A Wyche for £88.13 has bounced.

(a) What is the initial balance on A Wyche's account and on the bank account?
(b) Record the bounced cheque, following the instructions given above.
(c) What is the balance on the two accounts now?
(d) How is the transaction shown in A Wyche's customer's ledger account?

PART B   USING ACCOUNTING SOFTWARE

6 Refunding paid invoices

To cancel an *unpaid* invoice, you should issue a credit note for the same amount.

However, when an invoice has been paid, but it is subsequently decided that the customer should be given a refund in full, a different procedure is required. In Sage Line 50 and Instant Accounts Plus this procedure is as follows. (Sage Instant users should read this section but won't be able to follow the procedure on-screen.)

Click on **Tools**. Then choose **Write Off, Refund, Return** and proceed exactly as described in the previous section, except that this time you choose **Customer Invoice Refunds**.

Details of all *fully-paid* invoices for the chosen customer will appear on screen. Click on the item to which the refund applies to highlight it and then click on the **Next** button. You are then asked which bank account you want to post the adjustment to. Choose 1200 for the case study.

You are then presented with a summary of what you have said you want to do, and are asked to confirm it by clicking on **Finish** (or select **Back** if you need to make changes).

The effect of this is as follows.

(a) A sales credit note is posted to the account in the Customers ledger, with the same reference as the refunded invoice, and showing 'Refund' in the details column. A dummy sales invoice is posted to the same account, and is automatically allocated in full to the credit note. The details column shows 'Allocation – Refund'. The sales turnover to date on the account is reduced by the amount of the refund.

(b) The appropriate Nominal ledger account for sales is reduced by (debited with) the amount refunded. The nominal ledger bank control account, out of which the refund is being paid, will be credited with the amount refunded (in other words the bank balance will be reduced).

Activity 6.5

Load Assignment 6.

What is the balance on the accounts for Bridgford and Co and Sales – Contract cleaning?

On 31 October 2000 it has been decided that Bridgford and Co should be given a refund for invoice number 10003.

Post this transaction. What is the new balance on Bridgford and Co's account and on the Sales – Contract cleaning account?

How does this transaction appear in Bridgford and Co's account?

7 Account balances

You might be asked to find out what is the unpaid balance on a customer's account. A customer might telephone, for example, and ask how much he owes. Or your supervisor might ask how much a particular customer still owes. The simplest way of finding the unpaid balance on an customer's account is to use the **Activity** button.

This gives a window similar to the Suppliers Ledger Activity window, which allows you to find the current unpaid balance on any supplier account in the Suppliers Ledger. This option was described in Chapter 5.

8 Payments with order (bank receipts)

8.1 Receipts from 'Cash Sale' customers

Customers might pay by cheque or credit card for goods or services when they make their order. The customer is not asking for credit; any may not want or need an account in the Customers Ledger. The transaction should be recorded as a sale and a bank receipt.

To record a cheque or credit card receipt for items that will not be processed through the Customers ledger, click on the **Bank** button in the main Sage window, and then (after selecting the appropriate bank account if there is more than one) on the **Receipt** button.

To enter the details of the receipt, you will need the following information:

(a) The bank account to which the transaction will be posted (1200 in the Blitz case study).

(b) The transaction date.

(c) The reference number your company uses for cash sales transactions.

(d) The nominal account code to which the credit will be posted (ie the sales account or other income account in the nominal ledger).

(e) The department code, if any.

(f) A description of the item for which the payment has been received (also optional).

(g) The net value of the item (excluding VAT).

(h) The VAT code for the item.

PART B   USING ACCOUNTING SOFTWARE

8.2 Entering bank receipt details

When you click on the **Receipt** button, the following window will appear (or a similar window if you are using an earlier version of Sage).

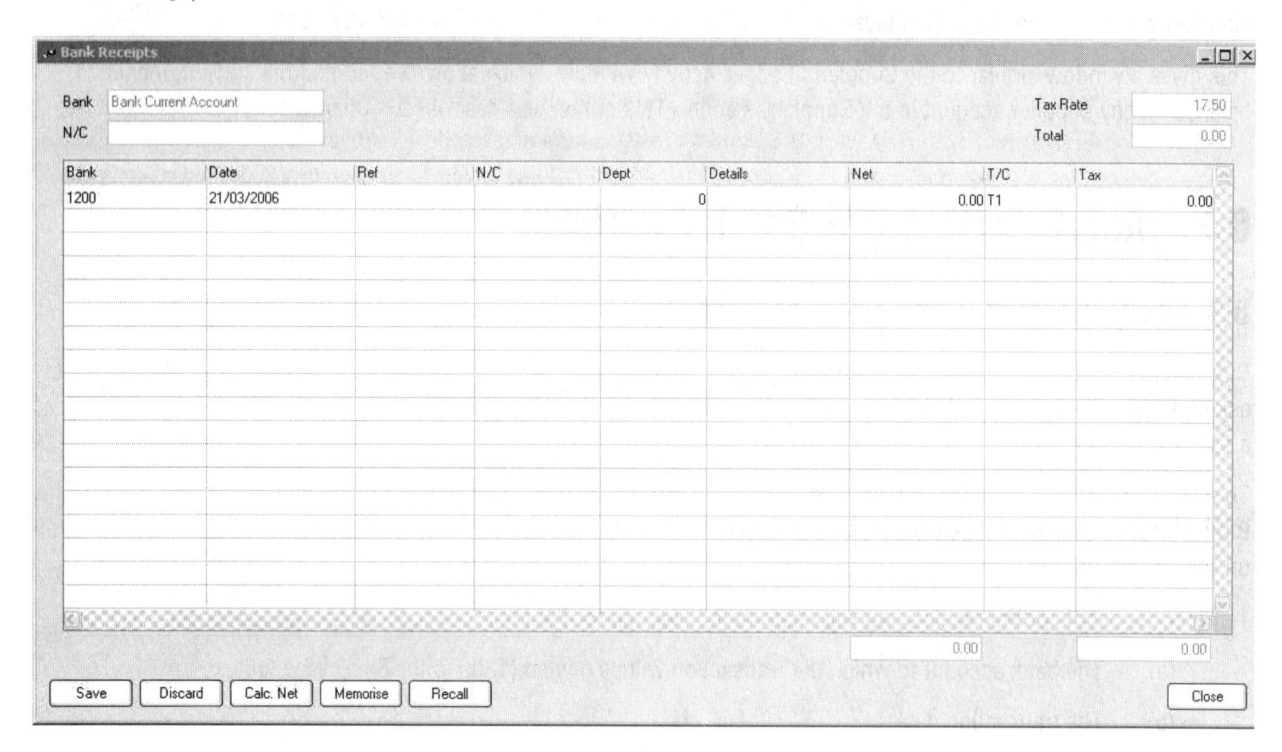

Enter the bank account code (1200 in Blitz) and the date as usual. For the **Ref** you can enter a reference for the transaction such as the customer's cheque number or your own paying-in slip number. Press Tab again.

Key in the code of the nominal ledger account (for sales or income) to which the receipt refers, then press Tab (the N/C name will then appear in the N/C Name box at the top of the window). In the Blitz case study, the code will be one of the following:

4000	Sales – contract cleaning
4001	Sales – window cleaning
4002	Sales – domestic services
4100	Sales – materials

In the **Dept** and **Details** boxes you can enter the code of the Department concerned if any and a description of the purpose of the payment from the customer.

132

You can enter either the net amount of the receipt (excluding VAT) or the gross amount (including VAT).

(a) If you enter the net amount, press Tab and the cursor will move to the T/c column. This may show a default code such as T1, but you can alter it if you wish. In the Blitz case study, the codes are:

T0 For zero-rated items

T1 For standard-rate items (currently taxed at the rate of 17.5%)

(b) If you key in the gross receipt in the Net column and click on **Calculate Net** (or press F9) this automatically deducts VAT at the standard rate (assuming tax code T1 applies). If you than press Tab you can change the tax code if you like and the amounts will be recalculated as appropriate. (If the code has to be altered from, say T0 to T1, you may need to Tab back to the Net box, re-enter the gross amount and click on Calculate net again.

Whichever method you choose for entering the net payment and tax code, the amount of VAT will be calculated automatically and displayed in the Tax column.

Press Tab to move to the next line on screen, where you can enter further details of the receipt if necessary (for example if a single receipt is being posted to more than one Nominal code).

8.3 Posting details of bank receipts

When you have entered all the details of a bank receipts click on the **Save** button. This will only be active if the amount in the Amount box is equal to the amount in the Analysis Total box. Once you have saved an entry the screen will clear, ready for the next entry. If you have finished all your entries click on **Close** or press Esc. (You will be asked if you are sure you wish to Exit. If you are, click on Yes.)

Activity 6.6

Load Assignment 1.

It is 8 October 2000. You have received the following amounts from non-sales ledger customers.

Gleamo Prize for shiny windows: £1,000 (N/C 4900; T/C T0)

D. Spenser, one-off payment for domestic services: £100 (gross)

Post these transactions using the paying-in slip reference 123478.

What is the balance on the bank account after you have done this?

PART B   USING ACCOUNTING SOFTWARE

9 Reports

A wide variety of reports are available to display and analyse receipts from customers. Again, the process for producing reports differs slightly depending upon the version of Sage you are using.

Explore the options available under the **Reports** button in the **Bank** window. Ensure you are able to print the Day Books: Bank Receipts (Detailed) Report.

10 Conclusion

When you feel you have a reasonable understanding of this chapter, you should be ready to attempt **Assignment 4**.

Key learning points

- When customers make payments for invoices, the **receipt** should be recorded in the **Customers ledger**, sometimes known as the Sales ledger.

- Receipts can be posted in Sage from the **Bank** button in the main Sage window. The user selects the bank account the payments will be made from (usually the Bank Current Account) and then clicks on the **Customer** button.

- Details of the receipt are **entered on-screen**, and there is the opportunity to **allocate** the receipt to outstanding transactions.

- Customer receipts will usually comprise the value of outstanding **invoices**, less any **credit notes** issued and **discount** agreed.

- Occasionally, a cheque issued by a customer may not be paid after they have been submitted for banking. Such cheques are often said to have '**bounced**'. Modern accounting packages such as Sage include facilities for processing bounced cheques.

- Accounting packages such as Sage also **simplify** the **accounting procedures** for issuing refunds for previously paid invoices and accounting for sales paid for immediately.

- A range of **reports** are available from within Sage that allow you to analyse receipts from customers.

Quick quiz

1. List the information required to post a receipt to the Customers ledger.
2. What is 'settlement discount'?
3. What is the most common reason for a cheque to 'bounce'?
4. In Sage, how would you record a transaction involving a new customer who pays with cash and does not want or need an account in the Customers Ledger.
5. How would you print a listing of bank receipts from Sage?

PART B USING ACCOUNTING SOFTWARE

Answers to quick quiz

1. The information required is:

    - The nominal ledger code (or at least the nominal ledger account name) of the bank account into which the receipt will be banked.
    - The name of the customer or the customer's account reference code.
    - The date of the receipt.
    - The customer's cheque number (not essential).
    - The cheque amount.
    - The amount of early settlement discount taken, if any.

2. 'Settlement discount' is the amount that can be deducted from the total owed if payment is received before a specified date. For example, a customer may purchase an item for £100, but the supplier states that if they make payment within 7 days (example only), £95 will be accepted as full payment. In this case, £5 settlement discount must be accounted for.

3. The most common reason a customer's bank refuses to pay a cheque is because there are insufficient funds in the customer's bank account. Other reasons could include an unauthorised signature on the cheque or only one signature when two are required.

4. The transaction should be recorded as a sale and a bank receipt. To do this in Sage, you would click on the Bank button from the main Sage window, and then (after selecting the appropriate bank account if there is more than one) on the Receipt button. You are required to enter a range of details, including the code of the nominal ledger account (for sales or income) to which the receipt should be posted.

5. To get a report on receipts, you would click on Bank from the Sage main window, ensure that the account you want is highlighted, and then click on Reports. You would select the Day Books: Bank Receipts (Detailed) report, and specify the criteria for your report.

Activity checklist

This checklist shows which knowledge and understanding point is covered by each activity in this chapter. Tick off each activity as you complete it.

Activity		
6.1		Knowledge and Understanding: Operation of computerised accounting systems
6.2		Knowledge and Understanding: Operation of computerised accounting systems
6.3		Knowledge and Understanding: Operation of computerised accounting systems
6.4		Knowledge and Understanding: Operation of computerised accounting systems
6.5		Knowledge and Understanding: Operation of computerised accounting systems
6.6		Knowledge and Understanding: Operation of computerised accounting systems

PART B USING ACCOUNTING SOFTWARE

chapter 7

Other cash transactions

Contents

1 Introduction
2 Petty cash transactions
3 Nominal ledger journal entries and bank-cash transactions
4 Bank transactions not involving sales or purchases
5 Bank reconciliations
6 Conclusion

Range statement

Relevant computerised records
Computerised records
Computerised ledgers

Knowledge and understanding

Operation of computerised accounting systems

PART B   USING ACCOUNTING SOFTWARE

1 Introduction

In this chapter we explain the procedures for processing a range of cash transactions not related to receipts from customers.

2 Petty cash transactions

2.1 Petty cash account

A petty cash account is a record of relatively small cash payments and cash receipts. The balance on the petty cash account at any time should be the amount of cash (notes and coins) held within the business. Petty cash is commonly kept in a locked metal box, in a safe or locked drawer. The box will contain notes and coins, vouchers recording amounts of cash withdrawn (and the reasons for using the cash) and vouchers for petty cash receipts.

The accounting records for petty cash are often maintained in a book, or a spreadsheet. Transactions are recorded from the petty cash vouchers into the petty cash book.

A petty cash account must also be maintained in the nominal ledger. The person responsible for petty cash needs to ensure entries from the petty cash book are entered into the into 'main' accounting system. Requests for petty cash **must be authorised** in line with stated policy.

For payments of cash out of petty cash, details must be entered of

(a) The amount withdrawn.

(b) The purpose. This will be used to allocate the nominal ledger account to which the item of expense relates.

Similarly, for receipts of cash into petty cash, details must be entered of

(a) The amount received.
(b) The reason for the receipt – used to allocated the nominal ledger account.

2.2 Recording petty cash transactions

The information you need to record a cash payment or cash receipt is as follows.

(a) The code of the nominal ledger account to which the payment will be debited or the receipt credited.

(b) The transaction date.

(c) If appropriate, a reference number such as the petty cash voucher number.

(d) A description of the reason for the payment or receipt unless the nominal account code used means this is obvious.

(e) Either the net value of the item (excluding VAT), or the gross amount of the item (including VAT).

(f) The appropriate VAT code.

7: OTHER CASH TRANSACTIONS

The petty cash account is included in the list in the Bank window. Just select the Petty Cash account (code 1230) instead of the main bank account (code 1230).

Transactions are posted **exactly as for Bank receipts and payments**. Try the following Activity.

Activity 7.1

Load up Assignment 3.

Post the following transactions to the petty cash account. Transactions are numbered consecutively, beginning at PC013. VAT receipts have not been obtained, so no VAT applies.

25 Oct   Stationery: £5.26.

28 Oct   Refreshments: £4.45

24 Oct   Present for new baby: £27.99 (N/C 6202)

25 Oct   Loan (Joan Davies): £50 (N/C 9998)

31 Oct   Received from Joan Davies: £50.

What is the balance on the petty cash account and on account 7504 now?

3 Nominal ledger journal entries and bank-cash transactions

3.1 Nominal ledger journal entries

A nominal ledger journal entry is used to record transactions and accounting entries that will not be recorded in any other book of prime entry.

Although a journal can be thought of as a 'book' for recording transactions to be posted to the nominal ledger, it is common for journal transactions to be recorded on sheets of paper, known as journal vouchers.

Entries in the journal must subsequently be posted to the appropriate accounts in the nominal ledger. For every journal transaction, there will have to be:

(a) A debit entry in one nominal ledger account.
(b) A corresponding credit entry in another nominal ledger account.

In other words, there are two sides to every transaction, the debit entry and the credit entry.

A transaction recorded in the journal, for example, could relate to a transfer between accounts in the nominal ledger. In the Sage system, a journal entry is used, for example, to record transfers of petty cash from the bank account to the cash account.

Movements of money between the bank account and petty cash are known as bank-cash transactions.

3.2 Recording bank-cash transactions

To record a movement of money from the bank account to cash (that is, a cash withdrawal) or to record the payment of notes and coin processed through petty cash into the bank, click on the **Nominal** button in the main Sage window (or select **Modules**, **Nominal Ledger** from the main menu) and then click the **Journals** button in the Nominal Ledger window. The window shown below will be displayed (or a similar window depending upon the version of Sage you use).

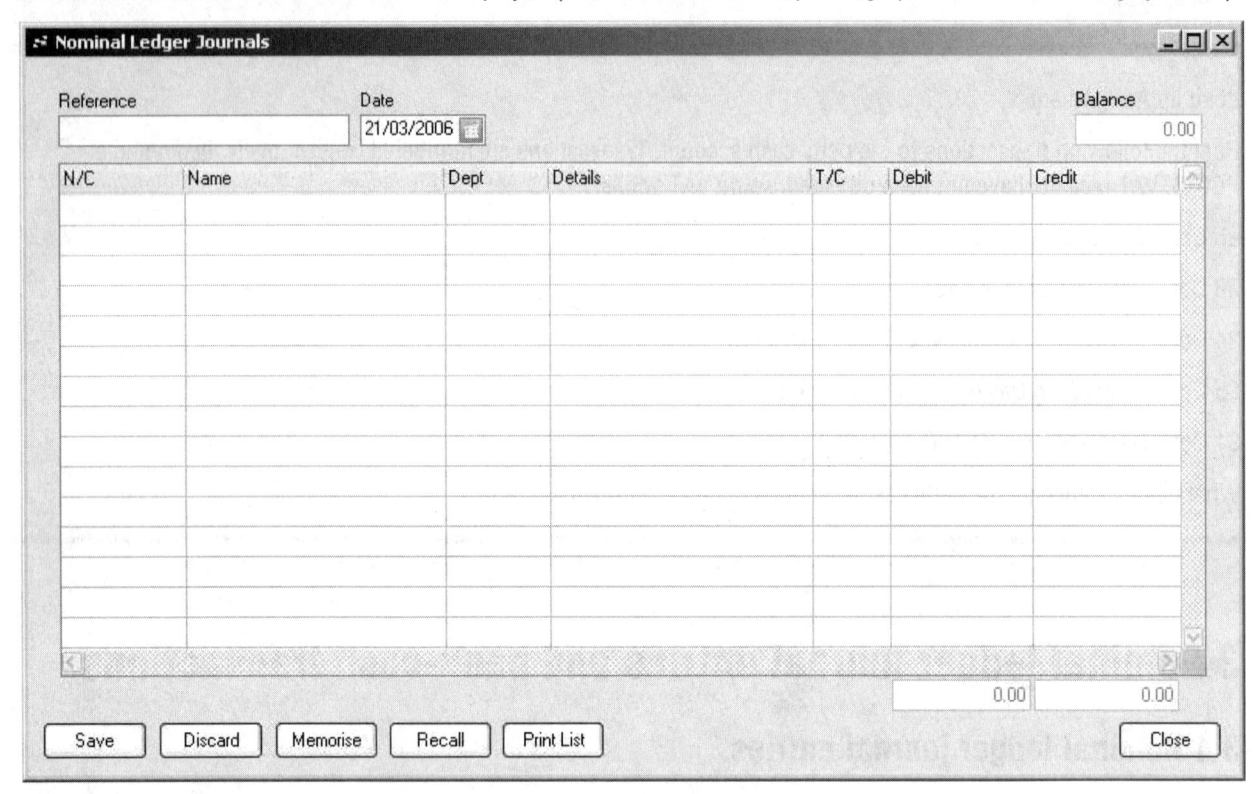

3.2.1 Reference

This is an optional item, which can be used to identify the transaction. The journal voucher number could be inserted here (up to a maximum of six characters).

3.2.2 Date

If necessary, enter the transaction date, as an eight-digit code in the format DDMMYYYY or use the calendar button. The cursor will then move past the box labelled Balance, down to the main part of the screen. Here, you enter the details of the debit item and the credit item, one per line, for the transaction.

For a bank-cash transaction, the debit and credit entries are as follows.

(a) When *cash is withdrawn* from the bank.

		Nominal ledger code
DEBIT	Petty cash	1230
CREDIT	Bank current account	1200

(b) When *cash is paid into* the bank from petty cash.

		Nominal ledger code
DEBIT	Bank current account	1200
CREDIT	Petty cash	1230

3.2.3 N/C and Name

Enter the nominal ledger code of the bank account (1200) or the petty cash account (1230). It does not matter which code you enter on the first line. You will need to enter both, one per line, to complete the input details. When you enter the code, the account name will appear in the Name box automatically. (To find other codes you can use the Finder button in the normal way: click on it or press function key F4 when the cursor is in this box.)

For our purposes we can ignore the Dept box and Tab through to Details.

3.2.4 Details

You can enter brief details of the transaction. For example:

N/C	Name	Description	T/c	Debit	Credit
1230	PETTY CASH	Received from bank a/c	T9	100.00	
1200	BANK CURRENT A/C	To petty cash float	T9		100.00

The description for one side of the entry should always indicate the other nominal ledger account to which the transaction relates. In the example above, the details for the withdrawal of £100 from the bank (the credit of 100.00 for N/C 1200) refer to petty cash which is the recipient of the money.

3.2.5 T/c (Tax Code)

A bank-cash transaction does not involve VAT. Enter tax code T9.

3.2.6 Debit/Credit

Enter the amount of the transaction, in the debit or the credit column, according to whether the nominal ledger account should be debited or credited.

Remember that there must be two entries for a bank-cash transaction, one a debit and one a matching credit, to complete a journal entry. In fact the system will not allow you to post your journal until Debits equal Credits and the amount shown in the Balance box is nil.

When you have completed the entry, Click on **Save** as usual and the nominal ledger accounts will be updated with the transaction details.

PART B   USING ACCOUNTING SOFTWARE

Activity 7.2

Load Assignment 6.

A payment of £1200 has been incorrectly analysed as Legal Fees. In fact £500 of this related to consultancy fees and £300 was advertising. All figures are stated net.

Post a journal to correct this (reference J23) dated 6 November 2000. What is the balance on the advertising account now?

4 Bank transactions not involving sales or purchases

A business will occasionally receive or make payments by cheque (that is, through its bank account, not in cash) that do not involve sales or purchases, receipts from customers or payments to suppliers. These cash payments or receipts should be recorded using the **Payment** and **Receipt** buttons in the **Bank** window. These options were described in Chapter 5 (payments) and Chapter 6 (receipts).

Examples of transactions you could be expected to record are suggested below.

(a) Payment of PAYE income tax to the Inland Revenue authorities.
(b) Payment of a court fine (eg a parking ticket fine).
(c) Payment for a road vehicle licence (car tax).
(d) The receipt of a loan.

5 Bank reconciliations

5.1 The Sage bank reconciliation

Sage includes a facility for performing a bank reconciliation – ie checking the bank account records in the nominal ledger against transactions recorded on bank statements issued by the bank.

If a transaction is the same in both the bank statement and the nominal ledger account it is said to be 'reconciled'. The reconciliation process therefore involves matching items on bank statements against transactions listed in the nominal ledger bank account. Any differences should be identified to complete the reconciliation.

The starting point is the nominal ledger account. *Unreconciled* items are those that have *not yet appeared in the bank statement*, even though they have been recorded in the nominal ledger account (items that appear in the bank statement before they appear in the nominal ledger are less common and are usually adjusted for fairly quickly eg bank charges).

5.2 Documents for checking

You need the bank statements from the bank to carry out a reconciliation. Paying in slips will also probably be needed, as we shall see. An activity listing of transactions from the nominal ledger bank account may also be useful.

5.3 Performing the bank reconciliation

Click on the **Bank** button in the main Sage window, Select the account you want to reconcile then click on the **Reconcile** button. If you are using **version 11** (or earlier), you will be taken to the main Bank Reconciliation window (see next page). Users of **more recent versions** are presented first with a Statement Summary window, as shown below.

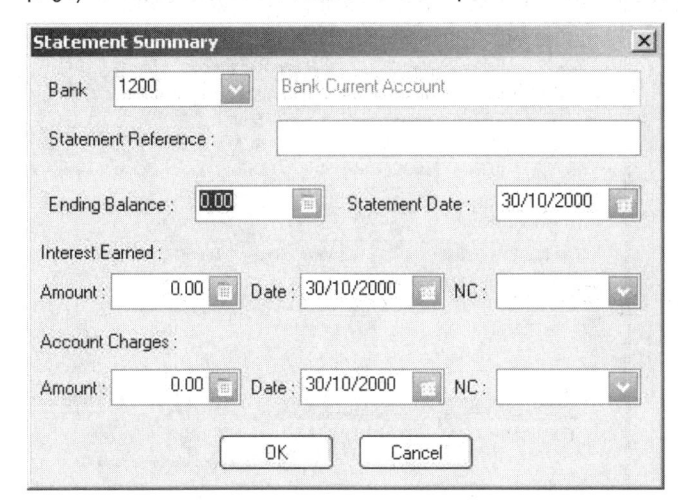

The Statement Summary window allows you to enter the following statement information.

Statement Reference. Enter a reference to enable you to associate the reconciliation with your bank statement (eg statement page number).

Interest Earned Amount. If the statement shows interest earned, enter the amount. The amount is committed to the bank account when as a bank receipt. This amount is added to the reconciliation as a fixed amount, which cannot be split up. If you have several interest payments you want to record separately, add them using an adjustment.

Date. The date the interest was applied to your account.

NC. Use the drop-down list to select the correct nominal code to post the interest to.

Ending Balance. If this is the first time the bank account is to be reconciled the account's opening balance is displayed, otherwise the reconciled balance from the previous reconciliation is displayed. Enter the balance shown on the bank statement. To record a negative (overdrawn) amount place a minus (-) at the beginning of the value.

Account Charges. If any bank charges appear on your statement, enter an amount for charges. The amount is committed to the bank account as a bank payment. The amount is added to the reconciliation as a fixed amount. If you have several charges you want to record separately, add them using an adjustment.

Date. Enter the date the charges were applied to your account.

NC. From the drop-down list, select the correct nominal account to post bank charges to.

Statement Date. The current system date appears here. You should change this to the date of the bank statement, so that only those transactions up to and including the date are available for reconciliation.

When you have entered your statement information, click OK.

Note: You can ignore the Statement Summary window and enter the bank information using the Bank Reconciliation window. To skip the Statement Summary window, leave the boxes blank and click OK.

PART B USING ACCOUNTING SOFTWARE

The main Bank Reconciliation windows for version 11 and later versions are shown below.

Version 11 | Later versions

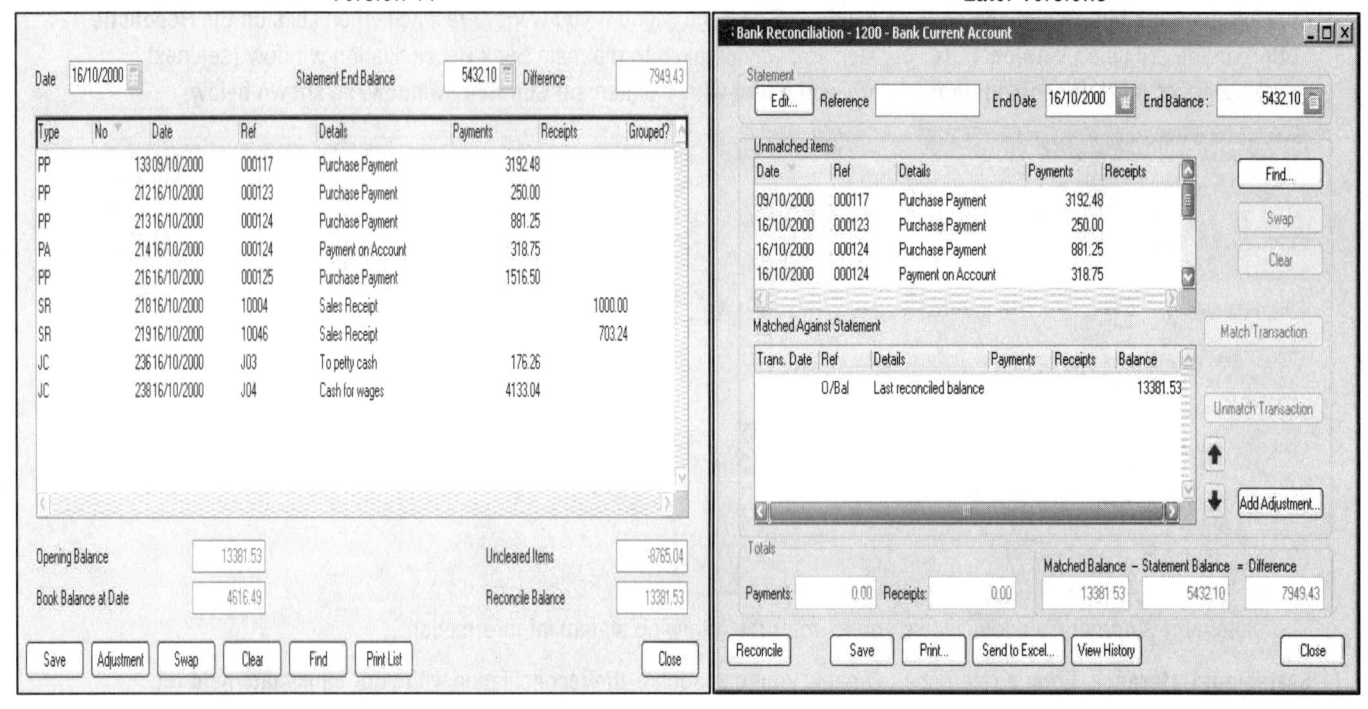

5.3.1 End Balance / Statement End Balance

Key in the **Date** of the bank statement and the **Statement End Balance**.

5.3.2 Opening Balance / Last reconciled balance

This is the bank Reconcile Balance brought forward from the last time a bank reconciliation was done. It should reflect the opening balance on the bank statement. If there has not been a previous bank statement, or if the procedure has never been carried out before, the balance brought forward will be 0.00.

5.3.3 Book Balance at Date (version 11)

The version 11 window displays the balance of the bank account from the nominal ledger.

5.4 Reconciliation procedure

The reconciliation involves **matching transactions** listed on the **bank statement** with transactions recorded in the **nominal ledger bank account**.

In **version 11**, you match a transaction on the bank statement with a transaction in the nominal bank account by clicking on it to highlight the transaction on the screen. The figures in the Reconcile Balance box and the Uncleared Items box will change by the amount of the transaction that you just highlighted. If you make a mistake, and want to de-select a transaction, just click on it again.

In **later versions**, you select the item to be matched, then click Match Transaction. As you move transactions from the unmatched to the matched portion of the screen, the 'Matched Balance' and 'Difference' values change automatically. To move a transaction back from the 'Matched Against Statement' area to 'Unmatched Items', select the transaction then click Unmatch Transaction.

5.4.1 Items made up of several transactions

You may have a problem in matching items because there may be some that are the total of several smaller transactions. This happens on both the bank statement and on the screen listing.

If several receipts were paid into the bank on a single paying-in slip the **bank statement** will only show the total. You may need to consult the paying-in slips to see how these items are made up, and match individual receipts.

The **reconciliation screen** lumps together transactions of the same type posted together with the same date, unless they were given a unique *reference* number. For this reason, it's important to give receipts a unique reference number.

5.4.2 Items in the bank statement but not in the ledger account

There could be some items in the bank statement that have not been entered in the nominal ledger bank account. For example, there could be some bank charges that have not yet been recorded in the account.

You can make an adjustment, and post the receipt or payment to the bank account in the nominal ledger. To do this click on the **Adjustment** button (**Add Adjustment** in later versions). A new window will appear, as shown below.

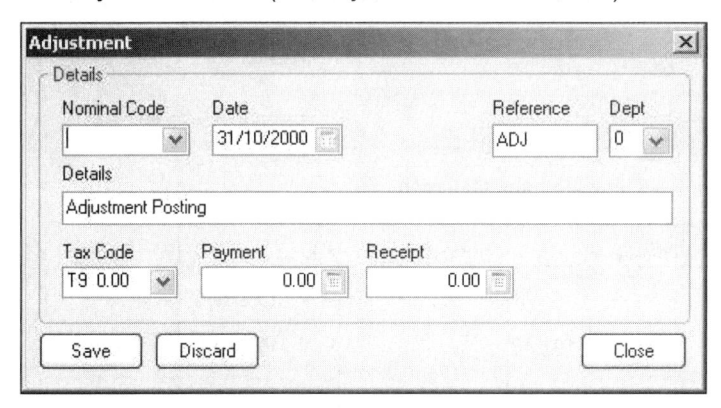

The entries to make are as follows.

(a) *N/C (Nominal Code).* Enter the appropriate nominal ledger code. In the Blitz case study, for example, a deduction of bank interest would be coded 7900 and a deduction of bank charges would be coded 7901.

(b) *Date.* Enter the date of the receipt or payment.

(c) *Details.* Enter brief narrative details of the item.

(d) *Tax Code.* The VAT code would be T9 for bank charges, but for other items (for example, some direct debits) it would be T1. Check with your supervisor if you are not sure.

(e) *Payment / Receipt.* Enter the gross value of the receipt or payment, in the appropriate box.

Click on **Save** when you are satisfied that your adjustment details are correct. The transaction will be posted in the appropriate nominal ledger accounts.

PART B USING ACCOUNTING SOFTWARE

5.5 Completing the reconciliation

In **version 11**, after you have matched all items in the bank statement against the nominal bank account, click on the **Save** button. This will clear the reconciled transactions (ie the transactions that you have matched). The unreconciled items will be displayed on screen the next time you do a bank reconciliation. A listing of unreconciled payments and receipts is available under the Bank Reports option.

In **later versions**, when you have completed the reconciliation (all transactions are selected, the 'Statement Balance' = 'Matched Balance' and the 'Difference' balance is zero) click **Reconcile**. The transactions are marked as reconciled (displayed as 'R' in the audit trail) and they will not appear for reconciliation again.

If the end and matched balances are not equal you can choose to **Investigate and rectify the problem**. You also have the option of putting the bank reconciliation on hold until later. Any transactions you add to Line 50 to rectify the problem will be made available for reconciliation provided their date does not exceed the reconciliation's 'Statement (End) Date'. To put the bank reconciliation 'on hold' click **Save**, and then OK.

The Nominal Activity Report referred to earlier should help investigate the difference. This report lists all the transactions that have been made to and from the bank, both reconciled and those that have not been reconciled. To produce this more recent versions choose Company, Nominal Ledger, click Reports and then select Nominal Activity Reports. Select the criteria for the bank account you are reconciling (eg 1200).

You also have the option of to **Save the reconciliation with a known discrepancy**. If this is selected, the reconciliation is saved as usual, however the next time you reconcile the bank account the opening balance displayed for the bank will be in doubt.

Activity 7.3

Load Assignment 6. On 20 October you receive the following bank statement.

Date	Details	Withdrawals	Deposits	Balance
10-Oct-2000	Balance from sheet 5			13,381.53
11-Oct-2000	000117	3,192.48		10,189.05
14-Oct-2000	BGC		1,000.00	11,189.05
18-Oct-2000	000124	1,200.00		
18-Oct-2000	000125	1,516.50		8,472.55
20-Oct-2000	BACS	4,133.04		4,339.51
20-Oct-2000	Bank interest	74.50		4265.01

Perform a bank reconciliation as at 20 October 2000, following the procedures explained in the preceding section. What are the outstanding items, if any?

6 Conclusion

Further bank reconciliation practice is included in **Assignment 5**, which you should now attempt.

Key learning points

- ☑ Organisations often keep a relatively small amount of cash in a locked metal box, in a safe or locked drawer. This is known as '**petty cash**' and is used for small cash purchases and receipts.

- ☑ A **petty cash account** must be maintained in the nominal ledger. Records of individual petty cash transactions are recorded using **petty cash vouchers**, which may be entered into a **book** or a spreadsheet – from which the **nominal ledger journal** is prepared.

- ☑ In Sage, the petty cash account is included in the list in the Bank Accounts window. After selecting the petty cash account (rather than the main bank account), transactions are posted exactly as for Bank **receipts** and **payments**.

- ☑ Transactions and accounting entries that are not recorded in any other book of prime entry are entered using **nominal ledger journal entries**. Each journal entry comprises two sides – a debit entry and a credit entry.

- ☑ Sage Line 50 includes a facility for automating the process of conducting a **bank reconciliation**.

Quick quiz

1. How are the notes and coins that make up the petty cash usually stored?
2. No record of petty cash is required to be kept in the nominal ledger. TRUE or FALSE?
3. As petty cash amounts are small, there is no need to know the purpose of the funds. TRUE or FALSE?
4. What are journal entries used for?
5. How do you access the bank reconciliation function in Sage?

Answers to quick quiz

1. Petty cash is commonly kept in a locked metal box, in a safe or locked drawer.
2. FALSE. A petty cash account must be maintained in the nominal ledger.
3. FALSE. The purpose of the funds is required so the transaction can be posted to the correct nominal ledger account – and to prevent fraud.
4. Nominal ledger journal entries are used to enter transactions and accounting entries that are not recorded in any other book of prime entry.
5. You click on the Bank button in the main Sage window, select the account you want to reconcile, then click on the Reconcile button.

PART B USING ACCOUNTING SOFTWARE

Activity checklist

This checklist shows which knowledge and understanding point is covered by each activity in this chapter. Tick off each activity as you complete it.

Activity		
7.1	☐	Knowledge and Understanding: Operation of computerised accounting systems
7.2	☐	Knowledge and Understanding: Operation of computerised accounting systems
7.3	☐	Knowledge and Understanding: Operation of computerised accounting systems

chapter 8

Other credit transactions

Contents

1 Introduction
2 Contra entries
3 Credit limits
4 Writing off bad debts
5 Chasing overdue customer payments
6 Correcting errors
7 Conclusion

Range statement

Relevant computerised records
Computerised records
Computerised ledgers

Knowledge and understanding

Operation of computerised accounting systems

PART B USING ACCOUNTING SOFTWARE

1 Introduction

This chapter explains the procedures for processing a range of other transactions that may occur on customer and supplier accounts.

2 Contra entries

2.1 What is a contra entry?

Contra is an accounting term that means against, or on the opposite side. A contra entry is made in the accounts of a business when a debit entry can be matched with a credit entry so that one cancels out the other. A common type of contra entry occurs when a supplier is also a customer. The amount owed as a supplier and the amount owing as a customer can be offset, to leave just a net amount owed or owing.

For example, suppose that ABC Limited is both a customer of your business, currently owing £1,000, and a supplier to your business who is currently owed £700. ABC Ltd pays £300 to settle the debt. The £700 owed has been offset against the £1,000 owing, and ABC Limited has simply paid the net debt of £300. This would be recorded in the accounts as a

- (a) A cash receipt of £300; and
- (b) A contra entry for £700, to cancel the debt to ABC as a supplier and the remaining £700 owed by ABC as a customer.

The accounting entries done for contra transactions are as follows.

- (a) In the sales ledger, the customer's account is credited with the amount of the contra entry. This reduces the customer's outstanding debt.
- (b) In the purchase ledger, the supplier's account is debited with the same amount.
- (c) In the nominal ledger, the double entry transactions are:

    CREDIT   Debtors Control Account (code 1100)
    DEBIT   Bank Current Account (code 1200)
                  (or any other specified bank account)
    DEBIT   Creditors Control Account (code 2100)
    CREDIT   Bank Current Account (code 1200)
                  (or any other specified bank account)

Sage Line 50 includes a facility that automates contra entries (Sage Instant does not include this function).

2.2 Posting a contra entry

2.2.1 Post the payment or receipt first

Before you post a contra entry, you should record the actual cash payment (or receipt) in the purchase ledger (or sales ledger). For example, suppose that your company owes ABC Ltd £700, ABC Ltd owes your company £1,000 and ABC Ltd sends you a cheque for £300 to settle the difference. Your first step should be to record the £300 received as a part payment of an invoice in the account for ABC Ltd in the sales ledger. This will make the outstanding balance on the customer account (£700) equal to the outstanding balance on the supplier account (£700).

You can find out the balances on the two accounts by looking at them in the windows that appear when you click on the **Customers** button and the **Suppliers** button. Subtract one from the other to find out the amount due.

In Line 50 it is *not* essential that there are equal amounts owed and owing before you post a contra entry, but it is good accounting practice, so always post the payment (and/or) receipt that brings this about *first*.

2.2.2 Making the contra

Users of Line 50 can post a contra entry as follows (Sage Instant does not include this facility). Click on the word **Tools** at the top of the screen. A menu will appear from which you should select **Contra Entries**. A window will display, as shown below. Check the correct Bank account is displayed (eg Current Account), then Tab into the Sales Ledger A/C Ref box.

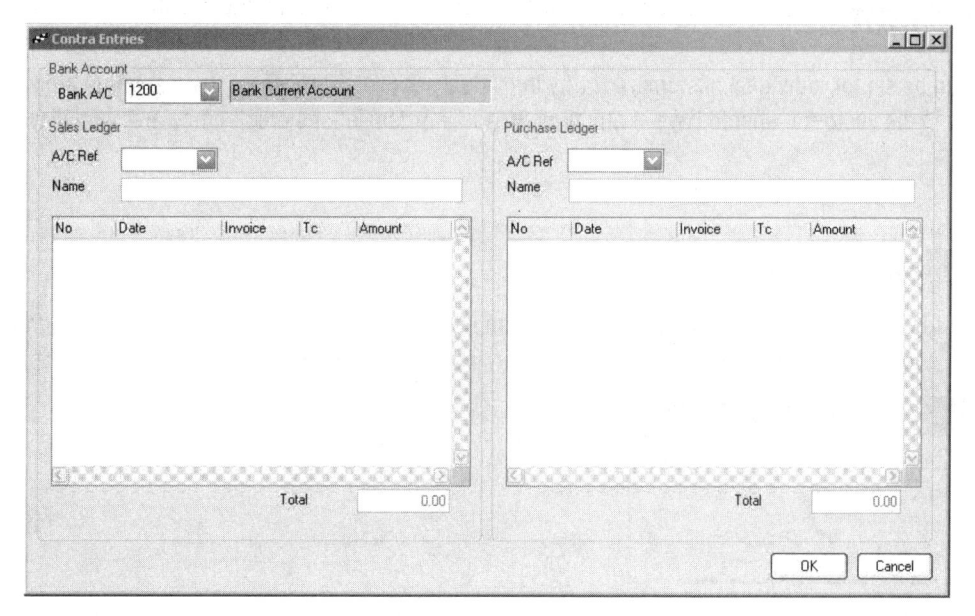

2.2.3 Sales Ledger A/C (Customer Account)

Enter the customer's account reference code if you know it (or use the Finder button or press function key F4 if not). When you press Tab the customer's name will be displayed automatically, and a list of outstanding invoices on that customer's account will appear in the left-hand box below. (Credit notes and payments on account are not listed.)

PART B USING ACCOUNTING SOFTWARE

2.2.4 Purchase Ledger A/C (Supplier Account)

Enter the supplier's account reference code. This would normally be the same as the customer's code, but not necessarily so – for instance, a customer might trade under a different name when making supplies. When the code is entered, pressing Tab brings up the supplier's name and a list of outstanding invoices appears in the right hand box below it.

Now that the two accounts are shown side-by-side, you should be able to identify the matching transactions for which you want to make the contra entry.

To make the contra entry, select the appropriate transaction (sales invoice) in the customer account, by clicking on it. The amount in the Total box for sales invoices at the bottom of the screen is increased by the value of the transaction. (Note: you can de-select an invoice by clicking on it again.)

When you have selected the appropriate sales invoice find the appropriate purchase invoice in the other box, and select it by clicking. The amount in the Total box for purchase invoices at the bottom of the screen is increased by the value of the transaction you have selected.

So long as you first posted any payment that was due or receipt that had been received the two totals will now be equal.

Click on OK to save the transaction, which will be posted to the appropriate accounts in the sales, purchase and nominal ledgers.

3 Credit limits

Credit limits can be set for individual customers (or by individual suppliers). These fix the maximum amount of credit (unpaid invoices) the customer should have at any time. In some organisations credit limits are not always strictly observed.

3.1 Exceeding a credit limit

A warning message will be displayed on screen whenever an invoice you are processing takes the outstanding balance on the account above its current credit limit. This is the warning you see if you are using the **Invoicing** option.

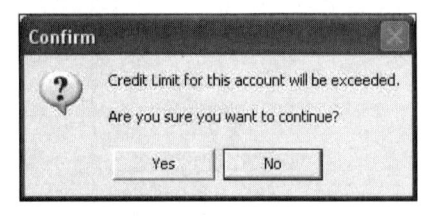

```
Confirm
    ?   Credit Limit for this account will be exceeded.
        Are you sure you want to continue?
            Yes         No
```

You should be aware of your organisation's policy regarding credit limits. You should ask your supervisor what to do whenever you are not sure.

If you know that you should proceed, perhaps on instructions from your supervisor, you can select the **Yes** option. The program will then allow you to continue with the entry, despite the warning.

If your supervisor instructs you to increase the customer's credit limit, click on **No** and then (without closing the current **Invoice** window) click on the **Customers** button, select the Customer's account from the list and then click on **Record**.

Activate the Credit Control Tab and click into the Credit Limit box, key in the new limit and then click on **Save.** Then press Esc twice to get back to the invoice window. The invoice will now be accepted without the warning.

A customer who is over their credit limit is listed *in red* in the main Customers window.

Activity 8.1

Load Assignment 3.

Post an invoice for £400 (net) to School of Dance. The invoice is for Window cleaning, is numbered 21785, and is dated 14 November 2000.

By how much is School of Dance over its credit limit and what is the new balance on the Sales – Window Cleaning account?

4 Writing off bad debts

4.1 Bad debts

Occasionally, a customer who has been invoiced will fail to pay, and the debt must eventually be 'written off' as uncollectable. There are various reasons why a debt could become a 'bad debt'. Three common reasons are:

- (a) The customer proves unreliable and is unlikely to pay.
- (b) The customer goes out of business.
- (c) There is a dispute with the customer relating to items billed on a particular invoice.

In each of these situations, it may eventually be decided to write off the money owed as a bad debt.

When a debt is written off as uncollectable, one of two possible situations could apply.

- (a) The customer will not be granted credit ever again. The customer's entire debt is written off, and the customer's account will eventually be deleted from the sales ledger.
- (b) An individual transaction is written off, but the company will continue to sell on credit to the customer. A dispute about one transaction is not allowed to affect the long-term relationship with the customer.

Sage Line 50 automates the process of writing off bad debts (**Sage Instant does not include this feature**).

PART B USING ACCOUNTING SOFTWARE

4.2 Writing off an account

To write off all the outstanding debts in a customer's account, users of Line 50 **version 11** start by clicking on the word **Tools** at the top of the screen, on **Write Off, Refund, Return** and then selecting the **Sales ledger** option and clicking Next.

In later versions, access the same 'Wizard' through the main **Customers** module, by clicking **Write Off / Refund** in the **Tasks** list in the upper left area of the screen.

You will then see the following box.

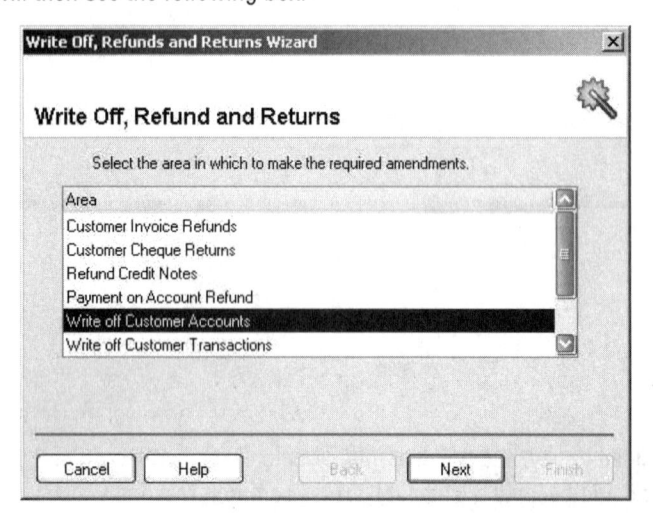

This gives you a number of options (a similar list appears if you select the Purchase ledger). The one we want on this occasion is **Write Off Customer Accounts**. Select this and then click on **Next**. Select the account you want and then click on **Next**.

This option writes off Customer Accounts rather than individual transactions, so clicking on **Next** will write off *all* the transactions listed.

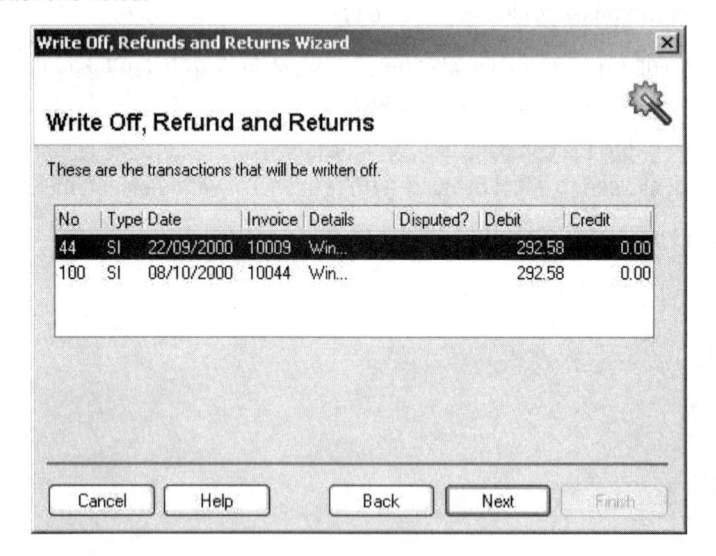

You will be asked to select a date for the write off. Enter the appropriate **date**, then click Next again, and you will see the following.

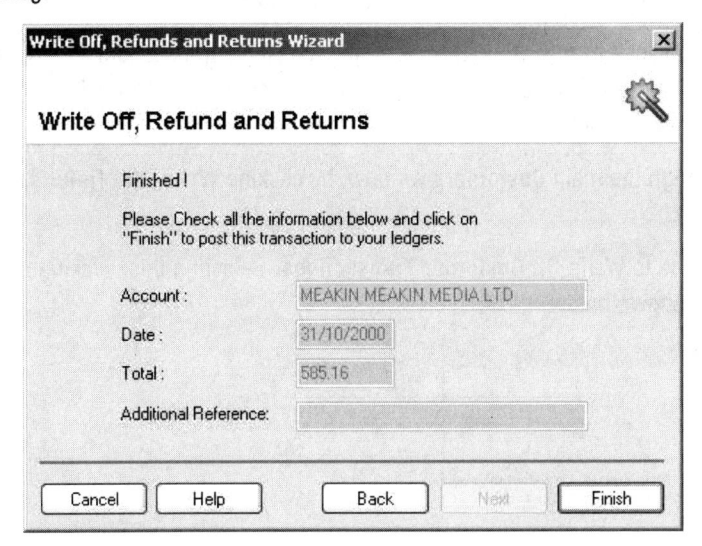

```
Write Off, Refunds and Returns Wizard

Write Off, Refund and Returns

Finished !

Please Check all the information below and click on
"Finish" to post this transaction to your ledgers.

Account:              MEAKIN MEAKIN MEDIA LTD
Date:                 31/10/2000
Total:                585.16
Additional Reference:

    Cancel    Help         Back     Next     Finish
```

Click on **Finish** and you are returned to the main screen. The effect of all this is as follows.

(a) The customer's account in the Customers ledger will be updated automatically when you select the Yes option to write off the outstanding debts on the account. The account will remain, however, in the sales ledger and will not be deleted.

(b) The appropriate accounts in the nominal ledger will also be updated automatically:

CREDIT   Debtors control account (N/C code 1100)

DEBIT   Bad debt write off account (N/C code 8100)

If you check the Customers account and Nominal accounts Activity records you will see the entry that has been made.

You could be forgiven for thinking that, having chosen the option **Write off Account,** the account will no longer appear in the ledger. However, the customer account will not be completely removed. This is because it is needed to provide a complete record of transactions, and for auditing purposes. The customer record therefore remains on the system.

Activity 8.2

Load up Assignment 2.

It is 15 November 2000. Write off the account of the customer named Vice Versa.

What entries are shown in the customer's Activity record once you have done this?

What accounts are affected in the nominal ledger?

PART B USING ACCOUNTING SOFTWARE

4.3 Writing off a transaction

The same 'Wizard' used to write off an account balance may also be used to write off a single transaction. As explained earlier, users of Line 50 **version 11** start by clicking on the word **Tools** at the top of the screen, on **Write Off, Refund, Return** and then selecting the **Sales ledger** option and clicking Next.

In later versions, access the same 'Wizard' through the main **Customers** window, by clicking **Write Off / Refund** in the **Tasks** list in the upper left area of the screen.

The amendment selected in this scenario would be to **Write Off Customer Transactions.** Selecting this, clicking on Next and selecting the account brings you to the box shown below.

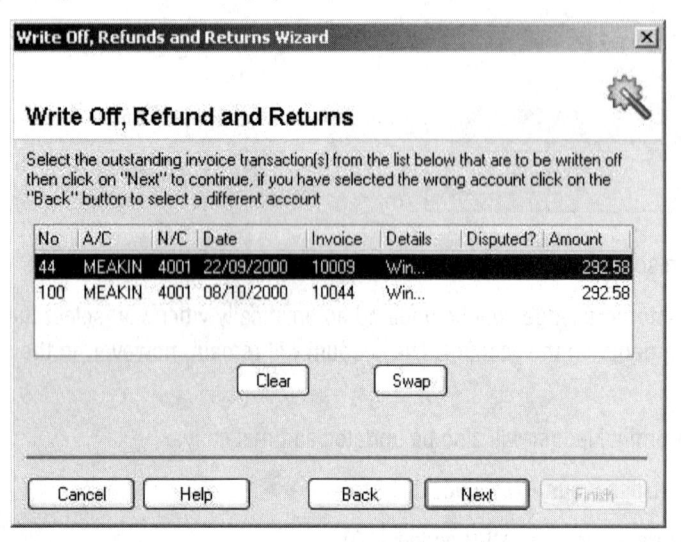

Write Off, Refunds and Returns Wizard

Write Off, Refund and Returns

Select the outstanding invoice transaction(s) from the list below that are to be written off then click on "Next" to continue, if you have selected the wrong account click on the "Back" button to select a different account

No	A/C	N/C	Date	Invoice	Details	Disputed?	Amount
44	MEAKIN	4001	22/09/2000	10009	Win...		292.58
100	MEAKIN	4001	08/10/2000	10044	Win...		292.58

[Clear] [Swap]

[Cancel] [Help] [Back] [Next] [Finish]

In the example above, to write off Invoice 10009, click on this to select it, then enter the **date** for the write off, click Next again then click on Finish.

Activity 8.3

Users of Line 50 should now load Assignment 5 and follow the instructions below. (Users of Sage Instant should skip this activity.)

It is 20 November 2000. Write off invoice number 10025, following the instructions above as appropriate.

What is the amount of the write off and the new balance on the Debtors Control account?

5 Chasing overdue customer payments

It is an unfortunate fact of business life that many customers delay payment of invoices. They will pay eventually, and there will not be a bad debt. However, unless a determined effort is made to collect the unpaid invoice or invoices, the customer might continue to delay payment for as long as possible. In most businesses, there are procedures for:

(a) Producing a regular list of unpaid invoices, analysing the length of time for which each invoice has been outstanding (an 'aged debtors list').

(b) Producing statements of unpaid invoices for individual customers, for sending out to the customer as a reminder.

(c) Producing and sending reminder letters to customers whose invoices are overdue for payment.

5.1 Aged debtors list

To produce a list of unpaid debts, analysed by age, print out an Aged debtors analysis (Detailed) using the **Reports** option in the Customers window. The procedures for producing an aged debtors were described in Chapter 6.

5.2 Statements

A printed statement of account shows the transactions and balance outstanding on an account at the date the statement was issued. Statements are sent to customers to assist with debt collection.

For the case study in this book, a standard layout provided by Sage (Statement With Tear Off Remit Advice) is used. This shows the following details.

(a) Customer name, address and account code.
(b) The statement date.
(c) Brought forward figures at the beginning of the period covered by the statement.
(d) Details of transactions in the period (date, invoice number, description, amount).
(e) An analysis of outstanding amounts by age.
(f) A total of the amounts outstanding.

To produce statements, use the **Statement** button in the **Customers** window (if Statement isn't showing click on the small >> symbol in the top right of the main Customers screen). The following window will appear (or a slightly different window depending upon the version of Sage you use).

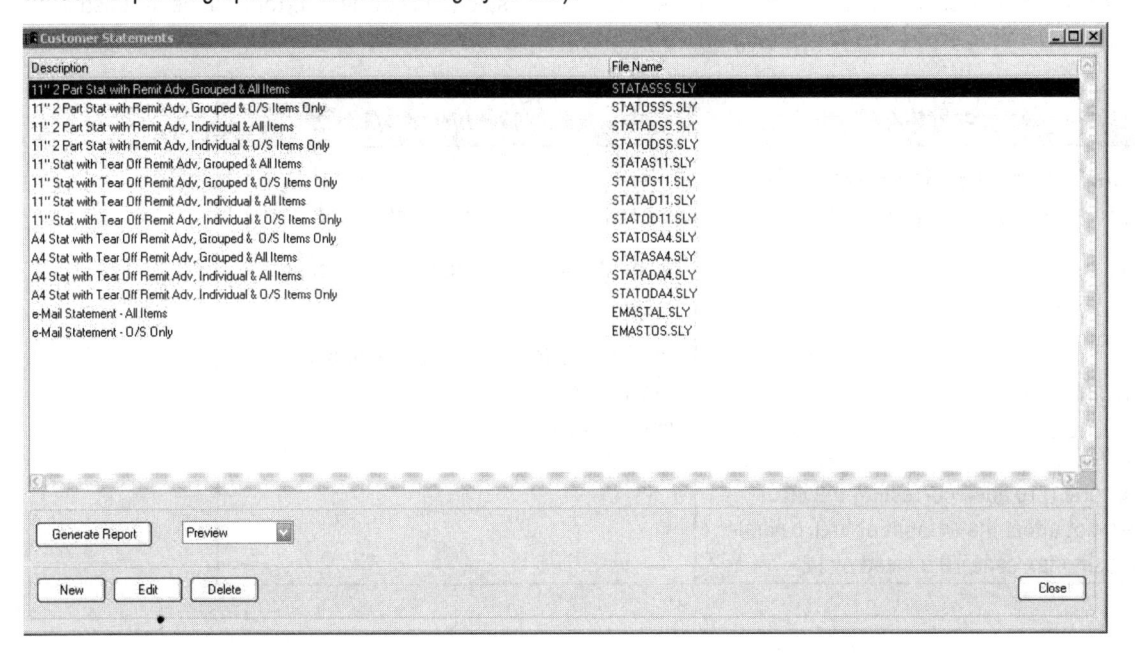

Description	File Name
11" 2 Part Stat with Remit Adv, Grouped & All Items	STATASSS.SLY
11" 2 Part Stat with Remit Adv, Grouped & O/S Items Only	STATOSSS.SLY
11" 2 Part Stat with Remit Adv, Individual & All Items	STATADSS.SLY
11" 2 Part Stat with Remit Adv, Individual & O/S Items Only	STATODSS.SLY
11" Stat with Tear Off Remit Adv, Grouped & All Items	STATAS11.SLY
11" Stat with Tear Off Remit Adv, Grouped & O/S Items Only	STATOS11.SLY
11" Stat with Tear Off Remit Adv, Individual & All Items	STATAD11.SLY
11" Stat with Tear Off Remit Adv, Individual & O/S Items Only	STATOD11.SLY
A4 Stat with Tear Off Remit Adv, Grouped & O/S Items Only	STATOSA4.SLY
A4 Stat with Tear Off Remit Adv, Grouped & All Items	STATASA4.SLY
A4 Stat with Tear Off Remit Adv, Individual & All Items	STATADA4.SLY
A4 Stat with Tear Off Remit Adv, Individual & O/S Items Only	STATODA4.SLY
e-Mail Statement - All Items	EMASTAL.SLY
e-Mail Statement - O/S Only	EMASTOS.SLY

Clicking on **Generate Report**, or **Run**, in earlier versions, will bring up the **Criteria** window which requires you to specify an Account Range and a Date Range. The dates you enter affect how the information is shown. All transactions dated before the first date in your range will be lumped together in a single brought forward figure. After entering the dates, clicking **OK** will produce the statements.

5.3 Reminder letters

Reminder letters can be sent to customers to urge them to settle invoices that are overdue for payment. The Sage package includes standard letters and also allows users to create their own.

The Letters function is accessed through the **Letters** button in the Customers window. We will not be explaining this feature further as it is not included in the AAT Foundation Standards. However, you may wish to experiment with the function yourself.

Activity 8.4

Load Assignment 3. It is 31 December 2000 (change the Program Date to 31/12/2000).

Print out a statement and as stern a reminder letter as you can for Townend Angus Ltd.

How many days overdue is payment of the invoice?

6 Correcting errors

6.1 Errors

Sometimes, errors are noticed after transactions have been input and posted to the system. Errors can be grouped into two types; **Non-accounting errors** and **Accounting errors**.

Non-accounting errors	Accounting errors
Errors in descriptive items, not affecting account code or money amounts	**Errors in amount or account**
Date	Account – ie input of the wrong account code
Reference items	Amount – ie the amount or value of a transaction, such as entering £1,100 instead of £1,000
Transaction details	
Department number	
Tax code (provided correcting the error does not affect the amount of VAT payable, eg. using tax code T0 instead of T2)	

If you notice an error, you should note down the details, including the transaction number. This may involve you looking through a list of sales invoices (call up the **Activity** of the Debtors Ledger Control Account or the Creditors Ledger Control Account), or looking through a particular customer or supplier account (again using the **Activity** option).

Locate the transaction in the appropriate ledger and, if possible, select the relevant account and print out an Activity report for that account. If you cannot get a print-out, note down:

- Transaction number
- Date
- Account codes concerned (customer/supplier and nominal accounts)
- Invoice number or other reference number
- Details
- Amount (net and VAT)

6.2 Correcting non-accounting errors

We will now explain the feature available within Sage to edit existing transactions Many organisations may prefer not to use such a feature – preferring to use traditional journal entries or new transactions to correct errors. If you use Sage at work, do not use this function without the approval of your manager.

To use the corrections facility provided within Sage, first close any windows that are currently open until you have only the main Sage window in front of you.

At the top of the screen you will see the word **File.** Click on this and a menu appears. The item you want is **Maintenance**. If you click on this window the same as, or similar to, the following appears.

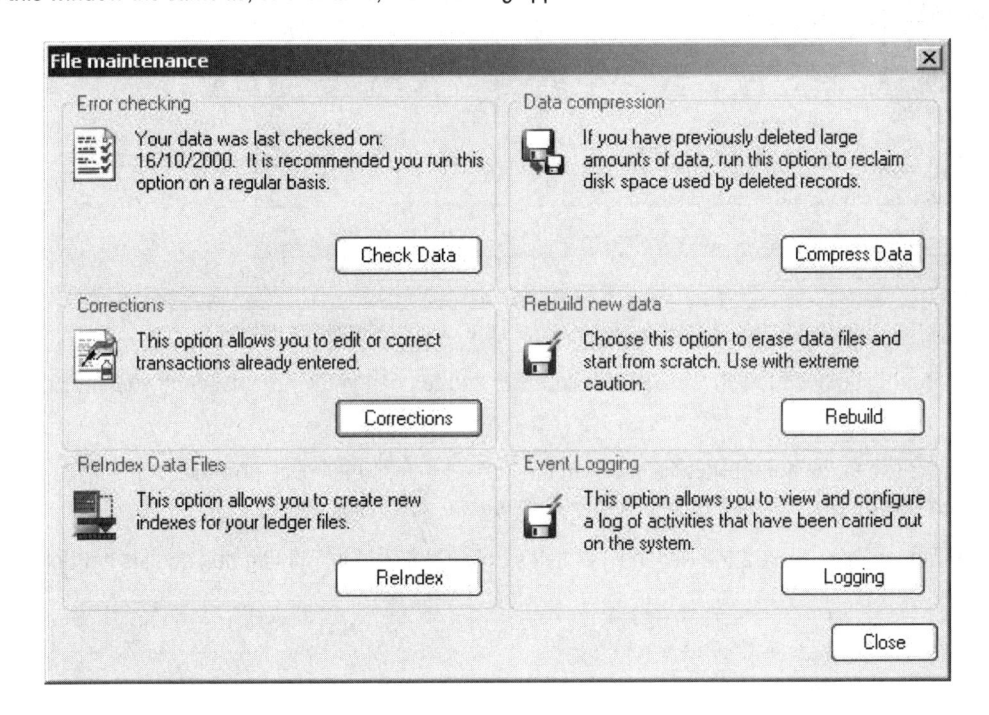

6.3 Posting error corrections

To correct errors you use the **Corrections** button. If you click on this the following screen will appear. This lists all the transactions currently on the system, in transaction number order.

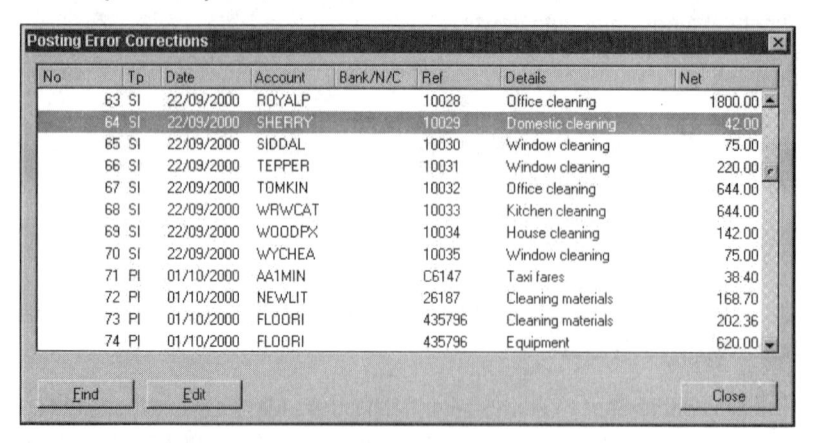

No	Tp	Date	Account	Bank/N/C	Ref	Details	Net
63	SI	22/09/2000	ROYALP		10028	Office cleaning	1800.00
64	SI	22/09/2000	SHERRY		10029	Domestic cleaning	42.00
65	SI	22/09/2000	SIDDAL		10030	Window cleaning	75.00
66	SI	22/09/2000	TEPPER		10031	Window cleaning	220.00
67	SI	22/09/2000	TOMKIN		10032	Office cleaning	644.00
68	SI	22/09/2000	WRWCAT		10033	Kitchen cleaning	644.00
69	SI	22/09/2000	WOODPX		10034	House cleaning	142.00
70	SI	22/09/2000	WYCHEA		10035	Window cleaning	75.00
71	PI	01/10/2000	AA1MIN		C6147	Taxi fares	38.40
72	PI	01/10/2000	NEWLIT		26187	Cleaning materials	168.70
73	PI	01/10/2000	FLOORI		435796	Cleaning materials	202.36
74	PI	01/10/2000	FLOORI		435796	Equipment	620.00

Your first job is to locate the transaction. If you noted down the transaction number this should be easy enough. Highlight the transaction and click on the **Edit** button. A new window will appear, the same as or similar to the following.

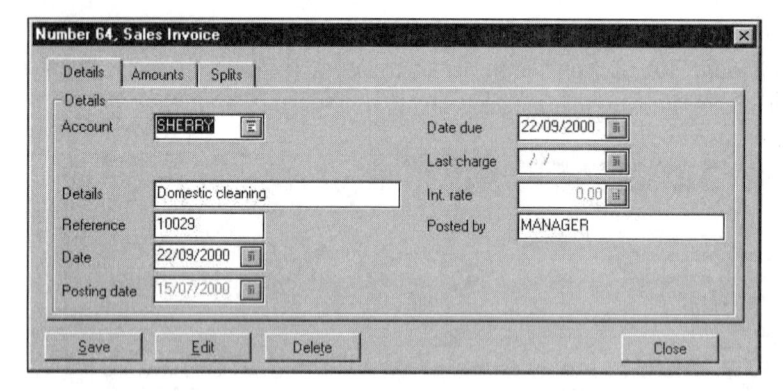

Number 64, Sales Invoice

Details | Amounts | Splits

Details
- Account: SHERRY
- Details: Domestic cleaning
- Reference: 10029
- Date: 22/09/2000
- Posting date: 15/07/2000
- Date due: 22/09/2000
- Last charge: / /
- Int. rate: 0.00
- Posted by: MANAGER

The **Details** section of the transaction will now be on screen and are available for editing.

To change the Amount you need to activate the **Amounts** Tab and to change the nominal code you should activate the **Splits** Tab.

To correct an error, Tab to the appropriate field, key in the correct details then click on **Save**. A message will appear asking you if you 'Do you wish to post these changes?'. If you are sure, click on Yes.

In the **Amounts** Tab you may correct the Net and Tax fields only if the Paid in Full flag box does is not ticked.

6.4 Correcting errors in account code or amount

You may only correct an *accounting* error using the **Maintenance** option if the transaction has not already been settled: in other words if a receipt or payment relating to the invoice has not yet been recorded on the system.

Journal entries will be required to correct errors in transactions that have been recorded as being paid. Two entries would be required, a reversing entry to cancel out the existing entry and another to input the transaction correctly.

Activity 8.5

Load the data for Assignment 3.

The details for a purchase invoice from the Ironcliffe Group posted on 26 August 2000 should have read 'Rent to 31 October 2000'.

Correct the details, as described above.

Activity 8.6

Still with Assignment 3 loaded, find the balance on each of the sales accounts. Then alter the amount of invoice number 10018 to £1000 plus VAT, and alter the details and nominal code to that for Window Cleaning.

What appears in the Activity record of the relevant customer's account after you have done this?

How have the balances on the sales accounts changed?

7 Conclusion

You should now be ready to attempt **Assignment 6**.

PART B USING ACCOUNTING SOFTWARE

Key learning points

- ☑ A **contra entry** is made in the accounts of a business when a debit entry can be matched with a credit entry. A common type of contra entry occurs when a supplier is also a customer – the amount owed as a supplier and the amount owing as a customer can be offset.

- ☑ Modern accounting software packages such as Sage allow **credit limits** to be set for customers. Credit limits show the maximum amount of credit (outstanding balance) the customer is allowed.

- ☑ A **warning message** will be displayed on screen whenever an invoice you are processing takes the outstanding balance on the account above its current credit limit.

- ☑ Occasionally, a customer who has been invoiced will fail to pay, and the debt must eventually be 'written off' as a **bad debt**.

- ☑ A range of reports are available from within Sage to help establish the effectiveness of credit control activities, for example an **Aged debtors analysis**.

- ☑ A **statement** of account shows the transactions and balance outstanding on a customer's account at the date the statement was issued.

- ☑ **Errors** can be corrected through reversing the transaction, for example posting a correcting **journal** or issuing a Credit Note to cancel an invoice. Sage allows some errors to be corrected by **editing existing transactions** through the File, Maintenance, Corrections option.

Quick quiz

1. What is a contra entry?

2. How do you access the contra entries facility for offsetting Customer and Supplier accounts in Sage Line 50 (the automated contra feature is not included in Instant Accounts)?

3. How would you increase a customer's credit limit?

4. List three reasons why a customer may not pay an invoice.

5. Give two examples of accounting errors.

Answers to quick quiz

1. A contra entry is an accounting entry that is offset by an opposite entry. A common type of contra entry occurs when a supplier is also a customer – the amount owed as a supplier and the amount owing as a customer can be offset.

2. From the main Sage Line 50 menu, you select Tools from the top of the screen and then select Contra Entries. You can then choose the relevant accounts and transactions.

3. You would click on the Customers button, select the Customer's account from the list and then click on Record. Activate the Credit Control Tab and click into the Credit Limit box, key in the new limit and then click on Save.

4. Three common reasons are: The customer proves unreliable and simply refuses to pay; The customer goes out of business; There is a dispute with the customer relating to the goods or services supplied and billed on a particular invoice.

5. Two examples are mistakes relating to the account number such as input of the wrong account code, and entering the wrong amount or value of a transaction.

PART B USING ACCOUNTING SOFTWARE

Activity checklist

This checklist shows which knowledge and understanding point is covered by each activity in this chapter. Tick off each activity as you complete it.

Activity		
8.1		Knowledge and Understanding: Operation of computerised accounting systems
8.2		Knowledge and Understanding: Operation of computerised accounting systems
8.3		Knowledge and Understanding: Operation of computerised accounting systems
8.4		Knowledge and Understanding: Operation of computerised accounting systems
8.5		Knowledge and Understanding: Operation of computerised accounting systems
8.6		Knowledge and Understanding: Operation of computerised accounting systems

Answers to Activities

Answers to activities

Chapter 1

Answer 1.1

(a) =SUM(B5:B6)

(b) =SUM(B6:D6)

(c) =SUM (E5:E6) *or* =SUM(B7:D7)

or (best of all) =IF(SUM(E5:E6) =SUM(B7:D7),SUM(B7:D7),"ERROR") Don't worry if you don't understand this formula when first attempting this Activity - we cover IF statements later in Chapter 1.

Answer 1.2

(a) For cell B7   =B6*0.175   For cell E8   =SUM(E6:E7)

(b) By using a separate 'variables' holding the VAT rate and possibly the Sales figures. The formulae could then refer to these cells as shown below.

	A	B	C	D	E	F	G	H
1	Taxable Supplies plc							
2	*Sales analysis - Branch C*							
3	*Six months ended 30 June 200X*							
4		Jan	Feb	Mar	Apr	May	Jun	Total
5		£	£	£	£	£	£	£
6	Net sales	=B12	=C12	=D12	=E12	=F12	=G12	=SUM(B6:G6)
7	VAT	=B6*$B$13	=C6*$B$13	=D6*$B$13	=E6*$B$13	=F6*$B$13	=G6*$B$13	=SUM(B7:G7)
8	Total	=SUM(B6:B7)	=SUM(C6:C7)	=SUM(D6:D7)	=SUM(E6:E7)	=SUM(F6:F7)	=SUM(G6:G7)	=SUM(H6:H7)
9								
10								
11	*Variables*							
12	Sales	2491.54	5876.75	3485.01	5927.7	6744.52	3021.28	
13	VAT rate	0.175						
14								

Answer 1.3

(a)
Cell	Formulae
C7	=SUM(B5:B6)
B12	=SUM(B9:B11)
B16	=SUM(B14:B15)
C17	=B12-B16
C18	=SUM (C4:C17)
C24	=C21+C22–C23

ANSWERS TO ACTIVITIES

(b) The finished spreadsheet follows. Further improvements could be made eg formatting numbers, clearer layout.

	A	B	C	D	E	F
1	**Ed Sheet**					
2	*Balance sheet as at 31 Dec 200X*					
3		£	£			
4	*Fixed assets*					
5	Plant	20000				
6	Vehicles	10000				
7			30000			
8	*Current assets*					
9	Stock	2000				
10	Debtors	1000				
11	Cash	1500				
12		4500				
13	*Current liabilities*					
14	Creditors	2500				
15	Overdraft	1500				
16		4000				
17	Net current assets		500			
18	**Net assets**		30500			
19						
20	*Represented by:*					
21	Opening capital		28000			
22	Profit for year		3500			
23	Drawings		1000			
24	Closing capital		30500			
25						

Answer 1.4

Tutorial note. This activity tests whether you can evaluate formulae in the correct order. In part (a) you must remember to put brackets around the numbers required to be added, otherwise the formula will automatically divide cell B8 by 4 first and add the result to the other numbers. Similarly, in part (b), the formula performs the multiplication before the addition and subtraction.

Solution

(a) =SUM(B5:B8)/4   An alternative is = AVERAGE(B5:B8).

(b) 59.325

Chapter 2

Answer 2.2

(a) AA1MIN

(b) 3DTECH

(c) 111111

(d) 3DTECH. You have a fresh copy of the assignment 2 data, free of any entries you made yourself.

This Activity is to encourage you to experiment with any entries you like, safe in the knowledge that you cannot damage the Blitz data.

Answer 2.4

The 000000 should disappear.

Answer 2.5

The query is from a credit customer, so you begin by clicking on the Customers button. To find Mr Newall's account use the down arrow in the scroll bar to the right of the list of accounts. When you see NEWALL, click on that name to highlight it, then click on the Activity button. Accept the Defaults suggested by clicking on OK. The next screen will show you the current balance on Mr Newall's account.

The display on screen should show you that there is only one invoice outstanding, an amount for domestic cleaning invoiced on 22/09/2000 for £77.55.

Answer 2.6

The supervisor has requested the Transactions on the Bank Current account. Select the Nominal button, scroll down to account 1200, highlight it, click on the Activity button and accept the Defaults. You should see the following.

1200 Bank Current Account

No.	Tp	Date	Ref	Details	Amount	Debit	Credit
1	BR	19/08/2000		M Green – shares	20000.00	20000.00	
2	BR	19/08/2000		T Nicholas – shares	20000.00	20000.00	
8	JC	16/09/2000		Wages and salaries	6053.93		6053.93
						40000.00	6053.93
						33946.07	

The Tp (Type) column shows the type of transaction. BR is a bank receipt. JC is a journal entry (credit entry). The three figures at the foot of the display show total debits and credits and the balance.

ANSWERS TO ACTIVITIES

Chapter 3

Answer 3.1

It should appear between LERWIC and MATTHI.

Answer 3.2

(a) N14 6TS
(b) Candy Spicer
(c) T Cooper (Stationery) Ltd, 01582 405592

Answer 3.3

Check the details you have entered on screen very carefully to make sure that all the spelling and numbers are exactly as you see them here. Have you got the right combination of letters and numbers in the post-code, for instance?

Answer 3.4

You should get BL OFFICE FURNISHING LTD and MUSWELL HILL COUNCIL.

Answer 3.5

(a) This is a hands on activity.

(b) FLOORI, HARDIN and LERWIC. This will only work if you follow the instructions given above and avoid the pitfalls.

Answer 3.6

You should get the answers £53.24, Materials Purchases and Office Machine Maintenance.

(Incidentally, unless we tell you otherwise, it does not normally matter whether you save information entered for activities or close without saving.)

Answer 3.7

These are the results you should get.

Account	With new transactions Dr	With new transactions Cr	Fresh Assignment 6 data Dr	Fresh Assignment 6 data Cr	Difference Dr	Difference Cr
2100		8034.78		7677.28		357.50
2202	7030.74		6977.50		53.24	
5000	6336.89		6236.89		100.00	
7701	204.26				204.26	
IRONCL		240.00		0.00		240.00
NEWLIT		789.63		672.13		117.50

The differences are entirely due to the transactions you posted in the Activity. You should trace through each figure until you are happy about this, using your knowledge of double entry from Units 1 and 2. Ideally, write out all the T-accounts.

This Activity is to reassure you that Sage follows the same principles of double entry as a manual system and to highlight how much easier it is to use a computerised package.

Answer 3.9

The last transaction listed should be number 194. You should get the following totals.

Net	Tax	Gross
54,742.89	8,119.29	62,862.18

Chapter 4

Answer 4.3

The screen should show the full details in the white box at the top left.
W R W CATERING LTD
11 STATION PARADE
BARNET
HERTS

BT5 2KC

Answer 4.4

You should have got an amount of £117.50 for ADAMSE (N/C 4001) and of £116.63 for GARDEN (N/C 4000). Although the net amount of both invoices is £100, GARDEN's record is set up to receive settlement discount of 5%, so the Sage package automatically charges VAT on the discounted amount (£100 – 5% = £95). £95 × 17.5% = £16.63

ANSWERS TO ACTIVITIES

You can check the records of ADAMSE and GARDEN to confirm that one is set up to receive settlement discount and the other is not.

Answer 4.5

You should have got the amount £122.51. First, set up the customer's record to receive 5% settlement discount. Delivery address, order number, telephone number and contact name should be entered on the Order Details tab, but not before you have checked why the phone number shown above is different to the one contained in the customer record (020 7734 2043). The number may have changed, or it may have been entered into the system incorrectly, or it may be an additional number. Likewise you should check whether the customer's record should be amended to show the contact name Jennifer. Other details are entered on the Footer tab.

Answer 4.6

The initial balance should be £0.00. The balance should still be £0.00 at the end of the activity, because you have not posted the invoice.

Answer 4.7

You should get the answer £50.20. The nominal code is 4100.

Answer 4.8

(a) Only eight invoices should appear.
(b) No invoices should appear.
(c) Did you get the result you expected and wanted?
(d) Credit notes 1 to 4 and invoices 10001 to 10052 should all appear.

Answer 4.9

The invoice is shown on the following page.

Answer 4.10

(a) It is the same as when you started because you have not posted anything yet.
(b) GOODMA now has a balance of £117.50. HASLAM has a balance of £117.50. The Sales – Window Cleaning account has increased by £200 to £2,834.40.

BLITZ LTD
25 APPLE ROAD
LONDON
N12 3PP

| Invoice | Page 1 |

D J HARGREAVES
6 COLLEGE PARK
LONDON
NW10 5CD

Invoice No.	10042
Invoice/Tax Date	08/10/2000
Cust. Order No.	
Account No.	HARGRE

Quantity Details	Disc%	Disc Amount	Net Amount	VAT Amount
Domestic services	0.00	0.00	43.50	7.61

Total Net Amount	43.50
Total VAT Amount	7.61
Carriage	0.00
Invoice Total	51.11

ANSWERS TO ACTIVITIES

Chapter 5

Answer 5.2

(a) The initial balances should be:

NEWLIT: £672.13
Bank £33,946.07

(b) You cannot print out a remittance advice after you have saved a bank transaction.

(c) The balances should now be:

NEWLIT: £198.22
Bank £33,472.16

Answer 5.4

The balances should be nil and £55.16.

Answer 5.5

View the Remittance advice on-screen if you don't have access to a printer.

Answer 5.6

The cheque is for £3,044.75. The discount has to be allocated between three separate items: £82.50 + £56.25 + £21.50 = £160.25. You should have used the (F4) calculator button.

There is no VAT on insurance. You could check this by finding the transaction numbers (Suppliers ... Activity), which are numbers 76, 77 and 78 and then looking up these numbers by clicking on Financials.

Well done if you got this activity right.

Answer 5.7

You should take advantage of the credit note.

Answer 5.8

(a) £300.25
(b) £399.75

ANSWERS TO ACTIVITIES

Answer 5.9

Ensure you process the cheque through the **Bank**, **Payment** option.

Chapter 6

Answer 6.1

The opening balance on the bank account is £4,616.49 and the closing balance is £6,615.10. the opening balance on the Debtors ledger control account is £25,486.83 and the closing balance is £23,488.22.

The receipt from ELITEC is likely to have been the most difficult to deal with: it does match up precisely to existing invoice amounts, however. Note that ROSEAL has underpaid by a small amount. You should be left with a balance of £0.88 on this account.

Here are the sort of details that your report on ELITEC should have contained. (This is an extract from a Customer Activity (Detailed) report.)

No	Tp	Date	Refn	N/C	Details	T/C	Value	O/S	Debit	Credit
56	SI	22/09/2000	10021	4000	Kitchen cleaning	T1	756.70 p	556.70	756.70	
96	SI	08/10/2000	10043	4000	KITCHEN CLEANING	T1	756.70		756.70	
97	SI	08/10/2000	10043	4100	OVEN CLEANER	T1	71.68		71.68	
98	SI	08/10/2000	10043	4100	FLAME DETERGENT	T1	84.60		84.60	
99	SI	08/10/2000	10043	4100	BRUSHES	T1	28.13		28.13	
161	SR	10/10/2000	10021	1200	Sales Receipt	T9	200.00			200.00
196	SI	16/10/2000	10054	4000	Kitchen cleaning	T1	223.25 *	223.25	223.25	
246	SR	15/11/2000	10043	1200	Sales Receipt	T9	941.11			941.11
							779.95	779.95	1,921.06	1,141.11

Answer 6.2

Follow the instructions in Section 3 of Chapter 6.

Answer 6.3

The customer should end up with £17 discount and a balance of £0.00 if you do all of this correctly.

Answer 6.4

(a) £0.00 and £4,616.49.

(b) Follow the instructions in Section 5 of Chapter 6.

(c) £88.13 and £4,528.36.

ANSWERS TO ACTIVITIES

(d) As follows. The cheque receipt on 10 October is now shown as a cancelled cheque and the invoice from 22 September is reinstated.

No	Tp	Date	Refn	Details	Amount	O/S	Debit	Credit
70	SI	22/09/2000	10035	Window cleaning	88.13		88.13	
150	SR	10/10/2000	CANCEL	Cancelled cheque	88.13			88.13
246	SI	31/10/2000	CANCEL	Cancelled cheque	88.13	88.13	88.13	

Answer 6.5

The initial balances are £0.00 and £27,167.80. The new balances are £0.00 and £26,752.80.

Here is the activity as recorded in Bridgford's account (shown on the following page).

No	Tp	Date	Refn	Details	Amount	O/S	Debit	Credit
38	SI	22/09/2000	10003	Office cleaning	487.63		487.63	
94	SI	08/10/2000	10041	Office cleaning at inv	493.50		493.50	
145	SR	10/10/2000	10003	Sales Receipt	981.13			981.13
246	SC	31/10/2000	REFUND	Refund – 10003	487.63			487.63
247	SI	31/10/2000	REFUND	Allocation – 10003	487.63		487.63	

Answer 6.6

It should be £35,046.07 (debit).

Chapter 7

Answer 7.1

You should get £262.30 (Dr) for petty cash and £415.10 (Dr) for account 7504.

Answer 7.2

The balance on the advertising account should be £3050.00

(Cr Legal Fees (7600) £800; Dr Consultancy (7602) £500, Dr Advertising (6201) £300.)

Answer 7.3

If you have ever performed a manual bank reconciliation you should find the computerised method much easier.

The outstanding items are as follows.

Cheque 000123		250.00
Cheque 000126		176.26
Receipt		(703.24)
Total		(276.98)

Chapter 8

Answer 8.1

School of Dance is £163.75 over the limit. The new balance on the Sales – Window Cleaning account is £2,920.40.

Activity 8.2

Here is what you should see in Vice Versa's account.

No	Tp	Date	Refn	Details	Amount	O/S	Debit	Credit
58	SI	22/09/2000	10035	Window cleaning	52.88		52.88	
84	SC	15/11/2000	BADDBT	Bad Debt Write Off	52.88			52.88

The write off affects the Debtors Control account (1100) and the Bad Debt Write Off account (8100).

Activity 8.3

The write off is for £2,714.25. The new balance on the Debtors Control account is £17,235.19.

Activity 8.4

More than 90 days.

ANSWERS TO ACTIVITIES

Answer 8.5

You should see the following activity.

No	Tp	Date	Refn	Details	Amount	O/S	Debit	Credit
53	SI	22/09/2000	10018	Window cleaning	1175.00	1175.00	1175.00	
107	SI	22/09/2000	10018	Deleted – see tran 53	940.00			

Answer 8.6

The balances change as follows.

Account	Before	After	Change
	£	£	£
4000	20,807.80	20,007.80	800.00
4001	2,520.40	3,520.40	1,000.00
4002	853.10	853.10	None
4100	980.14	980.14	None

PART C

Assignments

Assignments are designed to enable you to apply your Sage and Excel skills in realistic situations.

		Assignment	Answer to assignment	Done
1	Supplier invoices and credit notes	183	219	
2	Customer invoices and credit notes	187	223	
3	Payments to suppliers	195	231	
4	Receipts from customers	199	237	
5	Other cash transactions	205	243	
6	Other credit transactions	213	249	

Assignment 1:
Supplier invoices and credit notes

Loading and carrying out the assignment

Load assignment 1 into Sage now!

For instructions on how to load the data for assignments refer to Section 3 of Chapter 2. Check with your tutor in case special instructions apply to your college's system.

If you need to break off from this assignment part-way through, back-up your work, following the instructions given on screen when you quit the Sage program. You can restore your entries when you wish to re-start working on this assignment.

If you want to keep a permanent copy of your finished work, back it up and save the back-up file with a suitable name.

Purpose

Assignment 1 tests your ability to set up accounts for new suppliers in the purchase ledger, to process invoices and credit notes from suppliers, to post the entries to the appropriate accounts in the suppliers and nominal ledgers, to produce reports and to check the current balance on the creditors control account.

The **Tasks** for this assignment follow the **Information.** Read the information and all the tasks *before* commencing work.

PART C ASSIGNMENTS

Information

Your supervisor asks you to process eight invoices and two credit notes received from suppliers. Today's date is 2 October 2000. Details are as follows.

Invoices from existing suppliers

Invoice No	Supplier	A/C Ref	Details	Nominal ledger account	Net amount (excluding VAT) £	£
C6147	AA1 Mini Cabs	AA1MIN	Taxi fares	Travelling		38.40
26187	Newlite Cleaning Fluids	NEWLIT	Cleaning materials	Materials purchases		168.70
435796	Flooring Supplies Ltd	FLOORI	Cleaning materials	Materials purchases	202.36	
			Equipment	Plant and machinery	620.00	
						822.36
4821	First Steps Ladder Hire	FIRSTS	Ladder hire	Equipment hire		126.75

All these invoices are subject to VAT at the standard rate of 17.5%. All invoices are dated 1 October 2000.

Invoices from new suppliers

(a) Samurai Insurance Brokers
15 Osnabruck Street
London EC3 5JG
Tel: 020-7488 1066

A/C ref	Inv no	Inv date	Nominal ledger account	Net amount	VAT
SAMURA	02381	1 Oct 2000	Premises insurance	1,650.00	
			Vehicle insurance	1,125.00	
			Miscellaneous insurance	430.00	
				3,205.00	

This invoice has a Post-It note attached by your supervisor saying 'Insurance is exempt from VAT - code T2.'

(b) 3D Technical Bookshops
116 Albert Road
Wood Green
London N22 7RB
Tel: 020-8889 3539
Contact: Adrian

A/C ref	Inv no	Inv date	Nominal ledger account	Net amount	VAT
3DTECH	001462	30 Sep 2000	Books	179.95	0%

ASSIGNMENT 1: SUPPLIER INVOICES AND CREDIT NOTES

(c) Thames Water
Umbrella House
Weather Street
London WC1 9JK
Tel: 020-7837 4411

A/C ref	Inv no	Inv date	Nominal ledger account	Net amount	VAT
THAMES	132157	1 Oct 2000	Water rates	420.00	0%

(d) ANS Newspaper Group
19 Cecil Road
London NW10 4PP
Tel: 020-8453 2926
Contact: Mandy Walker

A/C ref	Inv no	Inv date	Nominal ledger account	Net amount	VAT
ANSNEW	621014	29 Sep 2000	Advertising	750.00	17.5%

For all invoices, you have been given details of the item purchased, and you have been instructed to allocate each item to an appropriate nominal ledger account. Refer to the nominal ledger codes in Appendix 1 of this book if necessary.

Credit Notes from Suppliers

Credit note no	Supplier	A/C ref	Net amount	VAT
K0320	B L Office Furnishing	BLOFFI	150.00	17.5%
C0259	Trojan Secretarial Service	TROJAN	60.00	17.5%

Both credit notes are dated 1 October 2000.

The credit note from B L Office Furnishing is for the return of office furniture supplied in damaged condition. The credit note from the Trojan Secretarial Service is for overcharging; a temporary secretary had been employed for two days, but Trojan, the agency supplying the secretary, had charged for three days.

Your supervisor has asked you to identify the nominal ledger accounts for the credit note transactions, but has told you that the credit note for B L Office Furnishing relates to fixed assets (furniture and fixtures) and the credit note for Trojan Secretarial Service relates to casual wages.

PART C   ASSIGNMENTS

Tasks

(a) Enter these transactions in the Suppliers Ledger and post the details. Use the tax code T0 for items with 0% VAT.

(b) Print a detailed suppliers invoices day book listing and suppliers credits day books listing covering *only* the transactions you have posted. If you do not have access to a printer, you should display these listings (one at a time) on your screen. Check that the number of entries in the system so far is 83. What is the total amount of transactions in each day book listing?

(c) Obtain the balance on the Creditors Control Account, after all the entries have been posted. (This is the total amount currently owed to suppliers for goods or services obtained on credit.) The nominal ledger code for this account is 2100. You can obtain the balance on the account either by looking at an appropriate screen display or by printing a copy of the Activity for the account.

Assignment 2:
Customer invoices and credit notes

Loading and carrying out the assignment

Load assignment 2 into Sage now!

For instructions on how to load the data for assignments refer to Section 3 of Chapter 2. Check with your tutor in case special instructions apply to your college's system.

If you need to break off from this assignment part-way through, back-up your work, following the instructions given on screen when you quit the Sage program. You can restore your entries when you wish to re-start working on this assignment.

If you want to keep a permanent copy of your finished work, back it up and save the back-up file with a suitable name.

Purpose

Assignment 2 tests your ability to set up accounts for new customers in the customers ledger, to process invoices and credit notes to customers, to post the entries to the appropriate accounts in the customers and nominal ledgers, to produce listings and to answer queries from customers by searching the ledger files. If you have access to a printer, the assignment also tests your ability to produce invoices and credit notes.

The **Tasks** for this assignment follow the **Information**. Read the information and all the tasks *before* commencing work.

PART C   ASSIGNMENTS

Information

It is now 8 October 2000. You have been asked to process a batch of invoices and credit notes, using the Sage Invoicing option from the main menu.

Invoices

The invoice details for processing are as follows. All invoices are subject to VAT at the standard rate (17.5%): code T1.

(1) Customer Name   R P Marwood
     New Customer?   Yes
     Address   17 Eton Villas
                           Harrow Road
                           London NW3 0JS
     Telephone   020-7722 4488
     Contact   Mr Marwood
     Credit Limit?   No

     Details   Net Amount
     Domestic services   £66.00

(2) Customer Name   School of Dance
     New Customer?   Yes
     Address   10 Underwood Street
                           London N1 6SD
     Telephone   020-7490 2449
     Contact   Bernice
     Credit Limit?   Yes, £600

     Details   Net Amount
     Cleaning school property   £250.00

(3) Customer Name   B & T Fashions Ltd
     New Customer?   Yes
     Address   8 Green Lanes
                           London N16 4LM
     Telephone   020-7226 2703
     Contact   Peter Bruce
     Credit Limit?   No

     Details   Net Amount
     Window cleaning   £144.00

ASSIGNMENT 2: CUSTOMER INVOICES AND CREDIT NOTES

(4) Customer Name   The Keith Group
    New Customer?   Yes
    Address   3 Sheringham Avenue
                             London N14 2TT
    Telephone   020-8360 7723
    Contact   Pat Walker
    Credit Limit?   Yes, £2,500

    Details   Net Amount
    Office cleaning at Grants Parade   £1,420.00
    London N14 and Spur House, Watford

(5) Customer Name   Rapid Pizzas
    New Customer?   Yes
    Address   90 Upper Street
                             London N10 4ZX
    Telephone   020-8444 4136
    Contact   Luciano Palmarozza
    Credit Limit?   No
    Settlement discount   5%

    Details
    5 cases of Flame detergent at £12 per case
    3 boxes of Bream cleaner at £30.40 per box
    50 pairs of cleaning gloves at £0.84 per pair

(6) Customer Name   Bridgford & Co
    New Customer?   No

    Details   Net Amount
    Office cleaning at invoice   £420.00
    address

(7) Customer Name   D J Hargreaves
    New Customer?   No

    Details   Net Amount
    Domestic services   £43.50

PART C ASSIGNMENTS

(8) Customer Name   Elite Caterers
     New Customer?   No

     Details   Net Amount
     Kitchen cleaning   £644.00
     In addition, supply of materials
     10 boxes of oven cleaner at £6.10 per box
     6 cases of Flame detergent at £12 per case
     7 brushes at £3.42 each

(9) Customer Name   Meakin Media Services Ltd
     New Customer?   No

     Details   Net Amount
     Window cleaning   £249.00

(10) Customer Name   A Rose Ltd
     New Customer?   Not sure
     Address   8 Mill Mead Road
                           London N17 7HP
     Telephone   020-8808 4204
     Credit Limit?   No

     Details   Net Amount
     Window cleaning   £125.00

(11) Customer Name   Gardeners Delight
     New Customer?   Not sure
     Invoice Address   212 Spa Road
                           London NW3 3DQ
     Delivery Address   Gardeners Delight Centre
                           Buckmans Road
                           London NW3
     Telephone   020-8368 2115
     Contact   Joe Grundy
     Credit Limit?   No
     Settlement discount   5%

     Details
     30 cases of window cleaning fluid at £21.00 per case

ASSIGNMENT 2: CUSTOMER INVOICES AND CREDIT NOTES

(12) | *Customer Name* | Payne Properties Ltd
| *New Customer?* | Yes
| *Address* | 18 Caledonian Road
| | London N1 9PN
| *Telephone* | 020-7837 3442
| *Contact* | Carl Megson
| *Credit Limit?* | Yes, £2,500
| *Settlement discount* | 5%

Details — *Net Amount*
Office cleaning at invoice address and 8 Richardson Street — £1,210.00

(13) | *Customer Name* | T P Paul
| *New Customer?* | Yes
| *Address* | 1 Arcola Street
| | London N8 1QB
| *Telephone* | 020-8348 5453
| *Contact* | Mrs Paul
| *Credit Limit?* | No

Details — *Net Amount*
Domestic services — £60.00

(14) | *Customer Name* | Siddall Wallis
| *New Customer?* | No

Details — *Net Amount*
Window cleaning — £182.00

(15) | *Customer Name* | Norris Hydraulics Ltd
| *New Customer?* | No

Details — *Net Amount*
Factory and office cleaning — £816.40

PART C ASSIGNMENTS

Credit Notes

The following service credit notes are to be produced. Make sure these are numbered 1, 2 and 3, and all dated 8 October 2000.

(1) Customer Details — Gelling Private Bank
Credit note for £250 (plus VAT), following a customer complaint about the poor quality of cleaning at one of the office premises.

(2) Customer Details — Royal Properties Ltd
Credit note for £300 (plus VAT), following an agreement with the customer that the scale of the office cleaning service provided was less than originally anticipated.

(3) Customer Details — DCS Roofing
Credit note for £150.00 (plus VAT), after customer complaint about a window broken by a Blitz window cleaner.

Tasks

(a) Enter the service invoice and credit note details into Sage. Make sure that the first invoice in the series is numbered 10036. Where appropriate, establish new customer accounts.

Check the nominal ledger accounts used by Blitz Limited to account for sales. These are included in the list in Appendix 1.

(b) Print (or Preview) the invoices and credit notes. If you can, back-up your work *before* posting the invoices, so that you can correct any errors discovered later without re-entering all the data.

(c) Post the invoice and credit note details to the appropriate accounts in the customers ledger and nominal ledger.

(d) Produce day book listings of customer invoices and customer credits for these transactions. Print the listings if you have access to a printer. Otherwise, display each listing on screen.

(e) Your supervisor wants to know the current balance on the Debtors Control Account in the nominal ledger. Find out what this is. If you have access to a printer, print out the details of this account.

(f) Your supervisor also wants to know the current debit, credit and net total balances on each of the four sales accounts (codes 4000, 4001, 4002 and 4100 in the nominal ledger). After you have entered the invoice and credit note details, find out what these balances are.

(g) *This task can only be carried out if you have access to a printer.*

The invoice you have produced for the School of Dance has been damaged accidentally. Coffee has been spilled over it. Produce another invoice for sending to the customer.

(h) You receive a telephone call from your contact at CCC Engineering Limited. They have not yet received an invoice for factory cleaning services, but need to know what the cost will be, for a management meeting that afternoon. Find out the amount of the invoice.

ASSIGNMENT 2: CUSTOMER INVOICES AND CREDIT NOTES

(i) *Word-processing exercise*

Unload the Word and Excel exercises from the CD-ROM onto your hard disk (see Chapter 2 for detailed instructions).

Without closing Sage switch to your word processing application such as Microsoft Word. Open the document A2FAX which will now be in the folder C:\AATF on your hard drive and *save* it with another appropriate name.

Prepare a fax to send to CCC Engineering in time for their management meeting this afternoon. The fax number is 01923 354071. Other details can be found from CCC Engineering's customer record or from an audit trail report. Copy from Sage and Paste into your word processing document if you wish to, and can work out how.

Note. To switch between applications use Alt + Tab.

(j) *Word-processing exercise*

For the purpose of this exercise we will assume that the missing invoice was one of an early batch that was prepared manually, not using the Sage system.

Open the document A2INV and prepare a duplicate invoice for CCC Engineering. The details are those you found for the previous task.

Mention the duplicate invoice in your fax produced for the previous task. (Alter it if you have saved and closed it already.)

If you have access to a printer, print out the fax and the duplicate invoice.

PART C ASSIGNMENTS

Assignment 3: Payments to suppliers

Loading and carrying out the assignment

Load assignment 3 into Sage now!

For instructions on how to load the data for assignments refer to Section 3 of Chapter 2. Check with your tutor in case special instructions apply to your college's system.

If you need to break off from this assignment part-way through, back-up your work, following the instructions given on screen when you quit the Sage program. You can restore your entries when you wish to re-start working on this assignment.

If you want to keep a permanent copy of your finished work, back it up and save the back-up file with a suitable name.

Purpose

Assignment 3 tests your ability to process payments to suppliers, to post the transactions to the appropriate accounts in the purchase ledger and nominal ledger, to deal with part payments, credit notes, settlement discounts and payments in advance, to deal with payments for cheque requisitions, to produce reports for payments, and to check the current balance on the bank account and creditors control account in the nominal ledger. If you have access to a printer, the Assignment also tests your ability to produce remittance advices.

The **Tasks** for this assignment will be found following the **Information.** Read the information and all the tasks *before* commencing work.

PART C ASSIGNMENTS

Information

(Read this information now, but don't post any transactions until attempting the tasks on the following page.)

It is now 9 October 2000. You have been asked to process a batch of payments.

(1) Your supervisor has provided you with a list of payment transactions.

Supplier	Code	Amount	Cheque no
AA1 Mini Cabs	AA1MIN	£117.50	000100
British Telecom plc	BTELEC	£540.50	000101
Capital Radiopaging	CAPITA	£376.00	000102
B L Office Furnishing	BLOFFI	£1,493.78	000103
First Steps Ladder Hire	FIRSTS	£332.23	000104
Samurai Insurance Brokers	SAMURA	£3,205.00	000105
3D Technical Bookshops	3DTECH	£179.95	000106
The Ironcliffe Group	IRONCL	£3,000.00	000107
Trojan Secretarial Services	TROJAN	£141.00	000108
Muswell Hill Council	MUSWEL	£1,240.00	000109
North London Advertiser	NORTHL	£1,175.00	000110
Sterling Supplies	STERLI	£642.37	000111
Uniform Workerwear	UNIFOR	£763.75	000112
Van Centre	VANCEN	£19,059.44	000113

The payments to B L Office Furnishing and Trojan Secretarial Services are net of credit notes outstanding on these accounts.

(2) You have also been asked to process a newly-received credit note of £235 (£200 plus VAT of £35) from the Chieftain Newspaper Group (because of an error in an advertisement printed in a newspaper), and a cheque (number 000114) to this supplier for the balance outstanding on the account of £1,175. The credit note number is SC0108. The nominal account code is 6201.

(3) You have been given the following note by your supervisor.

> We have received full credit notes and revised invoices from three suppliers because they offered us early settlement discounts over the phone but did not reflect this on their original invoices, which have already been posted. The suppliers and the relevant Nominal Codes are:
>
> Floorsanders (Equipment) (FLOORS)   0020
> Harrow Cleaning Supplies (HARROW)   5000
> Matthias Scaffolding (MATTHI)   0020
>
> Please proceed as follows.
>
> (a) Post the credit notes, which are each for the full amount currently shown as outstanding on these accounts. Use the reference 'Disc'.
>
> (b) Post the revised invoices shown below. Use code T3 and post VAT manually.
>
> (c) Pay the invoices taking advantage of the discounts.
>
> (d) We are still negotiating long-term terms, so hold off making any changes to the suppliers record settlement discount % until terms are finalised.

The revised invoice details are as follows.

Supplier	Invoice no	Gross	VAT	Net
FLOORS	34005	1,005.31	143.31	862.00
HARROW	HC1213	2,840.62	412.22	2,428.40
MATTHI	63041	3,335.48	475.48	2,860.00

(4) Blitz Limited will be purchasing more equipment from Highpile Cleaning Supplies (code HIGHPI). It has been agreed with the supplier that Blitz should make a payment of £3,500, to settle its outstanding debt and as a payment in advance for future purchases. You have been asked to record the payment. The cheque number is 000118.

(5) You have also been asked to prepare cheques and record the payments for the following cheque requisitions. The supplier names will be filled in manually.

Cheque no	Amount	Purpose	Nominal code
000119	£258.50 (inc VAT at 17.5%)	Training course	8203
000120	£105.50 (no VAT)	Train ticket	7400
000121	£98.70 (inc VAT at 17.5%)	Refreshments	8205

PART C   ASSIGNMENTS

Tasks

(a) If you haven't already done so, post the transactions listed at the start of this assignment to the appropriate ledger accounts.

(b) Print a remittance advice for Samurai Insurance Brokers and B L Office Furnishing.

(c) Print a report for the payments to suppliers and the bank transaction payments. If you do not have access to a printer, produce a screen display for the report. What is the total amount of payments?

(d) Print a copy of the bank account transactions (nominal ledger code 1200) to date (9 October 2000), and establish how much money, according to the records, is remaining in this account. If you do not have access to a printer, obtain a screen display of the account to establish the remaining cash balance.

(e) Establish the current balance on the creditors control account (nominal ledger account code 2100).

(f) *Spreadsheet exercise*

To do this exercise you require access to Microsoft Excel.

If you have not already done so, unload the Word and Excel exercises into the folder c:\AATF as explained in Chapter 2. Then open the spreadsheet file named A3SPRSHT and save it with a new name.

Your supervisor has manually keyed some information from Sage into a spreadsheet.

(i) Explain the meaning of the numbers in the columns headed No. and Ref.

(ii) Your supervisor cannot understand why the totals do not match those shown in your payments report. Can you work out why? Alter the spreadsheet so that it produces the correct totals. The *totals* are calculated automatically, but you can alter the other amounts.

(iii) Use the skills you have acquired in working with word processors to improve the appearance of this document. (If you are using both Word and Excel you will see strong similarities in the features available.)

(iv) If you have access to a printer, print out your revised version of the spreadsheet.

Assignment 4:
Receipts from customers

Loading and carrying out the assignment

Load assignment 4 into Sage now!

For instructions on how to load the data for assignments, refer to Section 3 of Chapter 2. Check with your tutor in case special instructions apply to your college's system.

If you need to break off from this assignment part-way through, back-up your work, following the instructions given on screen when you quit the Sage program. You can restore your entries when you wish to re-start working on this assignment.

If you want to keep a permanent copy of your finished work, back it up and save the back-up file with a suitable name.

Purpose

The purpose of this assignment is to test your ability to enter details of payments received from customers and to post these details to the appropriate ledgers. The transactions include payments in full and part payments, receipts with a deduction for a credit note, receipts with a deduction for an early settlement discount, payments on account, payments with order, writing off small unpaid balances on a customer account and a customer refund. The completeness and accuracy of your input will be checked by a further test of your ability to produce reports and listings, and to find the current balance on the bank current account and the debtors control account.

The **Tasks** for this assignment will be found following the **Information.** Read the information and all the tasks *before* commencing work.

PART C ASSIGNMENTS

Information

You are asked by your supervisor to process the following transactions. The transactions are for processing on 12 October 2000, unless otherwise indicated.

(1) You have been given the following two customer invoices to process. You have been asked to enter and post the invoice details. If you have access to a printer, you should also produce invoices for these customers, as well as posting the invoice details to the ledgers.

Customer name	Bradley Fashions Ltd
A/C Reference Code	BRADLE
New Customer?	Yes
Address	18 Hospital Bridge Road
	St Albans, Herts
	SA5 9QT
Telephone	01727 532678
Credit Limit?	Yes, £2,500
Contact	Lee
Details	For contract cleaning services, £820 plus VAT at the standard rate

Customer name	A Rathod
A/C Reference Code	RATHOD
New Customer?	Yes
Address	200 West Road
	London N17 4GN
Telephone	020-8808 7814
Credit Limit?	No
Details	For domestic services, £75 plus VAT at the standard rate

(2) The following payments have been received from existing customers. You have been asked to post the details to the ledgers. Your supervisor instructs you that you must use the relevant invoice number as the reference (or the first invoice number if several are being paid).

Customer	Code	Amount
E T Adams	ADAMSE	143.35
Farrar Air Tools Ltd	FARRAR	940.00
000D J Hargreaves	HARGRE	51.11
A Rose Ltd	ROSEAL	141.00
CCC Engineering	CCCENG	1527.50
Bridgford and Co	BRIDGF	981.13
Goodman Brickworks Ltd	GOODMA	141.47
Townend Angus Ltd	TOWNEN	1087.70
P Wood	WOODPX	166.85
P Leyser & Co	LEYSER	96.59
A Wyche	WYCHEA	88.13
D C Sherry	SHERRY	49.35

(3) You have been asked to cancel an invoice of £70.50 for T P Paul. This was an invoice for domestic cleaning services, nominal account code 4002.

(4) You have also been asked to post details of the following payments from customers, for which each customer has taken advantage of an early settlement discount of 5%.

Customer	A/C ref code	Cheque amount	Discount taken
Payne Properties	PAYNEP	1350.66	60.50 (1,210.00 x 5%)
Rapid Pizzas	RAPIDP	215.66	9.66 (193.20 x 5%)

(5) The following payments have been received, where the customer has reduced the payment to allow for a credit note.

Customer	A/C ref code	Cheque amount
Gelling Private Bank	GELLIN	1727.25
DCS Roofing	DCSROO	82.25

Note. It may be advisable to take a back-up at this point, if you are happy with all the entries you have made, in case you make an error in posting the remaining transactions.

(6) The following part-payments have been received:

Customer	A/C ref code	Cheque amount
Elite Caterers	ELITEC	200.00
Campbell Consultants	CAMPBE	70.00

(7) You have been asked to enter and post details of a payment of £828.75 by Clough and Partners. This payment is partly to settle an outstanding invoice and partly a payment in advance for services not yet provided by Blitz Limited.

PART C   ASSIGNMENTS

(8) A payment on account has been received from the following new customer.

Customer name	M Zakis Ltd
A/C Reference Code	MZAKIS
Address	43 Ballards Lane
	London N12 0DG
Telephone	020-8445 2993
Credit Limit?	No
Amount of payment on account.	£500

(9) The following payments have been received:

Customer	A/C ref code	Cheque amount
A T Haslam	HASLAM	42.00
R P Marwood	MARW00	77.50

In each case, the customer has not paid the full invoice amount, but it has been decided to write off the small unpaid amount in each case. Post the details of the amounts to be written off. (Hint. Take a note of the unpaid amount in each case. If you forget to do this, can you think of a way of searching for this information in the Customers ledger?)

(10) Immediate payments have been received (by cheque) for the following items, without a requirement to supply an invoice or give credit to the customer. Payments *include* VAT at the standard rate of 17.5% in each case.

Item	Amount received	Paying-in slip number
Window cleaning	47.00	500000
Domestic services	101.05	500001
Domestic services	61.10	500002
Materials sales	117.50	500003
Window cleaning	86.95	500004

These receipts must be entered and posted to the appropriate accounts.

Tasks

(a) Enter and post the transactions as described in information items (1) to (10) above. Make all the necessary entries, including the set up of new customer accounts where appropriate.

(b) Produce a report for:

 (i) Amounts received from credit customers on 12 October 2000.
 (ii) Bank receipts (ie amounts received from sources other than credit customers) on 12 October 2000.

 Print the report if you have access to a printer; otherwise produce a screen display. What is the total amount received?

(c) After you have printed these reports, you are asked to process a refund of £96.59 to P Leyser for a payment already received. The refund has been agreed by the chief accountant with the customer.

(d) As at the end of processing, establish the total debits, credits and overall balances on the following accounts in the nominal ledger

	Account Code
Bank current account	1200
Debtors control account	1100

(e) Your supervisor wants to know how much is still owed by the customer Elite Caterers. What is the outstanding balance on this account?

PART C ASSIGNMENTS

Assignment 5:
Other cash transactions

Loading and carrying out the assignment

Load assignment 5 into Sage now!

For instructions on how to load the data for assignments, refer to Section 3 of Chapter 2. Check with your tutor in case special instructions apply to your college's system.

If you need to break off from this assignment part-way through, back-up your work, following the instructions given on screen when you quit the Sage program. You can restore your entries when you wish to re-start working on this assignment.

If you want to keep a permanent copy of your finished work, back it up and save the back-up file with a suitable name.

Purpose

The purpose of Assignment 5 is to test your ability to post entries for petty cash in the nominal ledger and to make a small number of journal entries, and to carry out a bank reconciliation. In addition, the assignment includes a further test of your ability to post transactions for customer and supplier invoices, and customer and supplier payments.

The **Tasks** for this assignment will be found following the **Information**. Read the information and all the tasks *before* commencing work.

PART C ASSIGNMENTS

Information

(1) On 13 October 2000, Blitz Limited's directors decided to set up a petty cash system with a float of £300. A cheque (number 000122) for £300 in cash was drawn on the company's bank account that day.

(2) The following invoices have been received from suppliers.

Supplier	New supplier	Invoice number	Date	Details	Net amount £	VAT £
Hardin & Nobbs Chapel Place White Hart Lane London N17 4HA 020-8801 1907 A/C Ref HARDIN	Yes	2641	12 Oct 2000	Legal fees (N/C 7600)	1200.00	210.00
Flooring Supplies Ltd	No	435850	8 Oct 2000	Cleaning materials (N/C 5000)	762.00	133.35
Trojan Secretarial Services	No	03012	12 Oct 2000	Casual labour (N/C 7005)	210.00	36.75
AA1 Mini Cabs	No	C6281	15 Oct 2000	Taxis (N/C 7401)	134.70	23.57
Great North Hotel 75 Park Road Ealing London W5 6RU 020-8997 6005 A/C Ref GREATN	Yes	6601	7 Oct 2000	Hotel room (N/C 7402) Hotel meal (N/C 7406) Hotel telephone (N/C 7502) Total	110.00 26.00 3.40 139.40	19.25 4.55 0.60 24.40
Lerwick Cleaning Co Ryelands Road Norwich, NH7 4DB 01603 590624 A/C Ref LERWIC	Yes	S4031	14 Oct 2000	Cleaning materials (N/C 5000) Carriage (N/C 5100) Total	1400.00 20.00 1420.00	245.00 3.50 248.50

Continued on the following page

ASSIGNMENT 5: OTHER CASH TRANSACTIONS

Supplier	New supplier	Invoice number	Date	Details	Net amount £	VAT £
First Steps Ladder Hire	No	5024	8 Oct 2000	Ladder hire (N/C 7700)	81.00	14.18
Prairie Couriers Ltd	No	T34228	14 Oct 2000	Couriers (N/C 7501)	92.50	16.19
Amin Launderers 16 Southey Road London N15 3AK 020-8802 2541 A/C Ref AMINLA	Yes	0877	8 Oct 2000	Laundry (N/C 7802)	145.00	25.38

(3) The following invoices are to be sent out to customers, all dated 16 October 2000, with VAT charged at the standard rate.

Customer	New customer?	Invoice number	Details	Net amount £
Aspinall & Co	No	10053	Window cleaning	90.00
Elite Caterers	No	10054	Kitchen cleaning	190.00
S T Chana 78 Katherine Road London N9 8UL 020-8803 0147 No credit limit A/C Ref CHANAS	Yes	10055	Domestic services	135.00
L Haynes & Co 14 Millmead Road London N17 2XD 020-8885 3731 No credit limit A/C Ref HAYNES	Yes	10056	Window cleaning Materials sales Total	82.00 45.20 127.20
Brookes Acoustics Ltd	No	10057	Warehouse cleaning	670.00
CCC Engineering	No	10058	Factory cleaning	850.00
Tek Systems 115 Cricklewood Broadway London NW2 5ES 020-8452 9442 Credit limit £2,000 A/C Ref TEKSYS	Yes	10059	Contract cleaning Materials sales Total	450.00 63.00 513.00

Continued on the following page

PART C ASSIGNMENTS

Customer	New customer?	Invoice number	Details	Net amount £
Telefilm Latinamerica 100 Tower Bridge Road London SE1 6FJ 020-7403 2144 Credit limit £2,500 A/C Ref TELEFI	Yes	10060	Contract cleaning	830.00
GHH Commercial Bank	No	10061	Contract cleaning	950.00
The Keith Group	No	10062	Office cleaning	850.00
Owen of London 19 Piccadilly London W1 9CD 020-7734 2043 Credit limit £3,000 A/C Ref OWENLO	Yes	10063	Contract cleaning Window cleaning Materials sales Total	750.00 130.00 55.40 935.40
Biophysica Orbit Court 33 Fairfax Road London NW6 4LL 020-7624 2002 No credit limit A/C Ref BIOPHY	Yes	10064	Window cleaning Domestic services Total	63.00 45.00 108.00

(4) The following payments to suppliers were made on 16 October 2000.

Date	Supplier	Cheque number	Amount £	Details
16 Oct 2000	Ace Telephone Answering	000123	250.00	Part payment of invoice
16 Oct 2000	ANS Newspaper Group	000124	1200.00	Payment of invoice plus payment on account
16 Oct 2000	Wells Business Systems	000125	1516.50	Payment of invoice, net of credit note CN4245 for £387 (gross) dated 14/10/2000. Nominal code 0030.

(5) The following payments have been received from customers.

Date	Supplier	Amount £	Details
14 Oct 2000	Campbell Consultants	70.00	Part payment of invoice
15 Oct 2000	Brookes Acoustics Ltd	1000.00	Part payment of invoice
16 Oct 2000	Gardeners Delight	703.24	Payment of invoice, discount of £31.50 taken

ASSIGNMENT 5: OTHER CASH TRANSACTIONS

(6) The company has received a cheque from Mr V J Richardson, a relative of one of the directors, for £10,000. The money was banked on 12 October 2000. It represents a loan from Mr Richardson to the company. A journal voucher has been prepared as follows:

```
                JOURNAL VOUCHER                    J02

                      N/C        Debit      Credit
                                   £           £
      Cash           1200       10,000
      Loan account  2300                    10,000

              Loan from Mr V J Richardson
```

(7) In the period to 16 October 2000, petty cash vouchers for expenditure items were as follows. (VAT is only shown where the company has obtained a valid VAT invoice.)

Ref	Date	Item	N/C code	Net amount £	VAT £	Gross amount £
PC001	13/10/2000	Postage stamps	7501	24.00	0	24.00
PC002	13/10/2000	Biscuits, coffee	8205	32.49	0	32.49
PC003	13/10/2000	Milk	8205	15.20	0	15.20
PC004	13/10/2000	Taxis	7400	25.00	0	25.00
PC005	14/10/2000	Train fares	7400	9.20	0	9.20
PC006	14/10/2000	Washing up liquid	8205	1.75	0	1.75
PC007	14/10/2000	Photocopying	7500	24.00	4.20	28.20
PC008	15/10/2000	Stationery	7504	37.24	6.52	43.76
PC009	15/10/2000	Taxis	7400	15.00	0	15.00
PC010	16/10/2000	Sandwiches, cakes	8205	38.26	0	38.26
PC011	16/10/2000	Parking	7304	7.00	0	7.00
PC012	16/10/2000	Train fares	7400	8.40	0	8.40

Notes and coin totalling £72.00 were paid into petty cash on 16 October. This was money received for various small window cleaning jobs, for which VAT should be recorded at the standard rate.

PART C ASSIGNMENTS

(8) Blitz Limited has not yet set up a computerised payroll system. Wages were paid by bank transfer on 16 October 2000, and the following transactions need to be accounted for.

	Code	Debit £	Credit £
Bank account	1200		4133.04
PAYE	2210		2217.96
National Insurance	2211		975.20
Directors salaries	7001	1350.80	
Staff salaries	7003	475.75	
Wages – regular	6000	4859.65	
Employers NI	7006	640.00	
		7326.20	7326.20

(9) On 19 October 2000, the following bank statement was received from Blitz's bank.

Account 11765444

BLITZ LIMITED
25 APPLE ROAD
LONDON N12 3PP

Centre Bank
Apple Road Branch
38 Apple Road
London N22

Particulars	Date	Withdrawn £	Paid in £	Balance £
BGC	21 AUG		20000.00	
BGC	21 AUG		20000.00	40000.00
BAC	16 SEP	6053.93		
				33946.07
000100	12 OCT	117.50		
000103	12 OCT	1493.78		
000104	12 OCT	332.23		
000105	12 OCT	3205.00		
000107	12 OCT	3000.00		
000111	12 OCT	642.37		
000113	12 OCT	19059.44		
000114	12 OCT	1175.00		4920.75
000101	13 OCT	540.50		
000102	13 OCT	376.00		
000106	13 OCT	179.95		
000108	13 OCT	141.00		
000109	13 OCT	1240.00		
000112	13 OCT	763.75		
000116	13 OCT	2767.77		1088.22DR
BGC	13 OCT		143.35	
BGC	13 OCT		51.11	
BGC	13 OCT		1527.50	
BGC	13 OCT		981.13	
BGC	13 OCT		940.00	

ASSIGNMENT 5: OTHER CASH TRANSACTIONS

Particulars	Date	Withdrawn £	Paid in £	Balance £
BGC	13 OCT		1087.70	
BGC	13 OCT		88.13	
BGC	13 OCT		141.00	
BGC	13 OCT		141.47	
BGC	13 OCT		166.85	
BGC	13 OCT		49.35	
BGC	13 OCT		96.59	
BGC	13 OCT		1350.66	
BGC	13 OCT		215.66	
BGC	13 OCT		1727.25	
BGC	13 OCT		200.00	
BGC	13 OCT		70.00	
BGC	13 OCT		828.75	
BGC	13 OCT		82.25	
BGC	13 OCT		101.05	
BGC	13 OCT		42.00	
BGC	13 OCT		500.00	
BGC	13 OCT		47.00	
BGC	13 OCT		77.50	
BGC	13 OCT		86.95	
BGC	13 OCT		61.10	
BGC	13 OCT		117.50	9833.63
000110	13 OCT	1175.00		
000115	13 OCT	962.21		
000118	13 OCT	3500.00		
000119	13 OCT	258.50		
000120	13 OCT	105.50		
000121	13 OCT	98.70		
CASH WITHDRAWAL	16 OCT	300.00		
TRANSFER-LEYSER	16 OCT	96.59		3337.13
BGC	16 OCT		70.00	
BGC	16 OCT		10000.00	13407.13
BANK CHARGES	16 OCT	25.60		13381.53

Tasks

(a) Post the transaction for withdrawing cash from the company's bank account to set up a petty cash system. Use the cheque number as a reference for the transaction (information item [1]).

(b) Post the transactions for invoices received from suppliers (information item [2]).

(c) Post the transactions for invoices sent out to customers (information item [3]).

(d) Post the payments to suppliers (information item [4]).

(e) Post the receipts from customers (information item [5]).

PART C ASSIGNMENTS

(f) Post the receipt of the money as a loan from Mr V J Richardson, using the journal voucher as your source document. The transaction reference should be the journal voucher number. The tax reference code should be T9.

(g) Post the petty cash transactions to the nominal ledger, for both expenditure and income items. Enter the income items as a single transaction, with reference PCR001. Produce a listing for the petty cash payments. Print the listing if you have access to a printer.

(h) The company uses an imprest system for petty cash. On 16 October 2000, the money in petty cash should be topped up to £300. A cheque (number 000126) is to be drawn on the bank account to withdraw cash.

    (i) What should be the cheque amount?

    (ii) Assume that a cheque for this amount is drawn, and petty cash is restored to £300. Post this cash withdrawal transaction. Give it a reference code 000126 and a tax code T9.

(i) Post the wages and salaries transactions, shown in information item (8), to the appropriate nominal ledger accounts. Post the transactions by means of a journal entry. Give the transaction a reference of J04. Use tax code T9.

(j) Your supervisor wishes to know the balances on the following nominal ledger accounts after you have dealt with tasks (a) to (i).

	Nominal ledger account code
Debtors control account	1100
Bank - current account	1200
Creditors control account	2100
Staff salaries	7003
Travelling	7400
Equipment hire	7700
Sales – contract cleaning	4000
Sales – window cleaning	4001
Sales – domestic services	4002
Sales – materials	4100
Petty cash	1230
Discounts allowed	4009

Report the balances on these accounts.

(k) Carry out a bank reconciliation on 19 October 2000, after you have completed tasks (a) to (j). How many unreconciled transactions are there and what are the amounts for:
    (i) Statement balance.
    (ii) Uncleared items.
    (iii) Trial balance.

A word of advice - your supervisor has advised that an error was made when posting cheque 000118. The cheque was for £3,500.00, but was mistakenly entered into Line 50 as £2,364.69. A correcting entry has been made for £1,135.31. You should match these two entries from your nominal account listing of account 1200 against the £3,500.00 that will show on the bank statement for cheque 000118.

Assignment 6:
Other credit transactions

Loading and carrying out the assignment

Load assignment 6 into Sage now!

For instructions on how to load the data for assignments, refer to Section 3 of Chapter 2. Check with your tutor in case special instructions apply to your college's system.

If you need to break off from this assignment part-way through, back-up your work, following the instructions given on screen when you quit the Sage program. You can restore your entries when you wish to re-start working on this assignment.

If you want to keep a permanent copy of your finished work, back it up and save the back-up file with a suitable name.

Purpose

This assignment tests your ability to post contra entries and write-offs for bad debts and to correct errors. It also tests your ability to deal with a variety of customer problems: customers who exceed their credit limit and late payers, and chasing customers for payment by producing an aged debtors list, statements and reminder letters.

The **Tasks** for this assignment will be found following the **Information.** Read the information and all the tasks *before* commencing work.

PART C ASSIGNMENTS

Information

Tim Nicholas and Maria Green, the directors of Blitz Limited, are quite pleased with the first few months of trading by the company. They are very aware, however, that the company must continue to win more sales if it is to be successful. This could mean having to take the risk of selling services to customers who might not be creditworthy. In addition, cash flow could be a problem. The company has already borrowed £10,000 from Mr V Richardson, and has used a bank overdraft facility. The directors have therefore recognised a need to collect money from debtors efficiently, to make sure that cash keeps coming into the business.

(1) Credit limits have been set for some of Blitz Limited's customers. If a customer exceeds his credit limit, however, the company's policy from now onwards will be to supply the goods or services and increase the customer's credit limit by £1,000. However, the directors wish to be informed of any such change.

(2) On 21 October 2000, you have been asked to process the following transactions. All sales are subject to VAT at the standard rate.

Credit Sales

Customer	New customer?	Invoice number	Details	Net amount
ANS Newspaper Group 19 Cecil Road London NW10 5CD 020-8453 2926 No credit limit A/C code ANSNEW	Yes	10065	Window cleaning	150.00
Brookes Acoustics Ltd	No	10066	Window cleaning	120.00
CCC Engineering Ltd	No	10067	Contract cleaning	630.00
R C Chadwick	No	10068	Domestic services	50.00
South Sea Airtours Girton House 62 Appendale Road London N17 1RA 020-8885 5553 Credit limit £2,500 A/C code SOUTHS	Yes	10069	Contract cleaning Materials sales Total	480.00 75.00 555.00
Clough & Partners	No	10070	Window cleaning	70.00
GHH Commercial Bank	No	10071	Contract cleaning	500.00
The Keith Group	No	10072	Contract cleaning Window cleaning Total	350.00 140.00 490.00
D J Hargreaves	No	10073	Domestic services	60.00
Meakin Media	No	10074	Window cleaning	100.00
Norris Hydraulics Ltd	No	10075	Contract cleaning	620.00
K Ogden Property Co	No	10076	Contract cleaning	480.00
Owen of London	No	10077	Window cleaning	150.00
School of Dance	No	10078	Contract cleaning	320.00
R I Tepper	No	10079	Contract cleaning	250.00
B Walton & Co	No	10080	Window cleaning	150.00

Continued on the following page

Customer	New customer?	Invoice number	Details	Net amount
WRW Catering	No	10081	Contract cleaning	370.00
The Lapsley Agency	Yes	10082	Window cleaning	144.00
105 Thetford Road			Domestic services	105.00
London N9 0PB			Total	249.00
020-8803 0147				
No credit limit				
A/C code LAPSLE				

Cash sales

The following amounts were received from cash sales to customers.

Date	Details	Gross amount (including VAT)	Method of payment	Paying in slip
21 October 2000	Domestic services	51.70	Cheque	500005
21 October 2000	Domestic services	44.00	Cheque	500006
21 October 2000	Materials sales	37.60	Cheque	500007
22 October 2000	Materials sales	25.38	Notes and coin	
23 October 2000	Domestic services	35.25	Notes and coin	
23 October 2000	Materials sales	52.88	Cheque	500008

The cheque payments were banked on 23 October 2000. The two receipts in notes and coin were put into petty cash (with reference codes PCR002 and PCR003 respectively).

Invoices from suppliers

The following invoices were received from suppliers. All three suppliers are credit customers.

Supplier	New supplier?	Invoice number	Date	Details	Net amount £	VAT £
ANS Newspaper Group	No	621347	20 Oct 2000	Advertising (N/C 6201)	471.28	82.47
Elite Caterers 85B Crowland Road London N15 9KW 020-8800 2069 A/C ref ELITEC	Yes	2046	20 Oct 2000	Catering (N/C 7403)	250.00	43.75
Meakin Media Ltd 4 Nursery Road Ashford Middlesex, AF8 5TS 01784 358452 A/C ref MEAKIN	Yes	10035	20 Oct 2000	Advertising (N/C 6201)	200.00	35.00

PART C ASSIGNMENTS

Receipts from customers

The following receipts from customers were obtained on 22 October 2000.

Customer	A/C ref	Amount £	Details
A Rathod	RATHOD	88.13	
A Rose Ltd	ROSEAL	146.88	
S T Chanas	CHANAS	158.00	
Biophysica	BIOPHY	52.88	To settle a part of an invoice relating to domestic services
Aspinall & Co	ASPINA	105.75	
Elite Caterers	ELITEC	1427.31	
Meakin Media Ltd	MEAKIN	350.16	

Tasks

(a) Post the credit sales transactions using the Service invoice option from the Invoicing menu.

    (i) Prepare a list of customers who have exceeded their current credit limit.
    (ii) Increase the credit limit for each of these customers by £1,000 each.

(b) Post the cash sales transactions (both the bank transactions and the petty cash transactions).

(c) Post the three invoices received from suppliers.

(d) Post the receipts from customers. The accounts of Elite Caterers and Meakin Media should be settled by means of *contra entries*.

(e) A cheque is being prepared to settle the account with ANS Newspaper group (cheque number 000127, dated 22 October 2000). The amount owed by ANS Newspaper Group should be offset against amounts owed to ANS, and the amount of the cheque should be for the difference.

    (i) What is the amount of the cheque?
    (ii) Post this cheque, and settle the accounts in the Suppliers and Customers ledgers by means of a contra entry (Sage Line 50 only).

(f) On 23 October 2000, you are instructed to write off small unpaid balances in any customer's account. Unpaid balances of £1 or less should be written off.

    (i) Write off these small unpaid balances.
    (ii) What is the total amount of bad debts written off in this exercise?

(g) Information has been received that the following customers have gone out of business.

Name	A/C ref
E T Adams	ADAMSE
L Haynes & Co	HAYNES

You are instructed that if there are any unpaid debts outstanding on the account of E T Adams or L Haynes & Co, the debts should be written off.

ASSIGNMENT 6: OTHER CREDIT TRANSACTIONS

(h) A credit note (reference 004) was issued to Owen of London on 22 October 2000 for £150 (plus VAT). Post this transaction, giving it a N/C code of 4000. (You are not required to produce the credit note itself.) Preview on screen a statement showing all transactions to date for GHH Commercial Bank.

(i) An invoice from AA1 Mini Cabs for £158.27 in October was entered in the accounts with a nominal ledger account code of 7401. Your supervisor tells you that the code should have been 7400. You are required to alter the code.

(j) A badly printed invoice from Newlite Cleaning Fluids dated 12 September was entered in the accounts incorrectly as £473.91 including VAT. The net amount, which is all that can be seen on the invoice, was actually £403. You are required to correct the error. What is the corrected figure?

(k) What are the current balances on the following nominal ledger accounts?

	Code
Bank current account	1200
Debtors control account	1100
Creditors control account	2100
Bad debt write off account	8100
Advertising account	6201
Sales – contract cleaning	4000
Sales – window cleaning	4001
Sales – domestic services	4002
Sales – materials	4100

(l) *Spreadsheet exercise: Aged Debtors Analysis*

Suppose that no more payments are received from customers before 5 November 2000. On 5 November, it is decided to review the current state of debtors, and take action to chase late payers.

However, due to a small fire which affected some of Blitz's computer hardware, it proves impossible to use the Sage system on 5 November.

Fortunately, the data from an aged debtors analysis dated 4 November is available in a spreadsheet file called A6AGED.xls.

(i) Open A6AGED.xls and save it with a new name. (The file A6AGED.xls will be in the folder C:\AATF if you have unloaded the Word and Excel files from the CD. Refer to Chapter 2.)

(ii) Check that the total value of debtors outstanding agrees with the value on your Sage system now that you have posted all the transactions for this assignment.

(iii) Sort the data in order of value of overall balance: largest first. Which five customers owe the largest amounts? (See the note below if you don't know how to sort the data.)

(iv) Sort the data in order of largest balance outstanding for over 30 days. Make a list of customers with a balance of over £1,000 that has been outstanding for more than 30 days.

(v) Resort the data into customer account code order.

(*Hint.* In Microsoft Excel you can sort data by clicking on the word **Data** at the top of the screen and then on **Sort** in the menu that drops down.)

PART C ASSIGNMENTS

(m) *Spreadsheet exercise: Cash flow forecast*

Blitz has been asked to submit a brief cash flow forecast to the bank for the first six months of next year (which is 2001 as the case is set in the year 2000).

A colleague has started to prepare the forecast, but is not sure how to continue.

(i) Open the file CashFcastFirstHalf2001.xls from the folder C:\AATF.

(ii) The relevant figures are:

Cash Balance Jan 1 2001	5,500
Cash Receipts Jan – June	4,500
Collections from Credit Sales Jan - June	130,000
Payments (materials)	25,000
Wages and salaries	52,000
Rent	8,000
Other payments	22,000

Enter this data into the spreadsheet, and enter formula to correctly calculate the required subtotals and totals.

Save the file with a different name.

Answer to Assignment 1: Supplier invoices and credit notes

You can enter the new supplier accounts in the Suppliers Ledger using either the Invoices button or the Record button.

If you use the Record button, as suggested in Chapter 4, you should set up accounts for the four new suppliers before entering any invoice details. Having set up the new accounts, you can switch to the Invoices window to process the eight invoices.

Having processed and posted the invoice details, you should then close the Invoices window and open the Credits window to process and post the details of the two credit notes.

Points to check

You should check the following points.

Date

For each invoice (or credit note) you should enter the actual date of the invoice (or credit note), rather than simply using today's date.

Nominal ledger codes

Carefully check transaction details shown below in the two listings. These list the entry details for the transactions. Make sure that you have specified the correct nominal ledger code for each transaction. To find the correct N/C codes for the credit notes, you should have looked for the account codes for Furniture and Fixtures (0040) and Wages - Casual (7005).

When an invoice is for purchases or items of expense for more than one nominal ledger account, you should enter each part of the invoice separately. This means that you should have entered:

(a) 2 lines of details for the invoice from Flooring Supplies Ltd, one for the purchase of cleaning materials (code 5000) and one for the purchase of plant and machinery (code 0020); and

(b) 3 lines of details for the invoice from Samurai Insurance Brokers, one for the premises insurance (code 7104), one for the vehicle insurance (code 7303) and one for miscellaneous items of insurance (code 8204).

PART C ASSIGNMENTS

Listings

When you have entered and posted the details of the invoices and credit notes, you can print the 'day book' listings.

Use the Reports button in the *Suppliers ledger* window and select Day Books: Supplier Invoices (detailed) and then Day Books: Supplier Credits (detailed).

You should specify the date ranges 29/09/2000 to 02/10/2000 for supplier invoices and 01/10/2000 to 01/10/2000 for credit notes.

The printouts should appear as follows, with 11 entries in the purchases day book and 2 entries in the purchases returns day book. (However, the sequence of transactions and the transaction numbers can vary, according to the order in which you entered them in the system.) The gross value of transactions is shown at the bottom of each listing.

Blitz Limited

Day Books : Supplier Invoices (Detailed)

Date from: 29/09/2000
Date to: 02/10/2000

Supplier From:
Supplier To: ZZZZZZZZ

Trans From: 1
Trans To: 83

N/C From:
N/C To: 99999999

Dept From: 0
Dept To: 999

No	Tp	A/c	N/C	Date	Ref.	Details	Net	T/C	VAT	Total
71	PI	AA1MIN	7400	01102000	C6147	Taxi fares	38.40	T1	6.72	45.12
72	PI	NEWLIT	5000	01102000	26187	Cleaning materials	168.70	T1	29.52	198.22
73	PI	FLOORI	5000	01102000	435796	Cleaning materials	202.36	T1	35.41	237.77
74	PI	FLOORI	0020	01102000	435796	Equipment	620.00	T1	108.50	728.50
75	PI	FIRSTS	7700	01102000	4821	Ladder hire	126.75	T1	22.18	148.93
76	PI	SAMURA	7104	01102000	02381	Premises insurance	1650.00	T2	0.00	1650.00
77	PI	SAMURA	7303	01102000	02381	Vehicle insurance	1125.00	T2	0.00	1125.00
78	PI	SAMURA	8204	01102000	02381	Misc insurance	430.00	T2	0.00	430.00
79	PI	3DTECH	7505	30092000	001462	Books	179.95	T0	0.00	179.95
80	PI	THAMES	7102	01102000	132157	Water rates	420.00	T0	0.00	420.00
81	PI	ANSNEW	6201	29092000	621014	Advertising	750.00	T1	131.25	881.25
						Totals	5711.16		333.58	6044.74

ANSWER TO ASSIGNMENT 1: SUPPLIER INVOICES AND CREDIT NOTES

Blitz Limited

Day Books : Supplier Credits (Detailed)

Date from: 01/10/2000
Date to: 01/10/2000

Supplier From:
Supplier To: ZZZZZZZZ

Trans From: 1
Trans To: 83

N/C From:
N/C To: 99999999

Dept From: 0
Dept To: 999

No	Tp	A/c	N/C	Date	Ref.	Details			
82	PC	BLOFFI	0040	01102000	K0320	Damaged furniture	150.00 T1	26.25	176.25
83	PC	TROJAN	7005	01102000	C0259	Temp overcharge	60.00 T1	10.50	70.50
						Totals :	210.00	36.75	246.75

Creditors control account

The balance on the creditors control account is £50,517.10.

	£
Total credits (invoices)	50,763.85
Total debits (credit notes)	246.75
Balance	50,517.10

This can be obtained by Escaping from the Suppliers Ledger to the main screen, and clicking on the Nominal Ledger button. In the Nominal Ledger window, click on Clear to ensure that no accounts are selected, then scroll down to account 2100 and select it by clicking on it. Then click on the Activity button and accept the defaults you are offered. At the bottom of the screen you will find the total balances.

Answer to Assignment 2: Customer invoices and credit notes

Invoices

When using the Invoicing window options, you should *save* each transaction when you have input the details, print the invoices in batches, and then update the ledgers.

Make sure you specify the nominal account code correctly for each item in each invoice.

Code	Account
4000	Sales - contract cleaning
4001	Sales - window cleaning
4002	Sales - domestic services
4100	Sales - materials

Where appropriate, enter new customer details, following the screen prompts. The default tax code is T1 if you choose to set this (we recommend you do). The suggested reference codes to use are as follows:

Customer	Ref code
R P Marwood	MARWOO
School of Dance	SCHOOL
B & T Fashions Ltd	BTFASH
The Keith Group	KEITHG
Rapid Pizzas	RAPIDP
Gardeners Delight	GARDEN
Payne Properties	PAYNEP
T P Paul	PAULTP

You must decide whether invoices (or credit notes) should be entered using the Product button or the Service button. You may prefer to use the Service option for materials sales this is ok as long as you ensure the invoice is posted to the correct nominal ledger sales account. (A business that sold mainly products rather than services would obviously use the Product Invoice.)

PART C ASSIGNMENTS

Order details

You should insert order details into an invoice where appropriate. Clicking on the Order Details index tab will give you a pop-up window for adding information about the delivery address. In this assignment, you need to add order details for the invoice to Gardeners Delight - ie you need to add details of the delivery address, which is different from the invoice address.

Details

You should add details for the invoice, based on the information given in the assignment. If you prepared a Service invoice that includes materials (the Elite Caterers invoice), you should have calculated yourself the amount payable (net of VAT) for materials, and entered this amount in the invoice.

Use tax code T1 for every invoice. The VAT and total amount payable are calculated automatically.

Footer

There is no requirement on any invoice for footer details, and you will not need to use the Footer index tab (or button).

Printing

To print the invoices, you must first select the invoices and then click on the Print Invoices button in the Invoicing window. Ensure you select the correct layout and paper-size for your printer.

Posting

When you use the Invoicing window options, you must post the transactions to the ledgers using the Update Ledgers button. Select all of the items listed in the Invoicing window: you can do this by clicking on Clear and then on Swap. Decide whether you want a print-out when the Update Ledgers window appears, and then simply click on OK. Follow the screen prompt for printing. A part of a printed listing of the invoices that might be produced is shown below. The invoice numbers may not be the same as yours, depending on the order in which you entered the data. Columns for Stock Code and Quantity have been omitted for lack of space.

Blitz Limited

Update Ledgers Report

Inv/Crd	Audit	Date	A/C	N/C	Details	Net	VAT	Total
2	85	08102000	ROYALP	4000	Revised scale of cleaning	−300.00	−52.50	−352.50
					Invoice Totals:	−300.00	−52.50	−352.50
10041	94	08102000	BRIDGF	4000	Office cleaning	420.00	73.50	493.50
					Invoice Totals:	420.00	73.50	493.50
10042	95	08102000	HARGRE	4002	Domestic services	43.50	7.61	51.11
					Invoice Totals:	43.50	7.61	51.11
10043	96	08102000	ELITEC	4000	KITCHEN CLEANING	644.00	112.70	756.70
	97			4100	10 BOXES OF OVEN CLEANER	61.00	10.68	71.68
	98			4100	6 CASES OF FLAME DETERGENT	72.00	12.60	84.60
	99			4100	7 BRUSHES	23.94	4.19	28.13
					Invoice Totals:	800.94	140.17	941.11
10044	100	08102000	MEAKIN	4001	Window cleaning	249.00	43.58	292.58
					Invoice Totals:	249.00	43.58	292.58

Credit notes

In older versions use the SrvCredit option, in newer versions specify Service and Credit Note during processing.

PART C ASSIGNMENTS

Listings

Click on the reports button in the *Customers* window.

(a) Use the Day Books: Customer Invoices (Detailed) option to preview or print the sales day book listing for invoices.

(b) Use the Day Books: Customer Credits (Detailed) option to preview or print the sales day book listing for credit notes.

In selecting the items for listing, you can specify the date range from 08/10/2000 to 08/10/2000.

Extracts from the listings are shown below. (The Dept column is omitted.) Check the totals shown. You should have obtained these same *totals* yourself (invoice numbers for particular customers may be different: it depends on the order in which you post the details).

Blitz Limited

Day Books : Customer Invoices (Detailed)

Date from: 08/10/2000 **Supplier From**:
Date to: 08/10/2000   **Supplier To**: ZZZZZZZZ

Trans From: 1   **N/C From**:
Trans To: 106   **N/C To**: 99999999

Dept From: 0
Dept To: 999

No.	Tp	A/c	N/C	Date	Refn.	Details	Net	VAT	T/c	Total
87	SI	MARWOO	4002	08102000	10036	Domestic services	66.00	11.55	T1	77.55
88	SI	SCHOOL	4000	08102000	10037	Cleaning school	250.00	43.75	T1	293.75
89	SI	BTFASH	4001	08102000	10038	Window cleaning	144.00	25.20	T1	169.20
90	SI	KEITHG	4000	08102000	10039	Office cleaning	1420.00	248.50	T1	1668.50
91	SI	RAPIDP	4100	08102000	10040	FLAME DETERGENT	60.00	9.98	T1	69.98
92	SI	RAPIDP	4100	08102000	10040	BREAM CLEANER	91.20	15.16	T1	106.36
93	SI	RAPIDP	4100	08102000	10040	CLEANING GLOVES	42.00	6.98	T1	48.98
94	SI	BRIDGF	4000	08102000	10041	Office cleaning	420.00	73.50	T1	493.50
95	SI	HARGRE	4002	08102000	10042	Domestic services	43.50	7.61	T1	51.11
96	SI	ELITEC	4000	08102000	10043	KITCHEN CLEANING	644.00	112.70	T1	756.70
97	SI	ELITEC	4100	08102000	10043	OVEN CLEANER	61.00	10.68	T1	71.68
98	SI	ELITEC	4100	08102000	10043	FLAME DETERGENT	72.00	12.60	T1	84.60
99	SI	ELITEC	4100	08102000	10043	BRUSHES	23.94	4.19	T1	28.13
100	SI	MEAKIN	4001	08102000	10044	Window cleaning	249.00	43.58	T1	292.58
101	SI	ROSEAL	4001	08102000	10045	Window cleaning	125.00	21.88	T1	146.88
102	SI	GARDEN	4100	08102000	10046	WIND. CLEAN FLUID	630.00	104.74	T1	734.74
103	SI	PAYNEP	4000	08102000	10047	Office cleaning	1210.00	201.16	T1	1411.16
104	SI	PAULTP	4002	08102000	10050	Domestic services	60.00	10.50	T1	70.50
105	SI	SIDDAL	4001	08102000	10048	Window cleaning	182.00	31.85	T1	213.85
106	SI	NORRIS	4000	08102000	10049	Factory and office	816.40	142.87	T1	959.27
						Totals	6610.04	1138.98		7749.02

ANSWER TO ASSIGNMENT 2: CUSTOMER INVOICES AND CREDIT NOTES

Blitz Limited

Day Books : Customer Credits (Detailed)

Date from: 08/10/2000
Date to: 08/10/2000

Supplier From:
Supplier To: ZZZZZZZZ

Trans From: 1
Trans To: 106

N/C From:
N/C To: 99999999

Dept From: 0
Dept To: 999

No.	Tp	A/c	N/C	Date	Refn.	Details	Net	VAT	T/c	Total
84	SC	GELLIN	4000	08102000	1	Poor quality cleaning	250.00	43.75	T1	293.75
85	SC	ROYALP	4000	08102000	2	Revised scale of cleaning	300.00	52.50	T1	352.50
86	SC	DCSROO	4001	08102000	3	Broken window	150.00	26.25	T1	176.25
						Totals	700.00	122.50		822.50

Balance on the debtors control account

Escape to the main window, and click on the Nominal Ledger button. Then select the Debtors Control Account (code 1100) and click on Activity. Accept the default transaction range you are offered. If you check the totals at the foot of the account, you should find that they are as follows.

	Debit	Credit
Totals:	30369.45	822.50
Balance:	29546.95	

Sales accounts

You can find the balances for each sales account using the Nominal Ledger Activity window. Click on the Nominal Ledger button, scroll down to the accounts concerned and highlight them, then click on Activity. Accept the defaults you are offered. Use the < and > buttons at the bottom of the screen to move from one account to the next.

The current balances shown in the box at the foot of each account's Activity window should be as follows:

Account		Debit	Credit	Balance
		£	£	£
4000	Sales - contract cleaning	550.00	21,357.80	20,807.80
4001	Sales - window cleaning	150.00	2,670.40	2,520.40
4002	Sales - domestic services	0.00	853.10	853.10
4100	Sales – materials	0.00	980.14	980.14

PART C   ASSIGNMENTS

School of Dance

(a) One method is to use the Search button in the Invoicing window where the Account Reference field Is Equal to SCHOOL. If you click on Apply and Close this will give you a window that includes only the relevant invoice.

(b) Select this invoice and click on the Print button in the Invoicing window.

CCC Engineering

Click on Customers and select the CCCENG account. Then click on the Activity button. You can find the amount currently owed by the customer, but not whether an invoice has been printed. The invoice amount is £1,527.50.

Word processing exercises

The next two pages show suggested solutions to the two Word exercises in this assignment.

For your duplicate invoice you will need to know the original invoice details including the VAT. An audit trail report for transaction number 40 is the best source. Use the Reports button in the main window and specify a transaction range 40 to 40 (and a date range ending on or after 8/10/2000). Alternatively you can look at CCC Engineering's transaction history and calculate the VAT manually.

To copy from one application to the other, select (highlight) the item press Ctrl + C to copy, switch to the other application and position your cursor, then press Ctrl + V.

Blitz Limited

25 Apple Road
London N12 3PP

Fax Cover Sheet

DATE:	October 8, 2000	**TIME:**	11:15
TO:	V Cockcroft CCC Engineering Ltd	**PHONE:** **FAX:**	01923 354022 01923 354071
FROM:	Your name Blitz Limited	**PHONE:** **FAX:**	020 8912 2013 020 8912 6387
RE:	Invoice number 10005		

Number of pages including cover sheet: Two

Message

This is in response to your telephone call earlier this morning.

The amount due is £1,527.50 (including VAT of £227.50). For your reference a copy of the invoice accompanies this cover note. Payment is due within 30 days of the date of the invoice.

PART C ASSIGNMENTS

Blitz Limited

25 Apple Road
London
N12 3PP
Tel: 020 8912 2013
Fax: 020 8912 6387

INVOICE

INVOICE NO: 10005
DATE: 22 September, 2000

To:
CCC Engineering Limited
28 Gardener Road
Watford
WF3 7GH

Deliver To:
Invoice address

QUANTITY	DESCRIPTION	UNIT PRICE	AMOUNT
	Factory cleaning	N/A	1300.00
		SUBTOTAL	1300.00
		VAT	227.50
		SHIPPING & HANDLING	-
		TOTAL DUE	1527.50

Make all cheques payable to: Blitz Limited
If you have any questions concerning this invoice, call: [Your name] 020 8912 2013

THANK YOU FOR YOUR BUSINESS!

Answer to Assignment 3: Payments to suppliers

Payments to suppliers

You should now process the payment transactions for the 14 payments shown in paragraph (1) in Assignment 3. Click on Bank in the main Sage window and then on the Supplier button. Follow the procedures described in Chapter 5.

It is simpler to use the Pay in Full button for these payments, rather than typing in the amount of the cheque (though it is worth trying both methods to see the difference). In the former case, press Tab when you reach the £ sign box. Click on Pay in Full when the cursor is in the Payment boxes until the £ sign box shows the correct amount.

Save each transaction.

Chieftain Newspaper Group

To process the payment to the Chieftain Newspaper group, you must first post the credit note transaction to the relevant account in the Suppliers Ledger. There is no need to close down the Bank option and return to the main Sage window if you do not want to. Just click on Suppliers and then Credit to input the credit note details – as explained in Chapter 3.

When you have entered and posted the credit note transaction, press Esc to return to the Supplier payments window (or open it up again if you closed it). You can then process the payment to the supplier.

PART C ASSIGNMENTS

Credit notes and early settlement discounts

You will first need to find out the amount of the credit notes by looking at the Activity for each of the accounts mentioned. The amounts you should have posted are as follows.

Account	Gross	VAT	Net
FLOORS	1,012.85	150.85	862.00
HARROW	2,853.37	424.97	2,428.40
MATTHI	3,360.50	500.50	2,860.00

Post the new invoices as you have done in previous assignments except that instead of accepting tax code T1 and letting the program calculate VAT at 17.5% on the full amount, use code T3 and type in the amount of VAT shown on the invoice.

To pay the new invoices, you will have to calculate the discount to establish what the amount of each cheque payment should be. You should have produced the following results:

Supplier code	Gross amount £	Net amount £	Discount %	Discount £	Cheque payment (gross less discount) £
FLOORS	1,005.31	862.00	5%	43.10	962.21
HARROW	2,840.62	2,428.40	3%	72.85	2767.77
MATTHI	3,335.48	2,860.00	5%	143.00	3192.48

To enter the payment details, Tab past the £ sign box and click on Pay in Full when you reach the Payment box. Then type in the amount of the discount in the Discount box.

Highpile Cleaning Supplies

Here, you are paying an invoice and also making a payment on account for invoices not yet received. Type 3500 in the £ sign box and then when you reach the Payment box click on Pay in Full.

Now click on Save. You will be told that there is an unallocated cheque balance of £1,135.31. Click on Yes to post it as a payment on account.

Bank transaction payments

To make the payments for the cheque requisitions, from the Bank Accounts window and click on Payment. For each payment that includes VAT (cheques 000119 and 000121) you can enter the gross payment in the Net column and then click on Calc Net. The VAT will be calculated automatically, and the Net amount adjusted to exclude VAT. The tax code for the train ticket (cheque 000120) should be T0.

Listing

You have processed payments to suppliers (Suppliers Ledger) and for three bank transactions (Nominal Ledger). There are several ways of doing this in Line 50. We suggest that you click on Reports in the Bank accounts window and select:

(a) Day Books: Bank Payments (Summary); and also
(b) Day Books: Supplier Payments (Summary).

Enter 09/10/2000 as the date in both date boxes, when making your specifications for the listing.

The output in printed form should be as follows. (Check that your totals match the totals shown here.)

Blitz Limited
Day Books: Supplier Payments (Summary)

Date from: 09/10/2000
Date to: 09/10/2000

Bank From:
Bank To: 99999999

Transaction From: 1
Transaction To: 136

Supplier From:
Supplier To: ZZZZZZZZ :

No.	Bank	A/c	Date	Refn.	Details	Net	VAT	Total
107	1200	AA1MIN	09102000	000100	Purchase Payment	117.50	0.00	117.50
108	1200	BTELEC	09102000	000101	Purchase Payment	540.50	0.00	540.50
109	1200	CAPITA	09102000	000102	Purchase Payment	376.00	0.00	376.00
110	1200	BLOFFI	09102000	000103	Purchase Payment	1493.78	0.00	1493.78
111	1200	FIRSTS	09102000	000104	Purchase Payment	332.23	0.00	332.23
112	1200	SAMURA	09102000	000105	Purchase Payment	3205.00	0.00	3205.00
113	1200	3DTECH	09102000	000106	Purchase Payment	179.95	0.00	179.95
114	1200	IRONCL	09102000	000107	Purchase Payment	3000.00	0.00	3000.00
115	1200	TROJAN	09102000	000108	Purchase Payment	141.00	0.00	141.00
116	1200	MUSWEL	09102000	000109	Purchase Payment	1240.00	0.00	1240.00
117	1200	NORTHL	09102000	000110	Purchase Payment	1175.00	0.00	1175.00
118	1200	STERLI	09102000	000111	Purchase Payment	642.37	0.00	642.37
119	1200	UNIFOR	09102000	000112	Purchase Payment	763.75	0.00	763.75
120	1200	VANCEN	09102000	000113	Purchase Payment	19059.44	0.00	19059.44
122	1200	CHIEFT	09102000	000114	Purchase Payment	1175.00	0.00	1175.00
129	1200	FLOORS	09102000	000115	Purchase Payment	962.21	0.00	962.21
131	1200	HARROW	09102000	000116	Purchase Payment	2767.77	0.00	2767.77
133	1200	MATTHI	09102000	000117	Purchase Payment	3192.48	0.00	3192.48
135	1200	HIGHPI	09102000	000118	Purchase Payment	2364.69	0.00	2364.69
136	1200	HIGHPI	09102000	000118	Payment on Account	1135.31	0.00	1135.31
		Totals		:		43,863.98	0.00	43,863.98

PART C ASSIGNMENTS

Blitz Limited
Day Books: Bank Payments (Summary)

Date from: 09/10/2000   Bank From:
Date to: 09/10/2000   Bank To: 99999999

Transaction From: 1   N/C From:
Transaction To: 133   N/C To: ZZZZZZZZ :

Dept From: 0
Dept To: 999

No	Tp	A/C	Date	Chq. No	Details	Net	VAT	T/c	
137	BP	8203	09102000	000119	Training course	220.00	38.50	T1	258.50
138	BP	7400	09102000	000120	Train ticket	105.50	0.00	T0	105.50
139	BP	8205	09102000	000121	Refreshments	84.00	14.70	T1	98.70
					Totals	409.50	53.20		462.70

Bank balance

You can print or display the Activity on the bank current account by selecting it in the Nominal Ledger (code 1200). Accept the default 'From' date and specify a 'To' date of 09/10/2000. You should get a credit balance of £10,380.61.

(Note: the Tp column indicates bank receipt [BR], purchase payment [PP], payment on account [PA], or bank payment [BP].)

Nominal Activity

Date from: 09/10/2000
Date to: 09/10/2000
N/C 1200
N/C To: 1200

Transaction From: 1
Transaction To: 133

No.	Tp	Date	Refn	Details	Value	Debit	Credit
1	BR	19082000		M Green - shares	20000.00	20000.00	
2	BR	19082000		T Nicholas - shares	20000.00	20000.00	
8	JC	16092000	xxxxx	Wages and salaries	6053.93		6053.93
107	PP	09102000	100	Purchase Payment	117.50		117.50
108	PP	09102000	101	Purchase Payment	540.50		540.50
109	PP	09102000	100102	Purchase Payment	376.00		376.00
110	PP	09102000	103	Purchase Payment	1493.78		1493.78
111	PP	09102000	104	Purchase Payment	332.23		332.23
112	PP	09102000	105	Purchase Payment	3205.00		3205.00
113	PP	09102000	106	Purchase Payment	179.95		179.95
114	PP	09102000	107	Purchase Payment	3000.00		3000.00
115	PP	09102000	108	Purchase Payment	141.00		141.00
116	PP	09102000	109	Purchase Payment	1240.00		1240.00
117	PP	09102000	110	Purchase Payment	1175.00		1175.00
118	PP	09102000	111	Purchase Payment	642.37		642.37
119	PP	09102000	112	Purchase Payment	763.75		763.75
120	PP	09102000	113	Purchase Payment	19059.44		19059.44
122	PP	09102000	114	Purchase Payment	1175.00		1175.00
129	PP	09102000	115	Purchase Payment	962.21		962.21
131	PP	09102000	116	Purchase Payment	2767.77		2767.77
133	PP	09102000	117	Purchase Payment	3192.48		3192.48
135	PP	09102000	118	Purchase Payment	2364.69		2364.69
136	PA	09102000	118	Payment on Account	1135.31		1135.31
137	BP	09102000	119	Training course	258.50		258.50
138	BP	09102000	120	Train ticket	105.50		105.50
139	BP	09102000	121	Refreshments	98.70		98.70
				Totals :		40000.00	50380.61
				History Balance :			10380.61

Balance on the creditors control account

You should repeat the same exercise but this time select the creditors control account - account code 2100. The balance on the account is now £6,113.86.

Spreadsheet

If you did this exercise you should fairly easily have been able to explain that the No. column lists the number of the transaction – the number allocated by the Sage package to each consecutive transaction that you post. The Ref column shows either the cheque number or the credit note number or, in the case of discounts, the original invoice number.

PART C ASSIGNMENTS

The problem with the totals is that some items have been included that should not have been included and one item has been omitted. To put things right you should have deleted the amounts shown in boxes ('cells') 16, 19, 21 and 23 in columns G and I, and you should have entered the amount 1,135.31 in cell I25.

As part of your tidying up exercise you could have changed the lines in capitals to small letters, made the headings italic, given the spreadsheet a title, and so on. No 'answer' is shown because many 'answers' are acceptable, although they will be different in appearance.

Answer to Assignment 4: Receipts from customers

The assignment requires you to process a variety of transactions.

Posting new invoices

The procedures for entering details of new customer accounts and producing invoices were described in Chapter 5. You should use the Invoicing option in the main window, and:

(a) The Service window to produce the invoice.

(b) The Print Invoices button to print the invoices.

(c) The Update Ledgers button to post the transactions to the ledgers.

The nominal account code should be 4000 for the invoice to Bradley Fashions (contract cleaning) and 4002 for the invoice to A Rathod (domestic services).

One of the two invoices is reproduced on the next page. If you have forgotten how to produce invoices, look again at Chapter 4.

Receipts - payment in full for invoices

Posting the 12 receipts transactions listed in item (2) in the information for the assignment should not present any difficulties. Click on the Bank button and then on the Customer button.

These are all payments in full for one or more outstanding invoices. In every case, you can use the Pay in Full button for allocating the receipt to an invoice. Make sure you include references for each receipt.

Click on Save when you have posted the details for each customer and move on to the next customer.

In the case of two customers (D J Hargreaves and A Rose Ltd) the amount received is in payment for just one invoice, when there are two outstanding invoices on the account. In cases where it is not clear what is being paid you should either allocate the payment to the earliest invoices on the account or record the payment as a payment on account - until it can be established which invoices are being paid.

```
                                    Invoice  Page 1
                                             10051
                                             12/10/2000


      BLITZ LTD
      25 APPLE ROAD
      LONDON
      N12 3PP



      BRADLEY FASHIONS LTD
      18 HOSPITAL BRIDGE
      ROAD
      ST ALBANS
      HERTS

                                                      BRADLE




      Quantity Details       Disc%   Disc Amount   Net Amount   VAT Amount
      Contract cleaning      0.00    0.00          820.00       143.50
         services










                              Total Net                      820.00
                              Total VAT                      143.50
                              Carriage                         0.00
                              Invoice Total                  963.50
```

ANSWER TO ASSIGNMENT 4: RECEIPTS FROM CUSTOMERS

T P Paul

The invoice of £70.50 for T P Paul can be cancelled by creating a credit note for £70.50. You can do this by using the SrvCredit option in the Invoicing window.

Discounts

Begin by checking that the discount has been correctly calculated. If you disagree with the customer's calculation, you would have to speak to your supervisor or (if authorised to do so) telephone the customer to query the mistake.

To check the calculation you first need to find out the transaction number(s) by looking up the customers' Activity and then the net amount due by looking at these transactions in the Financials listing.

The transactions are numbers 103 and numbers 91, 92 and 93. In the case of Rapid Pizzas, the discount of £9.66 must be divided into three chunks.

Transaction no	Net amount	Discount (5%)
103	1210.00	60.50
91	60.00	3.00
92	91.20	4.56
93	42.00	2.10
		9.66

Post this by returning to the Bank Customer receipts window and entering the relevant account code. In each case (Payne Properties and Rapid Pizzas) you should remember to follow these procedures.

(a) Make sure you enter a reference for the invoice being paid.

(b) Tab through the Amount box leaving it blank.

(c) Tab through the Receipt box leaving it blank.

(d) Enter the amount of the discount in the appropriate box and press Tab. The amount in the Receipt box will automatically be calculated.

(e) Click on Save.

Deductions for credit notes

Stay in the Bank Customer window. For each customer account, enter the invoice as the reference number. Leave the Amount box blank and Tab to the Receipt box. Click on Pay in Full in each case.

PART C ASSIGNMENTS

Part payments

The part payments by Elite Caterers and Campbell Consultants should be processed either:

(a) By *keying in* the amount of the payment in the Amount box, and then Tabbing to the Receipt box of the first invoice listed and clicking on Pay in Full; *or*

(b) By Tabbing through the Amount box and then *keying in* the amount of the payment in the first Receipt box you come to. Then you can just click on Save.

Clough and Partners

This payment of an invoice plus a payment on account must be processed by *typing* the amount received in the Amount box. When you click on Save after entering the receipt details, accept the Post as a Payment on Account message.

M Zakis Ltd

Before you process the receipt from M Zakis, you must set up an account for the (new) customer in the Customers ledger. Type in the code MZAKIS and press Tab. Click on **New** when the Customer Account window appears.

When you have set up and saved the account, return to the Bank Customer window and process the receipt.

Writing off small unpaid balances

Process the payments from A T Haslam and R P Marwood in the same way as the part payments from other customers. There will be unpaid balances of £0.18 and £0.05 respectively. (If you forgot to take a note of these amounts you can find the unpaid balance by searching the list in the Customers window.)

Click on Tools at the top of the screen, then on Write Off, Refund, Return. Choose the Sales Ledger amendments option. From the area list pick Write off Customer Transactions below a value. To be safe a good value to enter is 0.50, although you could put in a higher amount – say 1 (£1.00) – if you wish. Select both the accounts by highlighting them and click on Next. Confirm that you are writing off 23p by clicking on Finish.

Bank receipts

The five items of bank receipts from non-credit customers should be entered by using the Receipt button in the Bank Accounts window.

For each transaction, select the correct nominal ledger code (N/C). This should be 4001 for window cleaning, 4002 for domestic services and 4100 for materials sales. Enter the five transactions separately. Just key in the single number 4 and then click on the Finder button (or press F4) if you forget which nominal Sales account is which.

Reports

You should print, preview or display a *Day Books: Customer Receipts* Summary report and a *Day Books: Bank Receipts* Summary report, using the reports button in the Bank window.

The Reports window will allow you to specify the parameters for items to be listed. Specify a Date Range of 12/10/2000 to 12/10/2000.

The total amount for the report is as follows.

	Net £	Tax £	Gross £
Customer Receipts	10,508.25	0.00	10,508.25
Bank Receipts	352.00	61.60	413.60
Total	10,860.25	61.60	10,921.85

P Leyser refund

Click on Tools (at the top of the screen, then on Write Off, Refund, Return, and choose the Sales Ledger option. Choose Customer Invoice Refund from the list that appears as you click on Next. Scroll down to the LEYSER account and click on Next. The payment will appear in the window. Select it and click on Next again. You are asked which account you want to post the refund to the bank account 1200. Select this and click on Next. If the information given in the next window is correct, click on Finish.

Account balances - nominal ledger

You can establish these using the Activity button in the Nominal window. The balances should be:

Account	N/C code	Debit entries	Credit entries	Balance
Bank current account	1200	50,921.85	50,477.20	444.65
Debtors control account	1100	31,517.67	11,568.23	19,949.44

Account balances - sales ledger

Click on the Customers button and scroll down until you find the account ELITEC. You should find that the balance outstanding on this account is £1,497.81.

PART C ASSIGNMENTS

Answer to Assignment 5: Other cash transactions

Many of the tasks for this assignment are similar to tasks that were set in Assignments 1-4. There are invoices from new and existing suppliers, invoices to new and existing customers, and payments and receipts. In addition, however, some of the tasks relate to petty cash transactions, journal transactions and a bank reconciliation. Assignment 5 is therefore a wide-ranging test of your competence with Sage.

Setting up the petty cash system

The petty cash system is set up by withdrawing £300 in cash from the bank. This bank-cash transaction should be recorded in the nominal ledger as a journal entry. Click on the Journals button in the Nominal Ledger window. The fields should be completed as follows.

(a) Reference. Use the cheque number as a reference for the transaction. This is 000122.

(b) Date 13/10/2000.

(c) The double entry is as follows. (It doesn't matter whether you do the debit or the credit entry first.)

N/C	Details	T/c	Debit £	Credit £
1200	To petty cash	T9		300.00
1230	From bank account	T9	300.00	

Save the transaction, then press Esc or click on Close.

Invoices from suppliers

The invoices from suppliers can be entered using the Invoices button in the Suppliers window. This allows you to enter new supplier details, where appropriate. The transaction date should be the invoice date, not the date on which you are processing the transactions. Some invoices relate to different items of expense, and so different nominal ledger account codes. For example, the invoice from Great North Hotel should be recorded on three lines, for nominal ledger account codes 7402, 7406 and 7502 respectively. All the purchase invoice transactions should have a tax code T1. Your accuracy in entering the transactions is tested by a later task in the assignment. If you cannot remember how to process supplier invoices, refer back to Chapter 3.

PART C ASSIGNMENTS

Customer invoices

You should now be familiar with the procedure for entering invoices. Ensure you assign each sales item to the appropriate nominal ledger account code - 4000 for contract cleaning, 4001 for window cleaning, 4002 for domestic services and 4100 for materials sales. All transactions should have a T1 tax code, and a date of 16/10/2000.

Payments to suppliers

To record the payments to suppliers, Click on Bank and then on the Supplier button. Look up the supplier account reference codes if you need to, using the Finder button or the F4 function key to display the supplier accounts on screen.

For the Ace Telephone Answering and ANS Newspaper Group invoices, *key in* the amount paid in the Amount box, then Tab to the Payment box and click on Pay in Full. With the ANS Newspaper Group payment, confirm that the payment on account should be posted.

Before you record the payment from Wells Business Systems you should post the credit note. Use the Calc Net option to allocate the amount correctly.

Receipts from customers

Click on the Customer button in the Bank Accounts window. The receipts from the three customers can be processed in a similar way to the payments to suppliers. Don't forget that there *must* be a reference number. Use the number of the invoice being paid.

V J Richardson cheque

This transaction can be posted as a journal entry. Click on the Journals button in the Nominal Ledger window. The entries in the main part of the screen should be:

N/C	Details	T/c	Debit £	Credit £
1200	Loan – V J Richardson	T9	10,000.00	
1230	To bank account	T9		10,000.00

Alternatively, you can post the transaction as a bank receipt, using the Receipt button in the Bank Accounts window. The N/C code for the receipt should be 2300, the net amount 10000 and the tax code T9.

Petty cash transactions

Click on the Bank button and then select account 1230 Petty Cash.

To post the payments out of petty cash, just click on the Payments button and a window that will be familiar by now will appear.

To post the receipt into petty cash the N/C code 4001 should be used (for window cleaning sales). Enter 72 as the Net amount, then click on the Calc Net button to calculate the VAT automatically. The final entry should be for a net cash receipt of £61.28 and VAT of £10.72.

To produce reports of Cash Payments (or Receipts), click on the Reports button in the Bank window and scroll down until you find the appropriate option. Select the date range 13/10/2000 to 16/10/2000. Print the listing if you have access to a printer. Otherwise, display the listing on screen. An extract from the listing follows.

Blitz Limited

Cash Payments (Summary)

Date from: 13/10/2000
Date to: 16/10/2000
Bank From:
Bank To: 99999999

Transaction from: 1
Transaction To: 235

No.	Tp	A/C	Date	Refn	Details	Net	VAT	Total
223	CP	7501	13102000	PC001	POSTAGE STAMPS	24.00	0.00	24.00
224	CP	8205	13102000	PC002	BISCUITS, COFFEE	32.49	0.00	32.49
225	CP	8205	13102000	PC003	MILK	15.20	0.00	15.20
226	CP	7400	13102000	PC004	TAXIS	25.00	0.00	25.00
227	CP	7400	14102000	PC005	TRAIN FARES	9.20	0.00	9.20
228	CP	8205	14102000	PC006	WASHING UP LIQUID	1.75	0.00	1.75
229	CP	7500	14102000	PC007	PHOTOCOPYING	24.00	4.20	28.20
230	CP	7504	15102000	PC008	STATIONERY	37.24	6.52	43.76
231	CP	7400	15102000	PC009	TAXIS	15.00	0.00	15.00
232	CP	8205	16102000	PC010	SANDWICHES, CAKES	38.26	0.00	38.26
233	CP	7304	16102000	PC011	PARKING	7.00	0.00	7.00
234	CP	7400	16102000	PC012	TRAIN FARES	8.40	0.00	8.40
					Totals	237.54	10.72	248.26

PART C   ASSIGNMENTS

Topping up petty cash

Check the balance on the Petty Cash account (N/C 1230) by looking at the list of accounts in and balances in the main Nominal Ledger window. This should show a balance of £123.74.

A cheque for £176.26 cash (£300 - £123.74) must be drawn to top up the petty cash balance to £300.

To post this entry, click on the Journals button in the Nominal Ledger window. The main part of the entry is as follows:

N/C	Details	T/c	Debit £	Credit £
1200	To petty cash	T9		176.26
1230	From bank account	T9	176.26	

Check that the balance on the petty cash account (N/C 1230) is now £300 (look again at the list in the Nominal Ledger window).

Wages and salaries

These transactions can be entered in the nominal ledger accounts as a single journal entry. Click on Journals in the Nominal Ledger window. Key in the date 16/10/2000 and (as instructed) reference J04. The remaining entries should be as follows:

N/C	Details	T/c	Debit £	Credit £
1200	Cash for wages	T9		4133.04
2210	PAYE, 16 Oct	T9		2217.96
2211	Nat Ins, 16 Oct	T9		975.20
7001	Directors salaries	T9	1350.80	
7003	Staff salaries	T9	475.75	
6000	Wages	T9	4859.65	
7006	Employers NI	T9	640.00	

The total debits equal the total credits, therefore you can post these transactions as a single journal entry.

ANSWER TO ASSIGNMENT 5: OTHER CASH TRANSACTIONS

Account balances

You can just scroll through the Nominal Ledger window to search for the account balances required by your supervisor. Check that you have the following balances.

N/C		Debit £	Credit £
1100	Debtors control account	25486.83	
1200	Bank – current account	4642.09	
2100	Creditors control account		7677.28
7003	Staff salaries	951.50	
7400	Travelling	301.50	
7700	Equipment hire	503.75	
4000	Sales – contract cleaning		27167.80
4001	Sales – window cleaning		3060.68
4002	Sales – domestic services		1103.90
4100	Sales – materials		1243.74
1230	Petty cash	300.00	
4009	Discounts allowed	101.66	
5009	Discounts taken		258.95

Bank reconciliation

A bank reconciliation requires a careful, methodical approach. Performing the reconciliation requires a matching exercise between items on the bank statement and a corresponding entry in the nominal ledger bank account.

If you have access to a printer, print out a listing of activity on the Bank Account (1200). Then, ensure all Sage windows except the initial window are closed, and select **Settings**, **Change Program Date** from the main menu. Enter the date of the bank statement used in this exercise - 16/10/2000.

Now click on **Bank** and **Reconcile**. The window you are presented with will differ depending upon the version of Sage Line 50 you use. Refer back to pages 145-148 for instructions regarding how the reconciliation is performed.

You should be able to match nearly every item on the bank's statement against a transaction in the nominal ledger account. In this exercise, there is an additional item on the bank statement for bank charges. You should post this item to the nominal ledger (N/C code 7901 for bank charges) using the Adjustment button.

In **version 11**, after you have matched all items in the bank statement against the nominal bank account, click on the **Save** button.

In **version 12** or **2007**, when you have completed the reconciliation (all transactions are selected, the 'Statement Balance' = 'Matched Balance' and the 'Difference' balance is zero) click **Reconcile**.

PART C ASSIGNMENTS

Overall the position is as follows.

	£
Statement balance	13,381.53
Unpresented payments	(10,468.28)
Unpresented receipts	1,703.24
Trial balance	4,616.49

The trial balance figure is different (by £25.60) from the account balance figure you gave your supervisor earlier. This is because you have now posted the bank charges.

To print a list of Unreconciled Payments and Unreconciled Receipts, click on Reports from within the Bank window (you may need to click on the >> symbol to display the Reports button). Then **Expand** the **Unreconciled Transaction Reports** option (the last option on the list) and print the Unreconciled Payments and Unreconciled Receipts reports.

Extracts from these are shown below.

Blitz Limited

Unreconciled Payments

Date From: 01/01/2000   Bank From:
Date To: 31/12/2000   Bank To: 99999999

Tp	Date	Refn.	Details	Amount
PP	09102000	000117	Purchase Payment	3192.48
PP	16102000	000123	Purchase Payment	250.00
PP	16102000	000124	Purchase Payment	881.25
PA	16102000	000124	Payment on Account	318.75
PP	16102000	000125	Purchase Payment	1516.50
JC	16102000	000126	TO PETTY CASH	176.26
JC	16102000	J04	CASH FOR WAGES	4133.04
				10468.28

Unreconciled Receipts

Tp	Date	Refn.	Details	Receipts
SR	15102000	10004	Sales Receipt	1000.00
SR	16102000	10046	Sales Receipt	703.24
				1703.24

If you load up Assignment 6 you will be able to view the completed reconciliation. (Ensure you change the Program Date to 16/10/2000 or later – and in versions 12 and 2007 note that you will need to re-enter the Statement balance.)

Answer to Assignment 6: Other credit transactions

Posting credit sales transactions

Remember to code each item for the correct sales account in the nominal ledger, and use tax code T1 for every transaction. Whenever a customer exceeds the existing credit limit, make a note of the name, but continue to process the transaction.

The customers who have exceeded their existing credit limit are:

GHH Commercial Bank
The Keith Group
Norris Hydraulics Ltd
School of Dance
R I Tepper Ltd

Their credit limit should be increased by £1,000 in each case. To do this, after receiving the 'exceeding credit limit' warning and proceeding with the transaction, without closing the Customers Invoice window click on the Customers button, select the relevant customer account and click on Record. The customer details will then appear on screen. Move to the credit limit field (on the Credit Control tab) and key in a new credit limit (overwriting the old limit) by adding 1000 to the limit. Then click on Save and press Esc twice - you will be back in the Service Invoice Window.

Alternatively, you can post all the invoices first and then alter the credit limits of the Customers later.

Cash sales

The cheques received should be posted as Receipts in the Bank Accounts window. Enter each transaction in turn selecting the correct N/C code. The four entries should be as follows, if the tax code is entered as T1.

Deposit No.	N/C	Date	Amount	Description	Amount and tax code
500005	4002	21102000	–	Domestic services	51.7 then Calc Net button
500006	4002	21102000	–	Domestic services	44 then Calc Net
500007	4100	21102000	–	Materials sales	37.6 then Calc Net
500008	4100	23102000	–	Materials sales	52.88 then Calc Net

PART C   ASSIGNMENTS

Save each transaction when you have entered the details. You then get a blank window for the next transaction.

The cash receipts should be posted in account 1230 as Petty Cash Receipts. The two entries should be:

Ref	Date	N/C	Details	Net and Tax
PCR002	22102000	4100	Materials sales	25.38 then Calc Net
PCR003	23102000	4002	Domestic services	35.25 then Calc Net

Invoices received from suppliers

Click on the Service button in the Invoicing window. Enter the three transactions, setting up new supplier accounts where appropriate. The tax code is T1 for all three transactions.

Receipts from customers

Click on the Customer button in the Bank Accounts window. Post the seven transactions. Check the instructions in Chapter 7 if you have forgotten how to do this.

Tab through the main Amount box if you can see at a glance which invoice(s) are being settled. Just click on Pay in Full when you get to the relevant Receipt box (Plus2: Paid box). If it is not clear how the payment should be allocated, *type in* the amount received in the main Amount box and then click on Pay in Full in each of the Receipt boxes. When there is no more money to allocate, click on Save.

You should type in the amounts for S T Chanas, Elite Caterers, and Meakin Media.

Contra entries (Sage Line 50 only)

The accounts of Elite Caterers and Meakin Media can now be settled by contra entries. Take each customer/supplier in turn.

Click on Tools, then on Contra Entries.

(a) For Elite Caterers, enter both the Sales Ledger A/C and the Purchase Ledger A/C as ELITEC. The screen will display the unpaid invoice balances in the customer account (left-hand side) and the supplier account (right-hand side) for Elite Caterers. Click on each transaction in the sales account and then click on the supplier account transaction. The totals should be the same, and can therefore be set off in full against each other, so just click on OK to post the contra entry.

(b) For Meakin Media, repeat the procedure. The A/C code is MEAKIN for both the Customers Ledger account and the Suppliers Ledger account. The *first* entry in the customer account and the entry in the supplier account should be selected.

ANS Newspaper Group

Click on Bank, then on Supplier. Post a payment to ANSNEW for £58.75, dated 22 October 2000, cheque number 000127.

Note: The **£58.75** is made up of:

Invoice 621347	553.75
Less Sales invoice 10065 contra	(176.25)
Less payment on account (from assignment 5)	(318.75)
Balance outstanding	**58.75**

Key the amount 58.75 into the £ sign box, then tab down to the *invoice* for advertising (amount £553.75) and click on Pay in Full. Then Save this transaction.

Return to the Contra Entries window and process a contra entry for ANS Newspaper Group, accepting the offer to process a 'part contra'.

If you look at the balance of the ANSNEW account in both the Customers and Suppliers ledgers they should both show a nil balance.

Writing off small unpaid balances

Click on Tools, then on Write Off, Refund, Return and opt for the Sales Ledger. Choose Write Off Customer transaction below a value.

Enter a value of 1.01 (£1.01). The screen will display two unpaid balances.

    CAMPBE 1.00
    CHANAS 0.63

Click on both of these and then click on Next. Use a date of 31/10/2000, click Next and confirm the write offs when asked to do so. The total amount written off is £1.63.

Writing off accounts

Look at the Customers window to find the balances on the accounts ADAMSE and HAYNES. You should do this to establish that E T Adams currently owes nothing to Blitz.

With L Haynes & Co, however, there is an unpaid balance on the account. This must be written off as a bad debt.

To write off the bad debt for L Haynes & Co, click on Tools then on Write Off, Refund, Return, and choose the Sales Ledger. This time select the Write off Customer Accounts option. Choose the account reference HAYNES. Two lines are shown, but both relate to the same invoice. Click Next, enter the date of the write-off and click next again. The amount and date of the write-off will show, if these are correct click Finish.

PART C   ASSIGNMENTS

Credit note

The sales credit note to Owen of London should be posted using the SrvCredit button in the Invoicing window. The entry should be:

A/C	Date	Ref	N/C	Description	Amount	T/c
OWENLO	22102000	004	4000	Credit note	150.00	T1

Correcting the N/C code

A correction to an account code is an accounting error. You must first find the transaction reference number. Open the Suppliers window and select the account AA1MIN. Click on Activity. The transaction history of the account will show the October invoice for £158.27. (This includes VAT.) The transaction number is 186.

Click on File, then on Maintenance then on Corrections. In the window that appears scroll to transaction number 186, highlight it and click on Edit.

Activate the *Splits* tab, Click on Edit again and alter the N/C code. Then click on Close, then on Save and confirm that you wish to post the changes. If you scroll down to the end of the list you can see that the correction has been posted.

Newlite Cleaning Fluids

Check the Activity for NEWLIT in the Suppliers window. You should take a note of the transaction number (17) and the details of the invoice that has been posted incorrectly. Then use File ... Maintenance to correct the transaction as just explained.

The details should be:

A/C	NEWLIT
Date	12092000
Inv No	26115
N/C	5000
Details	Cleaning materials
Net Amount	403.00
T/c	T1

The corrected invoice figure is £403.00 net plus VAT of £70.53 giving a total invoice amount of £473.53.

ANSWER TO ASSIGNMENT 6: OTHER CREDIT TRANSACTIONS

Current balances

To find the current balances on the nominal ledger accounts, simply call up the Nominal Ledger window. Scroll through each account in turn and copy down the balances shown. These should be as follows.

	Code	Balance £	
Bank current account	1200	7073.03	(debit)
Debtors control account	1100	28369.34	(debit)
Creditors control account	2100	7995.65	(credit)
Bad debt write off account	8100	151.32	(debit)
Advertising account	6201	3421.28	(debit)
Sales - contract cleaning	4000	31017.80	(credit)
Sales - window cleaning	4001	4084.68	(credit)
Sales - domestic services	4002	1430.35	(credit)
Sales – materials	4100	1417.34	(credit)

Spreadsheet exercise - Aged Debtors Analysis

The customers owing the five largest amounts are:

A/C	Balance
GHHCOM	3,436.88
OGDENK	3,278.25
KEITHG	3,243.00
NORRIS	2,775.47
ROYALP	1,762.50

You could have found this information in Sage simply by clicking on the word Balance in the main Customers window. This re-sorts the data (smallest balance first), clicking on Balance again will sort in the opposite order (largest balance first).

Customers with a balance of over £1,000 that has been outstanding for more than 30 days are as follows.

A/C	Balance	Current	30 days
OGDENK	3,278.25	564.00	2,714.25
ROYALP	1,762.50	–352.50	2,115.00
GHHCOM	3,436.88	1,703.75	1,733.13
HARVEY	1,715.50	0.00	1,715.50
NORRIS	2,775.47	1,687.77	1,087.70

PART C ASSIGNMENTS

Spreadsheet exercise – Cash Flow Forecast

The spreadsheet is shown below – in normal format and with formulae displayed. This file is available within the data from the Word and Excel exercises unloaded from the CD (see Chapter 2 for full instructions).

This file is called CashFcastFirstHalf2001Ans.xls.

	A	B	C	D
1	Blitz Limited cashflow forecast			
2	January 2001 - June 2001			
3				
4				£
5				
6	Forecast cash balance, January 1, 2001			5,500
7				
8	Forecast receipts			
9	Cash receipts		4,500	
10	Collections from credit sales		130,000	
11	Total receipts		134,500	
12				
13	Forecast payments			
14	Payments for materials purchased		25,000	
15	Wages and salary payments		52,000	
16	Rent payment		8,000	
17	Power, phone and other payments		22,000	
18	Total payments		107,000	
19				
20	Cash balance, June 30, 2001			33,000

	A	B	C	D
1	Blitz Limited cashflow forecast			
2	January 2001 - June 2001			
3				
4				£
5				
6	Forecast cash balance, January 1, 2001			5500
7				
8	Forecast receipts			
9	Cash receipts		4500	
10	Collections from credit sales		130000	
11	Total receipts		=SUM(C9:C10)	
12				
13	Forecast payments			
14	Payments for materials purchased		25000	
15	Wages and salary payments		52000	
16	Rent payment		8000	
17	Power, phone and other payments		22000	
18	Total payments		=SUM(C14:C17)	
19				
20	Cash balance, June 30, 2001			=D6+C11-C18

PART D

Appendices

Appendix 1: The Blitz Nominal Ledger – account codes

The following is a list of the accounts in the nominal ledger of Blitz Limited.

Fixed assets
0010	FREEHOLD PROPERTY
0011	LEASEHOLD PROPERTY
0020	PLANT AND MACHINERY
0021	PLANT AND MACHINERY DEPRECIATION
0030	OFFICE EQUIPMENT
0031	OFFICE EQUIPMENT DEPRECIATION
0040	FURNITURE AND FIXTURES
0041	FURNITURE AND FIXTURES DEPRECIATION
0050	MOTOR VEHICLES
0051	MOTOR VEHICLES DEPRECIATION

Current assets
1001	STOCK
1002	WORK IN PROGRESS
1003	FINISHED GOODS
1100	DEBTORS CONTROL ACCOUNT
1101	SUNDRY DEBTORS
1102	OTHER DEBTORS
1103	PREPAYMENTS
1200	BANK CURRENT ACCOUNT
1210	BANK DEPOSIT ACCOUNT
1220	BUILDING SOCIETY ACCOUNT
1230	PETTY CASH
1240	COMPANY CREDIT CARD
1250	CREDIT CARD RECEIPTS

Current liabilities

2100	CREDITORS CONTROL ACCOUNT
2101	SUNDRY CREDITORS
2102	OTHER CREDITORS
2109	ACCRUALS
2200	SALES TAX CONTROL ACCOUNT
2201	PURCHASE TAX CONTROL LIABILITY
2210	PAYE
2211	NATIONAL INSURANCE
2230	PENSION FUND
2300	LOANS
2310	HIRE PURCHASE
2320	CORPORATION TAX
2330	MORTGAGES

Financed by

3000	ORDINARY SHARES
3001	PREFERENCE SHARES
3100	RESERVES
3101	UNDISTRIBUTED RESERVES
3200	PROFIT AND LOSS ACCOUNT

Sales

4000	SALES - CONTRACT CLEANING
4001	SALES - WINDOW CLEANING
4002	SALES - DOMESTIC SERVICES
4009	DISCOUNTS ALLOWED
4100	SALES MATERIALS
4101	SALES TYPE E
4200	SALES OF ASSETS
4400	CREDIT CHARGES (LATE PAYMENTS)
4900	MISCELLANEOUS INCOME
4901	ROYALTIES RECEIVED
4902	COMMISSIONS RECEIVED
4903	INSURANCE CLAIMS
4904	RENT INCOME
4905	DISTRIBUTION AND CARRIAGE

Purchases

5000	MATERIALS PURCHASED
5001	MATERIALS IMPORTED
5002	MISCELLANEOUS PURCHASES
5003	PACKAGING
5009	DISCOUNTS TAKEN
5100	CARRIAGE

APPENDIX 1: THE BLITZ NOMINAL LEDGER ACCOUNT CODES

5101	DUTY
5102	TRANSPORT INSURANCE
5200	OPENING STOCK
5201	CLOSING STOCK

Direct expenses

6000	PRODUCTIVE LABOUR
6001	COST OF SALES LABOUR
6002	SUB-CONTRACTORS
6100	SALES COMMISSIONS
6200	SALES PROMOTIONS
6201	ADVERTISING
6202	GIFTS AND SAMPLES
6203	PUBLIC RELATIONS (LIT & BROCHURES)
6900	MISCELLANEOUS EXPENSES

Overheads

7001	DIRECTORS SALARIES
7002	DIRECTORS REMUNERATION
7003	STAFF SALARIES
7004	WAGES - REGULAR
7005	WAGES - CASUAL TEMPORARY STAFF
7006	EMPLOYERS NI
7007	EMPLOYERS PENSIONS
7008	RECRUITMENT EXPENSES
7100	RENT
7102	WATER RATES
7103	GENERAL RATES
7104	PREMISES INSURANCE
7200	ELECTRICITY
7201	GAS
7202	OIL
7203	OTHER HEATING COSTS
7300	FUEL AND OIL
7301	REPAIRS AND SERVICING
7302	LICENCES
7303	VEHICLE INSURANCE
7304	MISCELLANEOUS MOTOR EXPENSES
7400	TRAVELLING
7401	CAR HIRE
7402	HOTELS
7403	UK ENTERTAINMENT
7404	OVERSEAS ENTERTAINMENT
7405	OVERSEAS TRAVELLING
7406	SUBSISTENCE
7500	PRINTING

PART D APPENDICES

7501	POSTAGE AND CARRIAGE
7502	TELEPHONE
7503	TELEX/TELEGRAM/FACSIMILE
7504	OFFICE STATIONERY
7505	BOOKS ETC
7600	LEGAL FEES
7601	AUDIT & ACCOUNTANCY FEES
7602	CONSULTANCY FEES
7603	PROFESSIONAL FEES
7700	EQUIPMENT HIRE
7701	OFFICE MACHINE MAINTENANCE
7800	REPAIRS AND RENEWALS
7801	CLEANING
7802	LAUNDRY
7803	PREMISES EXPENSES (MISC)
7900	BANK INTEREST PAID
7901	BANK CHARGES
7902	CURRENCY CHARGES
7903	LOAN INTEREST PAID
7904	HP INTEREST
7905	CREDIT CHARGES

Miscellaneous

8000	DEPRECIATION
8001	PLANT & MACHINERY DEPRECIATION
8002	FURNITURE/FIX/FITTINGS DEPRECIATION
8003	VEHICLE DEPRECIATION
8004	OFFICE EQUIPMENT DEPRECIATION
8100	BAD DEBT WRITE OFF
8102	BAD DEBT PROVISION
8200	DONATIONS
8201	SUBSCRIPTIONS
8202	CLOTHING COSTS
8203	TRAINING COSTS
8204	INSURANCE
8205	REFRESHMENTS
9998	SUSPENSE ACCOUNT
9999	MISPOSTINGS ACCOUNT

Appendix 2:
Shortcut keys

The table below shows the various functions assigned in Sage to the function ('F') keys along the top of the keyboard. You can view this from within Sage by selecting **Help**, **Shortcut Keys** from the main menu.

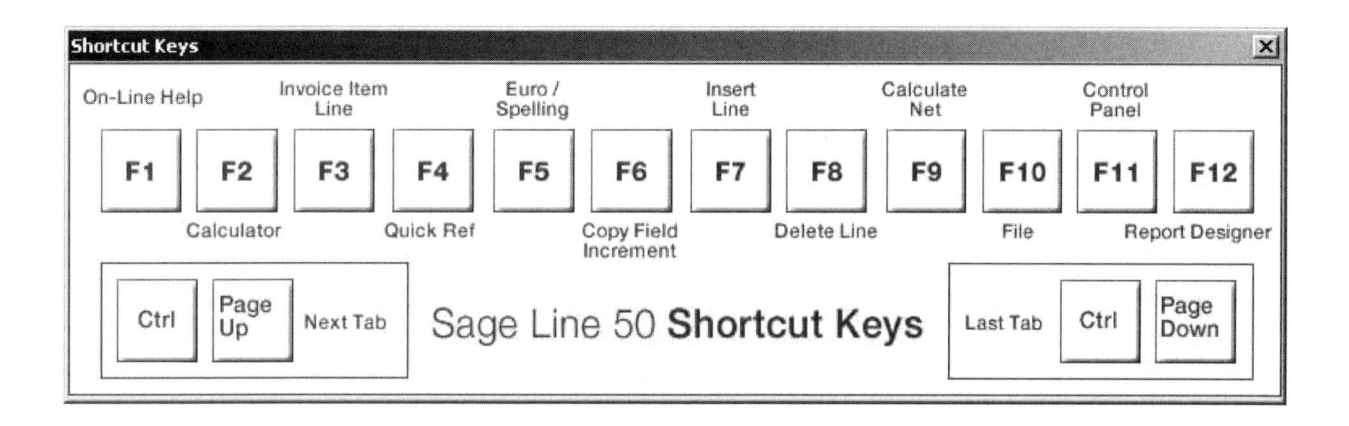

On-Line Help	Invoice Item Line	Euro / Spelling	Insert Line	Calculate Net	Control Panel
F1	F2 **F3**	F4 **F5**	F6 **F7**	F8 **F9**	F10 **F11** F12
Calculator	Quick Ref	Copy Field Increment	Delete Line	File	Report Designer

| Ctrl | Page Up | Next Tab | Sage Line 50 **Shortcut Keys** | Last Tab | Ctrl | Page Down |

Index

INDEX

Absolute cell references	18
Account balances	131
Account reference codes	52
Accounting errors	160
Active cell	4
Activity window	51
Aged debtors analysis	159
Aged debtors list	159
Allocating receipts	125
Analysis Total box	125
Assignments: loading data	45
Assumptions	30
Back ups	33, 45, 49
Back-up	33, 45, 49
Bad debt	155
Bank button	109, 124
Bank charges	147
Bank receipt	132
Bank reconciliations	144
Bank statement	147
Bank transactions	144
Bank-cash transactions	141
Blitz Limited	44
Book Balance (at Date)	146
Bounced cheques	128
Buttons	44
Calculate Net button	71, 118, 133
Calculator	88
Carriage	91
Case study	45
Cash flow projection	15
Cell	4, 5
Cell protection	33
Chart wizard	28
Charts	26
Cheque No.	110
Cheque printing	119
Collecting unpaid invoices	158
Column	4
Column width	13
Columns	12
Conditions	24
Contra entries	152
Control	33
Corrections button	162
Credit limit exceeded	154
Credit limits	83
Credit notes	95, 96, 115, 127
Credit notes received	73
Credits button	73

Criteria button	69, 96
Ctrl + Z	10
Currency	65
Currency format	31
Customer button (receipts)	124
Customer Order No.	90
Customer queries	100
Customer receipts	127
Customers: new	82
Customers window	51, 82
Date	70
Date Range	76
Day books	74
Debit and credit entries	142
Debit/Credit (journals)	143
Def N/C box	65
Def Tax Code box	65
Defaults	65
Delete	10
Delivery Address	90
Details	87
Discard option	92
Discounts	114, 128
Division	12
Duplicate copies	98
Duplicate invoices	101
Editing data	10
Errors	45, 160
Escape key	45, 51
F2 (edit)	10
F4 ('Quick Reference')	18, 51, 68, 70, 118
F8	67, 71
F9	71
File output option	75
File Maintenance	161
File View windows	77
Filling	11
Financials button	53
Finder button	68
Finish	157
Fixed format	31
Footer button	90
Formatting	31
Formatting numbers	31
Formula bar	5
Formulae	5, 17, 21
Formulae with conditions	25
Function key F2 (edit)	10
Function key F4	18, 51, 68, 70, 118

INDEX

Function key F8	67, 71
Function key F9	71
General format	31
Go To (F5)	10
Graphs	26
Gridlines	31
Headings and layout	16
Hidden format	31
Icons	44
Index of invoices	84, 91
Index tabs	63
Inserting	12
Invoice	67, 85
Invoice Date	86
Invoice details	91
Invoice number	70, 84, 86
Invoices: locating	106
Invoices: allocation of payments to	109
Invoices: duplicate	101
Invoices: printing	96
Invoices: refunding if already paid	130
Invoicing for the sale of goods	92
Invoicing window	83
Journal entries	141, 143
Journal vouchers	141
Journals button	142
Keyboard	44
Keyboard shortcut	13
Labels	30
Ledgers: updating	98
Letters	160
Linking worksheets	35
Loading the data for assignments	45
Maintenance	161
Microsft Excel	55
Microsft Word	55
Mouse	44
Multiplication	12
Multi-sheet spreadsheets	34
Net amount	71
New customers	82
Nominal accounts and codes	53
Nominal code	88, 91
Nominal ledger	53
Nominal ledger button	53

Non-accounting errors	160
Notes	90
Number format	31
Opening Balance	146
Opening data	50
Order Details	89
Output	75
Overdue payments	158
Page Width	98
Paid in Full	111, 125, 162
Part payment	112, 125
Password	34, 42
Pay in Full button	111, 125
Paying off the balance on an account	112
Paying specific invoices	112
Payment button	117
Payment on account	126
Payments:posting	109
Payments on account	116
Payments with order (bank receipts)	131
Percent format	31
Petty cash transactions	140
Posting invoices	72
Power (^)	6
Predetermined cheque amount	111
Preview	75, 98
Price box	88
Print button	96
Printer output option	75
Printing	97
Producing cheques	119
Producing invoices	83
Product button	83, 93
Product code	93
Purchase ledger (see Suppliers)	62
Queries	100, 120
Range	11
Receipt button (bank)	131
Receipts	124, 125, 132, 133
Reconcile Balance	146
Reconciliation procedures	146
Refunds	130
Relative cell references	18
Reminder letters	160
Reports	74, 119, 134
Reports for receipts	134
Returned cheques	128
Rounding errors	32
Rows	4, 12

INDEX

SA (sales payment on account)	125
Sales ledger	82
Sage software: quitting	44
Sales account codes	53
SC (sales credit note)	125
Service button	83
SI (sales invoice)	125
Spreadsheet calculations	23
Spreadsheet formatting	30
Spreadsheet formulae	6
Spreadsheet rounding errors	32
Spreadsheets and word processing software	34
Statement Balance	146
Statement button	159
Statements	159
Sum	5, 11
Supplier details	62
Suppliers: new	62
Suppliers button	50
Suppliers ledger data	50
Suppliers window	51
Tab key	44
Task bar	44

Tax code (VAT)	71, 91, 118
Three dimensional spreadsheets	34
Titles	30
Toolbar	13
Tp column	110, 125
Transaction numbers	76
Transaction Range	76
Trial balance	53
Uncleared items	146
Undoing actions (Ctrl + Z)	10
Unit Price	94
Unpaid invoices	158
Update Ledgers report	98
Updating the ledgers	98, 99
What if? analysis	21
Wildcard character	69
Word	55
Word processing software	56
Writing off a transaction	158
Writing off an account	156
Writing off bad debts	155
Zoom	98

INDEX

Review Form – Bookkeeping with Sage and Spreadsheets with Excel (4/08)

Name: _____ Address: _____

How have you used this Workbook?
(Tick one box only)

☐ Home study (book only)
☐ On a course: college _____
☐ With 'correspondence' package
☐ Other _____

Why did you decide to purchase this Workbook? *(Tick one box only)*

☐ Have used BPP Texts/Kits in the past
☐ Recommendation by friend/colleague
☐ Recommendation by a lecturer at college
☐ Saw advertising
☐ Other _____

During the past six months do you recall seeing/receiving any of the following?
(Tick as many boxes as are relevant)

☐ Our advertisement in *Accounting Technician* magazine
☐ Our advertisement in *Pass magazine*
☐ Our brochure with a letter through the post

Which (if any) aspects of our advertising do you find useful?
(Tick as many boxes as are relevant)

☐ Prices and publication dates of new editions
☐ Information on Interactive Text content
☐ Facility to order books off-the-page
☐ None of the above

Have you used other BPP Texts and Kits?   ☐ Yes   ☐ No

Your ratings, comments and suggestions would be appreciated on the following areas

	Very useful	Useful	Not useful
Files on CD	☐	☐	☐
Activities and answers	☐	☐	☐
Assignments and answers	☐	☐	☐

	Excellent	Good	Adequate	Poor
Overall opinion of this Workbook	☐	☐	☐	☐

Do you intend to continue using BPP products?   ☐ Yes   ☐ No

The BPP author of this edition can be e-mailed at: barrywalsh@bpp.com

Please return this form to Barry Walsh, BPP Learning Media, FREEPOST, London W12 8BR

Please note any further comments and suggestions/errors on the reverse of this page.

Review Form (continued)

Please note any further comments and suggestions/errors below